From Fear to Fraternity

FROM FEAR TO FRATERNITY

A Russian Tale of Crime, Economy and Modernity

Patricia Rawlinson

PlutoPress
www.plutobooks.com

First published 2010 by Pluto Press
345 Archway Road, London N6 5AA and
175 Fifth Avenue, New York, NY 10010

www.plutobooks.com

Distributed in the United States of America exclusively by
Palgrave Macmillan, a division of St. Martin's Press LLC,
175 Fifth Avenue, New York, NY 10010

British Library Cataloguing in Publication Data
A catalogue record for this book is available from the British Library

ISBN   978 0 7453 1868 4   Hardback
ISBN   978 0 7453 1867 7   Paperback

Library of Congress Cataloging in Publication Data applied for

This book is printed on paper suitable for recycling and made from fully managed and
sustained forest sources. Logging, pulping and manufacturing processes are expected to
conform to the environmental standards of the country of origin.

10   9   8   7   6   5   4   3   2   1

Designed and produced for Pluto Press by
Chase Publishing Services Ltd, 33 Livonia Road, Sidmouth, EX10 9JB England
Typeset from disk by Stanford DTP Services, Northampton, England
Printed and bound in the European Union by
CPI Antony Rowe, Chippenham and Eastbourne

*The book is dedicated to my parents,
Colin and Eileen, for their wisdom,
and my husband Glenn, for his enduring love.*

Contents

Acknowledgements

A book that has had such a long gestation as this has run up no inconsiderable number of debts. Back in the early days I was greatly supported by Gerald Brooke and Denis Ogden, Soviet (then Russian) friends including a select few from the St Petersburg police, not least Arkady Kramerev and Andrei Rogov. Many others are dead now – no fault of mine. As a PhD student at the LSE, my supervisor, David Downes, in his typically modest way, provided the advice and friendship without which there would have been no doctorate and no book. Current colleagues at the LSE whose input into papers, suggestions for reading or simply time given to talk through ideas include Nigel Dodd, David Frisby, Frances Heidensohn and Paul Rock from Sociology, Robert Reiner, Roxanna Bratu and other members of the Tuesday seminar group. Special thanks go to Dick Hobbs, whose mentoring and East End-style hectoring, even during his Eeyore moments, got me to finish this mother of all procrastinations. Colleagues from other institutions who have also offered support include (in no particular order) Frank Gregory, Keith Spence, Steve Tombs, Rob Hornsby, Mike Woodiwiss and Vincenzo Ruggiero.

Other thanks go to Penny Carnegie, for her constant source of encouragement, nephew Jake, the eternal idealist and fighter for justice, Dan and his extensive and ever available personal library and Hillary now Jones, for her sharp, constructive and typically humorous criticisms of my writing and sartorial disasters. To my editor, Roger van Zwanenberg, whose centuries-long patience and gentle hounding have finally paid off, you can tick me off your first Pluto list. And to the countless others I know I've forgotten (or will remember when it's too late), you're in there somewhere.

Finally, there are those who have shaped my life, knowingly or otherwise, and without whom this book would never have happened. My much-missed son Leon and his gentle wife Angela, who escaped to Sydney, have made the future seem even more precious after the recent birth of Caelan, our first grandson. My courageous, beautiful daughter and best friend, Taifa, who never let me give up, has been a constant source of inspiration. Granddaughters Kiara and Amber, equally beautiful in their different ways, give me hope that the next generation have so much to offer.

Introduction

Some stories never die. They are just retold with different characters and different settings. When the Berlin Wall came down and the Soviet Union collapsed in 1989 and 1991 respectively the looming 'threat' of communism was replaced by that of Russian organised crime (ROC) or the Russian 'Mafia'. The narratives constructed around each told of hostility to Western values and interests and an ever-present danger to global security. Neither threat materialised even remotely as predicted. The feared spread of communism was always dwarfed by that of its ideological nemesis. And nor has Russian organised crime, alongside other criminal organisations in a *Pax mafiosa*, achieved anything close to the global domination we were warned of by governments, law enforcement and journalists. That formidable task has been accomplished by 'freedom-loving' states themselves.

The current global economic crisis is a good time to reflect on these narratives of organised crime, in particular that which we call the Russian Mafia, to reassess the relationship between criminal and legal enterprise, to look more critically at the question of harm, to reconsider how issues of responsibility and morality are constructed and understood in a socio-economic context. Manichean narratives of good and evil, heroes and villains, 'us' and 'them', 'our' way of life and 'their' desire to destroy it appear less convincing when faced with the exploits of hedge fund managers and bank CEOs. (And yet, as a recent conference on Serious and Organized Crime demonstrated,[1] we still cling on to these simplistic dichotomies, perhaps as a means of comfort in an ever-growing world of uncertainty and threat from within.) Now, however, is a time for different narratives from those we are accustomed to hearing and delight in doing so. This book is an attempt to engage with some of them.

The most popular narratives on ROC, as with other 'mafia' groups, tell of gangsters, racketeers, godfathers, endemic violence, tightly structured hierarchies, underworld jargon, arcane rituals and global conspiracies. What makes them even more compelling in the Russian context is that they have become inextricably linked with Cold War thinking and its ideological binary vista, inculcating

1

the Manichean perspective even deeper into the reading of post-communist Russian society and its struggle with crime. These two *bêtes noires* were woven together during the global moral panic of the 1990s when the New World Order vision, the US blueprint for a post-Cold War future based on neo-liberal ideals, appeared increasingly vulnerable to attack from hostile elements, most notably transnational organised crime (TOC) dominated by the ferocious and increasingly ubiquitous Russian Mafia. Its strength, so we were told, lay in its access to resources (including nuclear) and powerful erstwhile communist networks. Succinctly described in the title of a popular publication on the subject, *Comrade Criminal*, a well researched but analytically limited account of the chaotic and lawless first few years of free market economic reform in Russia, this new global threat was seen as a terrifying fusion of communism and organised crime.

The majority of literature (English as well as Russian) explains ROC and its burgeoning in the new Russia as a consequence of the legacy of communism. Systemic corruption in the Communist Party and the endemic presence of the shadow economy in Soviet society were held responsible for the criminogenic environment in which 'shock therapy', a programme based on a *laissez-faire* model of economics, created in the West and sold to Russian reformers as the only path to economic stability, struggled to deliver its utopian promise. In fact, it delivered only a dystopian nightmare as Russia was thrown into social and economic chaos during the embryonic stages of what was now an officially sanctioned market. The repeatedly illicit and violent acquisition of newly privatised assets, and the unbridled exploitation of the country's most vulnerable citizens, confounded the predictions of Western neo-liberals who had presented shock therapy as a means of establishing rule of law, social justice and economic equity. This unexpected turn of events, so ran orthodox explanations, was an aberration of the 'real thing', a peculiarly Russian version of capitalism infected by its communist past. A new term was coined – 'gangster capitalism' – as a means of dissociating the cut-throat reality of Russia's economic transformation from its ideological foundations and the civilised version enjoyed by Western economies. The patient rather than the medicine was to blame.

With the exception of a few lone voices, the opportunity to interpret Russia's problematic transition to the market as a time for critical reflection on the development of capitalism, particularly the impact of increasing deregulation of global financial markets, became instead yet another round of scapegoating and a return to the alien conspiracy paradigm that had dominated US culture in the 1950s. Emphasis on the notion of the Russian gangster and highly organised, communist-linked (as much by behaviour as by relationship) crime groups brought a return of familiar stereotypes to a situation that threatened to expose the pathologies of capitalism itself. For, in the absence of a workable legal framework designed to curtail 'unacceptable' excesses of profit acquisition, the moral (or lack of moral) basis of the free market was increasingly exposed. Distinctions between the criminal entrepreneur and his or her legal counterpart became blurred, both hotly pursuing the same ideals and leaving behind a trail of harmful consequences. Hobbs's observation that 'Legality will be increasingly irrelevant in an international market immune to any other moral perspective other than profit'[2] resonated in the Russian context, especially as a flood of foreign businesses availed themselves of the Klondike conditions during these lawless times. Indeed, it was the *absence* of regulatory structures that made Russia so attractive for many foreign entrepreneurs. Deciding who was and who was not a 'criminal' thus became a political game, allowing the most powerful voices arbitrarily to locate and label a number of characters as dangerous and threatening, as 'gangsters' or 'Mafiosi'.

While the book understands the term 'organised crime' as a social construct, shaped according to historical, cultural, ideological, political and other considerations, it does not refute the brutal reality of the majority of illegal enterprise. Nor, however, does it subscribe to the fact that all illegal enterprise labelled 'organised crime' is necessarily harmful. It is this issue of harm, rather than legality, that frames the direction of the book and the unravelling of the familiar narratives on organised crime. For what is clear in the legally ambiguous background of Russia's experience of capitalism, but less so in the more sophisticated discourses of legality in advanced capitalist states, is the extent to which harmful acts are subjectively rather than rationally proscribed. 'Who' and 'what' rather than the level of injury perpetrated is often the primary determinant of unacceptable harm (a situation, we can argue, that also extends to how victimhood is acknowledged or not and to unacknowledged victims).

None of this is news to us. We know, for example, that statistically, deaths from illegal drug abuse are significantly lower than those from tobacco-related diseases.[3] Nonetheless, the 'unsavoury characters' behind the global illicit drugs trade continue to provoke outrage and harsh judicial responses while their legal counterparts in the tobacco trade, including erstwhile and serving government ministers on company boards, are given titles and bonuses for helping stimulate the economy and increase state revenue. What we refuse to accept, or perhaps is news to us, is that this is a *systemic* problem in which we are all involved to varying degrees as economic actors. Capitalism, like communism (in their manifest rather than idealised forms), is bad for our health.

The book argues that what is designated 'gangster' capitalism in Russia *is neither a deviation from nor an aberration of the free market*, but rather, when taken from a harm paradigm, a micro-version of capitalism as it operates on a global level. A closer examination of the social consequences of Russia's adoption of *laissez-faire*, the responses by Western advocates of shock therapy to political objections raised against fulfilling the programme, and the legal and ethical slack given to those supportive of the free market, expose a raft of harms to rival any of those attributed to organised crime. In the absence of effective legal guidelines to doing business in Russia, the difficulty in being able to distinguish between legal and criminal entrepreneurship thus not only exposes the extent to which, as Hillyard and Tombs write, 'crime has no ontological reality',[4] but, more importantly, underlines the fact that the pathologies present in so-called 'gangster' capitalism are also present in Western economies and cannot be ring-fenced as Russia's failure to embrace capitalism properly.

The issue of harm rather than legality introduces a different set of narratives, at the heart of which lies the question of morality and responsibility. These narratives find their way into the book by drawing, in part, on texts relating to similar debates on morality and responsibility related to the Holocaust. As critical texts they disturb the comfortable (and comforting) boundaries between perpetrator and victim, guilty and innocent, knowledge and ignorance by narrating the prickly moments of proximity and similarity which disable the facility to ringfence as 'evil' a single person, group or nation. The very techniques of disassociation critically examined in these texts are also employed by the official narratives on organised crime as a means of deflecting attention away from the diffusion or denial of harm inflicted by legal actors, that is by 'us' as well as 'them', or more alarmingly, by 'us' in collusion with 'them'. 'Have I as an individual, or us and our collective values, in some way contributed to this appalling act of exploitation or even killing?'

is a question that resonates through many critical analyses of the Holocaust, and one that I hope has equal resonance in this study.

As much as we would like to blame criminal entrepreneurs for the tragic human consequences of their pernicious business, or the bankers, hedge fund managers and politicians for their role in the global economic downturn, all of them can only (mal)function if the consuming public collaborate at some point and in some way with their schemes and operations. Clearly, there are different levels of consumer and political autonomy, varying degrees of freedom and responsibility according to which individuals can operate. A particular feature of Russia's history has been the absence and oppression of individual autonomy. Under Soviet communism, rather than in the historically workable communes of peasant ruralism, this enforced absence of individual economic accountability (and creativity) translated into apathy, often cruel indifference, corruption and the ever burgeoning presence of the second economy. Ultimately, it dragged the very system whose values it was supposed to materially sustain, down with it. Yet ideological barriers erected between state-run economies and their capitalist counterparts have little foundation when moral accountability, or the lack of it, is brought into the economic equation. The absence of individual accountability for the economic 'other', on and with whom we are each interdependent (in contrast to the hostile construction of the dangerous 'other'), as a central ethos of the modern economy, is as pertinent to the problems of capitalism as it was to the implosion of Soviet communism. The final aim of the book is to show why the story of crime, economy and modernity told by communist and capitalist Russia, framed by its historical and cultural denial of moral *individuality* (the other side of egotistical individualism), is a story for us all.

＊　＊　＊

A potted personal account of how the book came into being and the context of its genesis is the topic of Chapter 1, alongside the somewhat unconventional methods that shaped and were shaped by the research. Chapter 2 examines some of the main debates around the concept of organised crime, the agendas they bring with them and in particular those that have informed the Western and Russian perception of illegal and legal economy in the former Soviet Union (FSU). Chapter 3 places the illegal economy in Russia in its historical and cultural context, tracing how different perceptions of legal and illegal behaviour were manipulated by the ruling elites to disguise or reconfigure the nature of economic and social problems. Chapter 4 looks at the reform programme introduced to the Soviet Union under Mikhail Gorbachev and how this impacted on the illegal economy. It discusses how the problems Gorbachev faced went beyond the political and economic, ingraining themselves as moral issues to which there was clearly no quick policy 'fix'. As the country began to fall part, the term 'organised crime', as a foreign import, became an important weapon in the ideological battle provoked by Gorbachev's attempt to reinstate 'genuine' socialism.

The political, economic and moral legacy of the Soviet experiment has been blamed on Russia's failure to properly adapt to the free market, as delivered through the shock therapy programme, a failure which resulted in the explosion of 'organised crime'. Chapter 5 argues that this is only one reason for the economic chaos that followed the collapse of Soviet communism, and that the other, equally potent, problem was the nature of the 'medicine', that is, the free market. The conflicting narratives on organised crime, and how and when the label is applied, provide an insight into this problem and the ways in which advocates of the market have justified the harms it inflicted on Russian society. Chapter 6 looks behind the official narratives of organised crime and beyond the Russian context to identify a common and silent meta-narrative linking Soviet communism with the capitalist states of the West. This meta-narrative tells of the pathological condition of both economic models in the absence or erosion of individual account-ability for the harmful consequences promoted by each system. The chapter argues that despite upholding liberal values which promote the rights and interests of the individual, powerful neo-liberal states are in fact eroding the creative role of the individual as an economically accountable actor, for to adopt the position of being morally responsible is inimical to the competitive ethos of the market. Organised crime narratives function as a distraction away from the harms created by the legal economy, as well as actually nurturing illegal economic activity. The concluding chapter, 'From Fear to Fraternity', considers how a moral approach to the modern economy, born out of the lessons to be learned from Russia's experience of communism and capitalism, should shout down the narratives of organised crime which have hitherto deafened us to the possibility for radical change in economic thinking. By reassessing these narratives, we open up the possibility of transforming the misplaced fear of criminal shadows into genuine economic fraternity.

1
Telling Tales

The fate of the Russian people is to show the rest of the world how not to live.[1]
                                                                (Russian proverb)

A DAY IN THE LIFE ...

After the collapse of Soviet communism in 1991, Western eyes turned to their erstwhile enemy no longer with a sense of fear but rather with one of optimism tinged with triumphalism. They saw an ideology in tatters, a superpower brought to its knees and an opportunity to spread the word of the neo-liberal gospel with missionary zeal to a nation of willing converts. Barely one year after the euphoria of communism's demise, another enemy raised its head from the East. This was the subject of my PhD – Russian organised crime (ROC) – what the Western media, now awash with tales of guns and gangsters, termed 'the new communist threat'.[1] As ROC was then classed as a risk to global security, research on the subject tended to attract generous funding. So it was that in the autumn and winter of 1994 I found myself able to complete fieldwork (hitherto self-funded) in St Petersburg. Housed in the 'deluxe' (by Russian standards) section of a student hostel on the city outskirts, I was able to access and retreat from different aspects of Russian life at will.

I had painstakingly sketched out a research agenda – whom I would interview, where I would observe, which documents I needed to consult, library times for perusing through the limited but growing literature on the subject, and my timetable. Sometimes, however, the unexpected occurred, dramatic and overwhelming in an obvious way. One evening, on my way to dinner with British friends, I witnessed the beating of a young guy (a drug dealer as it turned out) by others of around the same age, on the ground floor of the hostel. Rushing to the *dezhurnaya*, the usual ferocious-looking babushka, whose job it was to keep an eye on the comings and goings of the hostel's residents, I shouted for her to do something about what was turning into a horrendously bloody affair. The response was typical:

7

'Not my business.' Nor was it mine, I decided. The drama, however, was to continue. As I got out onto the street, the door of the hostel flew open and the pulped victim came stumbling out behind me, immediately attended to by a couple of others who had obviously been waiting outside for him. Seconds later his assailants came flying out onto the street and the tables turned in an even more bloody manner. One of the assailants was grabbed by the victim's two associates, who promptly stretched out his arms on either side as a waiting car drove into him, reversed, and repeated the procedure. The body crumpled to the floor, and to my enduring shame I hurried away. I don't know whether he survived. On returning later that evening I asked the *dezhurnaya* what had happened. '*Narkotiki*' (drugs), was all she answered, and nothing more was said about the incident.

This was a tale of physical violence, gang warfare and drug dealing. Had a television crew or photojournalist been present it would have made exciting viewing and provided some darkly attractive pictures for a Sunday magazine. Here was the graphic reality of a society in chaos and confusion, one of the more familiar narratives of what has been designated 'organised crime' – two groups of young men, fighting over an illicit business, a trade that was destroying both them and their clients. This it was, as I and other Westerners thought, that was devastating the country and wrecking its path towards democracy and the free market. Some weeks later, I was not so sure.

If dramatic and unexpected cruelty is sharply memorable, commonplace, muted forms of violence, at times barely recognisable as such, can seep relentlessly into one's psyche producing equal levels of discomfort when recalled. There is, to turn around Hannah Arendt's famous phrase, an 'evil of banality', which allows us to tolerate, or, worse still, not even notice, the brutality and injustice of certain prosaic scenes and ubiquitous occurrences. St Petersburg in the mid 1990s, as in the rest of Russia, was suffering the effects of shock therapy, the free market antidote to the collapse of communism. Price liberalisation and rapid privatisation seemed a good idea at the time. It was working in other former European communist states, so we were told, so why not in the heartlands of the former Soviet empire? Its impact on the daily lives of the majority of Russian citizens, however, did little to endear the observer to its alleged merits, assuming, that is, it *was* observed in all its stark and tragic reality. For over two months I had walked past the human debris of the free market experiment, noticing but not wanting to register what was actually going on around me. Then one December day, not long after the bloody incident at the hostel, the reality of this mundane brutality hit home.

A Russian friend, Natasha, had been taken to hospital with a suspected brain tumour. In the privileged position of a Westerner, with easy access to hard currency, at that time an 'open sesame' to 'unavailable' essentials, I had agreed to accompany Natasha's mother, Svetlana, on the hunt for medication, using my magic dollars to buy what was 'out of stock' from the hidden shelves under the counter at the local chemist. Russian hospitals, starved of funds, relied on the families of patients not only to provide food but also to supplement the chronic shortage of drugs. So, on that cold winter's day, with the hostel thermometer reading −13 °C, I set off to work my privileged status. Natasha lived on the other side of the city and so the journey involved a metro change at Ploshad Vosstaniye, which served as the nearest underground stop for one of the city's railway termini, Moskovsky Voksal. The warmth and proximity of the metro to the main station attracted a growing number of homeless children, some could be seen sleeping against the walls. Others begged. Their main 'business' was conducted in and around the busy rail terminus. Economic opportunities were more plentiful there, begging, stealing or selling the only assets they had – their youthful bodies. In some cases older siblings honed their entrepreneurial skills and pimped their younger charges. There was no shortage of buyers either. For a country used to a state-run economy, the market dynamics of supply and demand were working at their most efficient. Most of the children were casualties of domestic abuse, the majority voluntarily homeless as they fled the violence of increasingly dysfunctional families. Some were literally dumped on the streets by parents who, finding themselves unemployed or having lost their savings as hyperinflation took hold, sold the family home and went off to live with relatives.[2]

That day, I *did* register what was happening, though why is difficult to say. It might have been the sleeping boy, pale and scruffy, likely no more than twelve, mouth covered in sores (terrible diet? oral sex?) his hand stretched out as if begging as I hurried along the metro subway; or perhaps, having scoured the polyclinics[3] and chemists for the required drugs and ending up with something that could have been a placebo rather than bona fide medication, there was a sense of defeat in knowing that even US dollars can fail to buy what simply isn't there; or the fact that in the absence of hospital equipment and transportation, Natasha's scheduled X-ray involved wrapping her up in her dressing gown and a blanket, Svetlana on one side, me on the other, forced to half-carry, half-drag the sick woman across a snow-covered square to the radiography unit at the other end of the huge decaying complex. This was violence of a different kind from the bloody conflict between drug dealers. It was random, indiscriminate harm; incidental, ubiquitous suffering, with no easily definable perpetrator. This was the fallout from legal economies, the legacy of one failed economic model and the impact of a newly implemented version of its ideological nemesis. A 'mistake', was how one Western academic, and one of the contributors to Russian economy reform, described it privately and with hindsight.

Suffering is more readily understood in the context of crime rather than the more ambiguous framework of harm. The former makes it easier to attribute blame, to identify those guilty of inflicting hurt through legislation and the criminal justice process. Crimes are the harms that society finds unacceptable and subsequently proscribe. As Nils Christie writes, 'Acts are not, they *become*. Crime does not exist. Crime is created.'[4] It was easy to place responsibility for at least some of the problems of Russia's transition to the market on gun-toting gangsters and smart, sleek, crime bosses. The hyperbole and rhetoric about the dangers posed by the 'Russian Mafia' (sometimes spelt 'mafiya' to distinguish it from the other mafias that were threatening global stability) caught the imagination of a Western public used to Hollywood-style representations of evil businessmen, or 'organised crime'. We wanted the pictures of bloodied corpses after a *razborka*, or shoot-out, and the glowering mug shot of a contract killer or drug trafficker, to feel aghast and morally distinct from the thugs who were tearing Russia part. But on that ordinary December day in 1994, the only smart and sleek businessmen I encountered in the late afternoon were sitting in the bar of the Grand Hotel, foreign and Russian entrepreneurs, shiny suits with shiny ideas, oblivious to or ignorant of the growing pile of human debris some barely metres from the hotel door, sharing their profit-making ideas over a bottle of imported red wine. No guns were to be seen (perhaps hidden in the jackets of unobtrusive bodyguards) and business was conducted in a civilised manner. Yet the power of the pen, scribbled on a contract here and there, the nod or handshake of a gentleman's agreement, wreaked more damage than an armoury of Kalashnikovs could have done. What suffering they might cause, would simply be a 'mistake'.

The limitations of my research back then are painfully clear now. As with so many commentators on Russia and crime, I was unknowingly trapped in the folds of official and similar narratives, understanding 'organised crime' according to, if not stereotypes, then concepts that I and other academics have tried best to fit the Russian context. What emerged in my findings was a half-truth at best, a distortion at worst, of the events and realities of Russia's experience not only of capitalism, free market style, but of Soviet communism. Constrained by these narratives, another more intriguing and important story, one which has particular resonance in the uncertain and nervous world of the present global financial crisis, remained out of vision. The meta-narrative behind the familiar tales of Russia, crime and economy brings with it another more appropriate lens through which to understand the 'Russian Mafia/mafiya/organised crime'. It challenges both the binary divide of traditional understandings of legal and illegal economy and the broader ideological dichotomy of communism and capitalism. To the now famous saying, 'It's the economy stupid', this meta-narrative presents the rider, 'and morality'.

Suffering and violence as a consequence of economic activity are all too evident to be ignored. Beyond Russia's experience of economically induced hardship are countless other stories, from the war-torn states of Africa to the dictatorial regimes of East Asia and South America. More recently, growing levels of economic distress and suffering are emerging in our own backyards, in those of the developed world which for so long has lived without the hardships of its more vulnerable neighbours. This economic vandalism is conducted not just by illegal actors and through illegal means but, and often inflicting greater suffering, by legal actors and legitimate means. Russia has an almost unique status of having experienced two major modern economic models, both of which have caused untold harm and both of which have nurtured immoral behaviour almost as a matter of course. Its culture and history, while for years regarded as distinct from the democratic path favoured by Western Europe, nonetheless holds lessons to which it would be wise to pay heed. Fourteen years on, and with hindsight and history to direct the way, I have returned to the subject of organised crime, from a new angle completely, in the spirit of Robert Skidelsky's observation that 'For quality of life, we have to rely on morals not markets.'[5]

NARRATIVES AND NARRATORS

... stories influence our ability to recall events, motivate people to act, modulate our emotional reactions to events, cue certain heuristics and biases, structure our problem-solving capabilities, and ultimately perhaps, even constitute our very identity.
(W. D. Casebeer, 2008)[6]

The most influential narratives of modern society, especially in the twentieth and twenty-first centuries, have been based on binary thinking. At its most fundamental this emerged in enlightenment thinking as debates about the individual and society, and notions of precedence and determination. 'Which came first, which has the greater influence on the other and to what extent?' eventually translated into two major streams of political economy, an ideological divide whose influence has defined our perceptions of society in the twentieth century. The two superpowers, the United States and the Soviet Union, stood as the representatives of the opposing values and aspirations of modern society; one in favour of an individual-oriented social order, the other emphasising the significance of the collective. Their different approaches were expressed most aggressively and vociferously in Cold War rhetoric, an exaggerated discourse in which the negative and threatening values of one's adversary became a justification for increased military spending or as a means of legitimising political interference in third countries. For the most part, it was with the aim of establishing a regime favourable to the appropriate economic model that their foreign policies were formulated and executed. When the Soviet Union finally collapsed in 1991 it came as no surprise that the death of communism was read as the triumph of capitalism.

These narratives of difference have been further encouraged by aspects of Russian history, and not just as ideology. Politically, for example, Russia has always stood apart from its European neighbours. Autocracy endured longer there than in any other European state, despite numerous attempts, largely by the intelligentsia, to impose more democratic forms of governance. Serfdom, abolished in Britain and France in the 1600s and 1789 respectively, was a major feature of the rural economy in Russia until the Emancipation Act of 1861.[7] Even when steps towards democratic reform were introduced, as in the establishment of the first Duma, or Parliament, at the beginning of the twentieth century, they stood on fragile ground. Barely four months after its opening in 1906, the Duma was unceremoniously dismantled as an 'unnecessary obstacle'.[8] Russia's peculiar position as a Janus culture, taking in the Asiatic and European simultaneously, alongside influences such as the Orthodox Church, have prompted many outsiders to view it as dangerously exotic. This enduring perception, intensified by its apparently willing conversion to Soviet communism, prompted Churchill's famous description of Russia as 'a riddle, wrapped up in a mystery, inside an enigma', a twentieth-century endorsement of the Marquis de Custine's observation 200 years previously that here was a country 'which differs from all others'.[9] It is a distinction often encouraged by the Russians themselves, formulated as the country's 'special destiny', or in the more aggressive tones of nationalism. And yet, on the other hand, its cultural influence and intellectual alignment with the West have been inspirational, as a gallery of figures from the arts and sciences – Dostoevsky, Tolstoy, Solzhenitsyn, Tchaikovsky, Shostakovitch, Diaghilev, Nureyev, Kandinsky, Eisenstein, Mendeleyev, Sakharov, to name but a few – have brought the universal into the distinct.

When former US President Ronald Reagan described the Soviet Union as 'the evil empire' during a resurgence of Cold War hostilities in the 1980s, he not only tapped into the historical and ideological aspects of the East–West divide, but appealed to an entrenched Manichean-style perception of reality *per se*. The mentality that understands the world in terms of good versus evil has been exploited by powerful elites in a number of areas, not least in how we evaluate economic behaviour and create 'crime'. The dominant narratives on organised crime are conspicuously pertinent to this view. Those labelled as 'organised criminals' are understood in similar terms, but for different reasons, to the 'evil communists'. In capitalist society, organised crime is short-hand for associations of 'bad people' engaged in 'bad business'. As with the anti-communist rhetoric, those thus described represent a threat to the value system underlying the healthy, civilised society of the narrators. They comprise, in the words of former United Nations Secretary-General Kofi Annan, 'terrorists, criminals, drug dealers, traffickers in people, and others who undo the good works of civil society', those who 'show no scruple about resorting to intimidation or violence. Their ruthlessness is the very antithesis of all we regard as civil.'[10] Delivered as the opening address to the Palermo Convention on Transnational Organised Crime in 2000, there would have been little doubt that Russian-speaking crime groups were one of the major references of the speech. A wave of interest in Russian crime had been prompted by the violence and chaos of the country's move to the free market and growing evidence of criminal activity by Russians abroad. A number of influential publications, mainly by Western journalists such as Claire Sterling and Stephen Handelman, had brought to the public's attention a phenomenon that combined the two *bêtes noires* (as interpreted largely by the US) of Western society: communism and the 'mafia'. Sterling warned that the Russian Mafia plans to 'stake out whole blocks of the planet, half a continent here, another there ... in a phase of stunning expansion, threatening the integrity and even the survival of democratic governments in America, Europe, everywhere'.[11] Handelman's book, a more restrained account of the crime problems mainly within Russia, played to the fears of the exotic and dangerous 'other' as understood by non-Russian readers in the alliterative and politically loaded title *Comrade Criminal*.[12]

The implicit message contained in the narratives of organised crime in general, and the Russian Mafia in particular, has been a resounding endorsement of the free market ethos, but only as understood and sanctioned by the narrators. 'Organised crime' thus describes those entrepreneurial activities and collaborations not approved of by the narrators. In its ambiguity (as Chapter 2 describes) it is open to broad forms of interpretation, to be expediently applied when required by law makers, the media, economic elites and others. It was this ambiguity that enabled its diverse and often contradictory application to life in post-Soviet Russia. The urgency of this message through those narratives which defined our understanding of Russian crime and economy, was prompted by the free-for-all that became the country's transition to market, a chaotic and violent response to *laissez-faire* that had the potential to seriously undermine the neo-liberal agenda being exported from Washington and London across the globe as part of a 'New World Order'.[13] The medicine could not be seen to be failing, and certainly could not be exposed as the toxic substance it really was. As Russian society struggled to stay afloat, its casualty count growing by the day, advocates of shock therapy distanced themselves from the economic carnage by engaging in a 'blame Russia and its communist legacy' game. What we were witnessing was a distorted form of capitalism, so the stories ran, a consequence of the endemic corrupting influence of the former regime, 'wild', 'gangster' or 'anarcho' capitalism, one which was infected with 'the pervasive presence throughout economic life of organized crime'.[14] Comrade criminal was screwing it all up. Some of the more optimistic amongst shock therapy supporters interpreted the chaos and violence as a necessary phase, albeit a peculiarly Russian one, in the evolution of capitalism. This 'robber baron' stage will be transitory, they pointed out, as it had been in the US during the nineteenth century. Given the self-corrective mechanism inherent in capitalism, the 'stationary bandit' would eventually see the rationale of conducting his business within a law abiding society.[15] How many of these shock therapy advocates would have predicted that the road to market would lead back to an authoritarian style of governance in the guise of former President Vladimir Putin and his titular successor, Dmitri Medvedev, and one in which capitalism is happily seated and thriving?

MORALITY AND ECONOMY

What, then, is the story behind the dominant narratives of organised crime in Russia, and does it have any relevance beyond the borders of this enigmatic and mysterious riddle of a country? Is it possible to compare crime narratives in a country 'dominated by the principle of autocracy' with those of the free world? If by autocracy/authoritarianism we understand the restriction of individual freedom, the erosion of conditions necessary for allowing choice-making by groups and individuals alike, of depriving one of accountability for one's activities, then yes, we can compare. Authoritarianism, as we shall see in later chapters, comes in many guises.

The dominant narratives of organised crime, like those describing communism and capitalism, have at their core a moral presence, or perhaps more accurately, a sense of the immoral in this bifurcation. The underlying assumption of these narratives behind 'organised crime' is that the activities and the actors targeted by this term are immoral because they are harmful and because those engaged in such activities either intend or have knowledge of the harmful outcomes of their economically driven activities. In other words, organised crime becomes an expression for, or symbolic of, economic immorality as understood by those who shape the dominant narratives. It works as a repository for an array of immoral economic activities and behaviours as defined by those who apply the label.

The tales we tell of organised crime in turn tell tales about the narrators, about our values, our sense of justice, what motivates us, and perhaps, as William Casebeer writes (above), 'even our identity'. It tells most especially of our moral priorities in the economic sphere, what we perceive as right and decent, and what we regard as its opposite. The two major streams of modern economy, communism and capitalism, speak through a variety of narratives, including those of organised crime, to the immorality of their ideological adversary. Representatives from each stream spent most of the twentieth century pointing to the pathologies of their foe. Capitalism was seen for its avarice and exploitation, communism for its repression and gross inefficiency.

After the collapse of Soviet communism the neo-liberal evolution of capitalism confidently took the moral high ground, leaving the Marxist body for dead. Its continuing survival and expansion was seen as an endorsement of those values condemned by its erstwhile enemy. And as China, the other great communist state, began to move towards the market, capitalism seemed to be the only game in town. But its claims to deliver democracy and wealth have been severely dented by the recent and continuing debacle in global financial markets, so much so that Marxist theory has once again found credibility amongst a small but wider audience. Even the Archbishop of Canterbury has endorsed the prescience of Marx on the flaws of capitalism and its propensity for immorality.[16] As Downes and Rock noted before the subprime mortgage fallout:

> Far from being over, the argument with Marxism is only just about to begin all over again, this time in the context of capitalism careering out of control and without the counterpoint of communism exerting a counter-pressure for egalitarian policies in welfare, income and wealth distribution and the equivalent in international terms of the controls exercised by nation-states over business and finance before the 'big bang' of global capitalism in the 1980s.[17]

And yet, as history and Marxist critics have pointed out, an even greater immorality has emerged in those regimes, which have adapted his theory of political economy. The majority of these have been spectacularly unsuccessful, bringing out the worst rather than the intended best of human nature, most notably in the widespread abuse of human rights, the endemic nature of corruption and the long-term malfunction of economic performance over short-term benefits. Despite endorsing the accuracy of the critique of capitalism, few actually believe a Marxist solution remains viable.

Might Russia, then, having experimented with both economic models, serve as a tragic example of the failures of communism and capitalism; in other words, of the failure of modern economy as it has developed thus far? Might also the diverse narratives on organised crime in Russia, stories told from both sides, have played a part in distracting attention away from the underlying pathology of the modern economy, a pathology recognised by each in the other, but in their own economic system ignored or obscured by these and other narratives of difference?

It is easy to blame Russia for these failed experiments and accuse it of distorting the principles of each economic system. Apologists for the free market have seized on the Soviet legacy as the corrupting (and corrupted) factor behind the chaos and violence of the 1990s, thwarting the path to democracy and equitable wealth distribution and leading to the emergence of 'market authoritarianism'. So, too, do Marxists claim that the Soviet communist state was a bastardised version of the 'real thing'. Historian Eric Hobsbawm criticised it as a pragmatic rather than ideological experience, bound to fail because it 'was not based on mass conversion, but was a faith of cadres'.[18] As far back as 1950, vociferous criticism of Stalin's manipulation of the principles of the Bolshevik Revolution with 'its noble sentiments, its noble ambitions, and its noble goal' created a distance between Soviet communism and some Western Marxists, such as Max Shachtman: 'Don't insult the good name of socialism by applying it to this brutal regime of exploitation and social inequality.'[19] All these accounts, however, tell only half-truths. The other unspoken half-truth reveals that while Russia has done communism and capitalism badly, in their turn, communism and capitalism have done Russia very badly.

This, then, is the story behind the narratives of organised crime in Russia, and one that I believe, can be extended to similar narratives of organised crime beyond the Russian context. This meta-narrative tells of the moral inadequacy of *both* communism and capitalism or modern economy, an inadequacy which manifests as an absence of accountability for the harms created by legal economic activity, by respectable people, by you and me. For neither economic model requires its participants to stand individually accountable for the consequences of their behaviour and *freely* think about and act on the impact their needs and desires might have on others. Indeed, freedom of thinking (and acting) as an economic-based activity is proscribed by one system and positively discouraged by another, the latter providing a convenient get-out clause known as the 'invisible hand'. The paradox of the modern economy is that while there is no longer economic autonomy, unless we live totally apart in a self-sufficient environment, this interdependence is based on individual material needs and desires which places a responsibility on each individual (to the degree at which we can act freely) for the harms inflicted by these needs and desires down. Further, when we acknowledge the imperative of this interdependency and take a look at the economy through the lens of harm, the divide between legal and illegal economies is in reality spurious. It becomes impossible for two parallel worlds to exist in a modern economy, which means we must look for the causes of harm and suffering in the dominant economy as well as the illegal.

We do not wish to know or see this. Instead, we engage in a number of strategies to distance ourselves from these outcomes. One of these strategies operates through the narratives of organised crime, and the creation of a world of evil individuals more threatening and awful because they work collaboratively – gangsters, drug dealers, pimps, racketeers, and so on. These narratives are constructed to create a moral distance between what they and we do. Theirs is an alien world of economy, distinct from ours, an aberration of the values we claim underlie the dominant economy. They are portrayed as the cancer, when in fact they are but the symptom. We cannot call them 'businessmen' or 'corporations', for that would reveal proximity to our world. They are 'organised crime' or a host of ethnically qualified mafias – Russian, Sicilian, Italian-American, Colombian, and so on. Narratives of organised crime are a form of denial, 'a way to keep secret from ourselves the truth we cannot face'.[20]

How can Russia, a country so historically and culturally at odds with its Western counterparts, so aptly expose this moral inadequacy inherent in communism and capitalism? What makes it especially apposite to a study of crime and modern economy? The irony, however, is that it is these very differences which provide a basis for comparison. Centuries of authoritarian rule have constrained the development of individual rights, the sense of 'self' as a primary source of motivation and behaviour. Russia's history is the story of the missing 'self', of 'individuality'. Repression of freedom and the individual have left it especially susceptible to deterministic models of economy in which accountability becomes peripheral to each economic actor, leaving a moral vacuum at the heart of the economic process. Where the central economy diffused accountability across the state as a collective body, leaving no one in particular to pick up the tab of responsibility for failure and harm, the free market experiment also had no need to engage with individuals as moral participants in the economy. Market forces would help fix the inconsistencies and address the moral vacuum. What emerged under both economic experiments was not a parody as advocates of each system claimed, but rather a highlighting of the pathologies intrinsic to economies that deny or daunt accountability as being centred within the individual economic actor.

Russia, we can say, has been a hothouse for modern economy, economy without moral responsibility. It reveals in all its tragedy what happens when the individual fails to act as a proactive moral force in economic relations. The narratives of organised crime in this context thus become a significant part of the Russian tale of crime, economy and modernity, a tale that, as the proverb at the beginning of the chapter notes, shows 'the rest of the world how not to live'.

MUSING ON METHODS[21]

Without 'being there', seeing and experiencing Russia as it imploded into a heap of economic chaos then bulldozed its way out of the ruins of communism into the dubiously stable edifice of capitalism, the questions and problems this book intends to address would not have arisen, certainly not in my case. Being in the field, variously described as 'ethnography', has clear advantages especially where hidden and dangerous communities are concerned. Despite the obvious problems associated with research into illegal economies a wealth of information has been acquired taking the fieldwork approach, reaching into the parts secondary research fails to reach.[22] Yet there is a tendency for ethnographers and like-minded researchers to believe too strongly in their ability to grasp reality through these methods, certainly in comparison to theorists. Perhaps this is a way of compensating for the years in which 'ivory tower' scholars dominated intellectual inquiry, especially in the social sciences, when empirical work was seen to be a poor cousin. 'Seeing', as we well know, however, is not always believing and can misconstrue reality as much as 'armchair philosophising'. What we want to see, or are trained to see, will determine the view we take and the understanding we make of a situation, a community or a nation. During 2008 I made a number of trips to the Urals city of Perm with a group of architects for a project on development (I was focusing on the impact of a master plan on deviance and crime). Where they observed spaces, I observed the people that occupied them. Our readings of a given scenario reflected the individual purpose of the visit, against which we interpreted reality.

My purpose in conducting fieldwork back in the 1990s was to observe 'organised crime' or at least, what I thought (wanted?) it to be, without sufficient questioning of the term and its meaning(s), its political and ideological connotations. This came much later, after a relatively long period of musing over the material in the doctorate, and observing, both from a distance and close up, the path Russia was taking and who was doing the steering. The long term, however, is not something that rests easily with research these days. Pressures on individuals to publish according to a centrally determined quota, to come up with five-year research trajectories (an arbitrary time period or one proven to provide maximum output from planning, something Stalin knew instinctively) are turning research into a production-line activity. Fieldwork periods become shorter, and papers hurriedly written to meet the quantifiable criteria of 'excellence'. Further, much of the funded empirical work, which facilitates a greater turnover of articles, requires a policy orientation. Political utility over critical thinking is a worrying trend in many disciplines. Theorists, those who do most of the musing, appear to be a dying breed in the social sciences. According to the *Oxford English Dictionary*, musing has another meaning beyond the more obvious 'thoughtful', 'pensive' or 'absorbed'. Its origins come from the Old French *muser*, 'to waste time', a somewhat appropriate alternative in a world where rapid turnover becomes an aspiration and the prime mover of promotion and success.

The current research climate also requires a more formulaic approach to methods. The scattergun approach of much of my own early research would not pass muster in the rigorous standards we apply today. (In many ways I would have welcomed a more controlled and focused environment, as opposed to the *ad hoc* nature of interviews and the occasional resort to doorstepping.) Russia can be a notoriously unpredictable environment in which to conduct research, especially on matters relating to crime and criminal justice. Access to data, whether interviewees or secondary material, was dependent on a series of negotiation strategies in a culture I had knowledge of but at times felt uncomfortably alien to. The methods chapter in Laura Piacentini's work on Russian prisons is especially illustrative of awkward gendered negotiation processes, some of which challenged the principled stance a female researcher might take in more culturally familiar settings.[23] But the momentum of change that enveloped Russia during the 1990s brought with it a chaos that even the native found difficult to fix and understand, let alone an outsider. Challenging situations sometimes require anarchic methods, which is perhaps why researchers often avoid uncertainty and messiness. Formulas can guide, but they can also restrict.

Conversations with those who worked as pimps, prostitutes, racketeers, the police, the 'straight' business world, journalists, academics and, most importantly, those whose professional status had no direct bearing on the research but whose lives were lived as the harsh reality of failed communism and failing capitalism – the hostel cleaners, local shop and kiosk staff, the (sociable) *dezhurniye*, bar staff, the adult students whom I taught English, and a decade later the younger generation I force-fed Politics 'A' level to as part of their British curriculum, school colleagues and friends – all played an important part in attempting to construct a picture with at least a modicum of coherence. As formal devices, interviews gave one story, but the more relaxed, social settings of casual talk provided a colour, and even altered the outlines, of data acquired elsewhere. In a society where authoritarianism has impacted deeply into the psyche of its residents, 'off the record' offers a valuable contribution to the hidden storyline. Crime correspondent Andrei Konstantinov insisted that to 'know' Russia one had to learn to read between the lines, to find significance in what was absent, especially in relation to criminality. Missing years in a Russian biography can be as crucial as the visible data. To understand the links between illegal business and the legitimate world, the latter being the support system of the former, one needs to discover, or at least have in mind, the connecting links and myriad characters involved. More important for the non-Russian is the necessity to divest oneself of certain habits of thinking, or at least have a conscious awareness of cultural difference, otherwise we are in danger of imposing our own narratives on the story Russia is trying to tell. As Zinoviev wrote, 'the monstrous mistakes' Westerners make in their assessment of Russia is because 'they measure our life too according to their own yardstick'.[24]

2
Crime-Time Stories

Now, in 1989, our readers are no longer shocked by such words as 'Soviet mafia' and 'Soviet racket'. But when I started investigating into the 'Amur Wars' in the summer of 1987, these words were still unheard of and did not even appear in the press. Back in 1987, I had to explain to my readers what 'mafia' and 'racket' meant in general and what was special about their Soviet versions.

(V. Vitaliev, 1990)[1]

To understand what was happening in its corrupt and crime-ridden society during the final years of Soviet communism Russians turned to the West seeking definitions and explanations for a criminal phenomenon the authorities had hitherto denied existed. Vitaly Vitaliev's education of his Soviet readership (above) into the terminology of the criminal underworld as business rather than political banditry was an indication of the success of Soviet propaganda in its denial not only of the pervasive presence of illegal business but, by extension, of the growing pathological state of the economy. Years of glossing over the problems of the state-run economy, of shortages and poor-quality goods created by its inefficiency, had produced a thriving second economy to which most of the population turned as a means of acquiring their daily necessities. This unofficial economy was populated by a diverse set of characters. Some worked solo, others in more structured forms. None of the latter were referred to as 'organised crime' until *glasnost*, or 'openness', gave voice to the media, previously the exclusive mouthpiece of the Party, and allowed them to lift the lid on the underbelly of Soviet society.

Ideologically, it would have been dangerous to use the term 'organised crime', for according to Soviet criminology, this could only manifest in a capitalist society. Indeed, the notion that crime in general would be eventually eradicated in a communist state meant that official statistics on offending were never published, so politically sensitive were such data. Crime, as Engels had stated in his famous passage from *The Condition of the Working Class in England in 1844*, was the result of economic exploitation: 'Under the brutal and brutalising treatment of the bourgeoisie, the working-man

... becomes an offender as certainly as water abandons the fluid for the vaporous state at 80 degrees Reamur.'[2] Economic forms of crime, especially those of a structured nature, must therefore stand as an indictment of the dominant system. Organised crime was absent from the vocabulary of Soviet criminologists and the state-controlled media unless as a means of emphasising the problems of the capitalist West; until, that is, the transparency of the late 1980s.

The problem facing the media, politicians and the public as they began to realise the extent of the illegal economy was how to understand it, to try and make sense of what for many had been an unspoken part of their daily lives but for whom the bigger question of what it 'meant' in terms of the health of Soviet communism could never have been articulated. Denied the vocabulary needed to make sense of this pervasive second economy and its main protagonists, Soviet journalists, academics and the more progressive law enforcement personnel looked to their counterparts in Western capitalist states for the lexicon they lacked. However, it was not only the glossary of terms they imported from the West, but the accompanying political and social constructions of 'organised crime' and the 'mafia'. Many of these were hardly appropriate for the Soviet Union, given that entrepreneurial activities *per se* were proscribed there. But these terms and concepts were also a distortion of reality in capitalist societies. Albini commented that the notion of the 'mafia' in the US was little more than a 'mythological belief that excites the imagination, entertains the public, and draws attention away from real social issues'.[3] Ironically, in the Soviet context, the borrowed lexicon drew awkward attention *to* rather than away from very real social issues, but the crucial question lay in how these social problems were being interpreted. 'Organised crime' and 'mafia' labels ended up becoming political tools in an emerging conflict between the reformist and conservative factions of the ruling elite, a means of discrediting one's opponent and, in the more extreme cases, ensuring the annihilation of their careers and even lives.

Soviet academics followed behind journalists in their willingness to engage with the problem of the burgeoning illegal economy. Ahead of their Western counterparts in many ways by being prepared to strip the terminology back to the fundamentals, sociologists such as Azalea Dolgova drew together an eclectic mix of academics and practitioners to debate the thorny issue of defining 'organised crime' and related terms. In a roundtable discussion in 1989, published later in book form as *Organizovannaya Prestupnost'* (Organised

Crime), definitions and cultural interpretations specific to the Soviet situation, of criminal organisations and their activities, were hotly discussed. There was a general agreement that the broad definition put forward by Dolgova herself aptly summed up the situation in Soviet Russia, describing organised crime as 'a product of society, and as such has its own specific characteristics and a strong *reciprocal* influence on social life' (emphasis added).[4] There was now sufficient evidence to uphold the idea that the Soviet economy was in a pathological state, almost every sector of which was infected by crime and corruption. Illegal business was understood as a *consequence* of the failing official economy, the symptom rather than the cancer itself. In other words, it functioned in almost a Durkheimian sense, as a barometer of economic ill-health and an indicator of societal decomposition.[5]

For many critics of Soviet communism, the proliferation of criminal business testified to the corrupt state of the system and the elites who ran it. Hence writers such as Arkady Vaksberg, author of *The Soviet Mafia*, wrote confidently at the time: 'The mafia is intact because it grew up with the system and has become an inseparable part of it, which means that the mafia will only collapse when the whole edifice, i.e. the system itself, collapses.'[6] The premise was simple: replace the old regime with the more democratic principles of the market and the mafia problem will be noticeably lessened.

Organised crime or the mafia was now understood as an ideological as well as criminal phenomenon. The symbiotic relationship between communism and the underworld brought together a number of perceptions that linked orthodox narratives of each as told in the West, especially by Washington. Each phenomenon was infused with similar traits. They were 'alien', that is, foreign in a literal and metaphysical sense, to the realities of the narrators; conspiratorial, insofar as each was set upon the destruction of the values and systems which underpinned capitalist democracies; and monolithic, in other words, of extensive and ubiquitous proportions, straddling the globe and therefore imminently threatening to freedom-loving states and their institutions. Underlying both communism and organised crime were shared characteristics: moral vacuity, intrinsic violence and ruthless exploitation.

After the collapse of communism the optimistic prognosis for the implosion of the mafia proved to be spectacularly off-centre. Against the expectations of the majority, there occurred a massive explosion of illegal business and violence against a background of unrestrained entrepreneurial activity. The free market at its freest, the supposed antidote to the criminogenic impulses of Soviet communism, nurtured an economic environment in which those characteristics deemed exclusive to illegal entrepreneurship found a natural home in the *laissez-faire* ethos advised by the West. Few were prepared to acknowledge that the narratives of organised crime enthusiastically applied to Soviet communism might have equal validity to the capitalist model of economy. Storytelling was to become notoriously complicated as orthodox understandings of organised crime were challenged by the 'new' Russia. So what were these familiar narratives?

NARRATIVES OF DISENGAGEMENT

The most influential narratives of organised crime have come from the US, both as fact and fiction, shaping government directives around the globe in the fight against international crime and moulding public perceptions through the silver screen. At the core of the majority of these diverse portrayals and representations lie fundamental traits which are adapted according to time and context. They can best be summed up by the definition of organised crime offered in the 1967 US *Task Force Report: Organized Crime*:

> Organized crime is a society that seeks to operate outside the control of the American people and their governments. It involves thousands of criminals, working within structures as complex as those of any large corporation, subject to laws more rigidly enforced than those of legitimate governments. Its actions are not impulsive but rather the result of intricate conspiracies, carried on over many years and aimed at gaining control over whole fields of activity in order to amass huge profits.[7]

Hierarchical, conspiratorial, monolithic, ruthless profit-seeking, hostile and at variance with the dominant norms of its indigenous society – these are the characteristics that have come to represent what is meant by 'organised crime'. These traits are not simply technical descriptions of illegal or criminal business, but assume a set of norms, values and aspirations intrinsic to the concept of organised crime. Further, they stand in contradiction to those existing across the legal divide. In other words, the dominant narrative of organised crime understands it as 'alien', or 'other', apart from and antithetical to 'decent', 'normal' society. It was not always thus.

Mike Woodiwiss's study of media representations in the US, one of the greatest influences on the public understanding of organised crime, noted little or no reference to crime structures, or that most popular manifestation of alienation – ethnicity in the Hollywood industry during the 1920s and early 1930s. Instead, high-profile actors such as Edward G. Robinson and James Cagney interpreted their gangster characters in a way that 'reinforced some of the country's most deeply held myths about individual, entrepreneurial success'.[8] Their ruthless entrepreneur image drew on a familiar rather than a conflicting set of values. Despite the 'crime doesn't pay' message behind films such as *Little Caesar* and *The Public Enemy*, it was the brutality of business as much as its underworld setting that the characters played to. As Woodiwiss explains, this sympathetic portrayal appealed to an audience whose relationship with illegal business had been inadvertently encouraged by Prohibition. Seizing the numerous business opportunities available from the ban on alcohol, the entrepreneurial-minded provided bootleg liquor for a thirsty population, endearing rather than alienating the public. All this changed following the repeal of the Volstead Act (Prohibition) when criminal business ceased to function as an important complement to the official market. Media portrayals increasingly adopted a propagandising tone, garnering support in the fight against crime. There was a sea change too in official discourses. Dwight Smith looked into the focus and rhetoric of early government investigations into illegal business in the US. The Wickersham Commission of 1929 was tasked with looking at 'law observance in the whole country' and to determine 'In what section is there an undue condition of lawlessness?'[9] An attempt was also made to discover where the cost of crime might be the greatest. As part of its conclusions, the Commission noted:

It must be emphasized that the criminal frauds which cause the largest losses are organized schemes, carried on as regular business, and, in many of the more serious cases, masquerading as legitimate business enterprises. Such criminal schemes shade off by imperceptible degrees into enterprises which are so conducted as to avoid criminal liability although employing unethical or even illegal methods of doing business. And the *line between criminal and non-criminal activity is thus frequently a rather arbitrary one* ... the typical criminal of this class is not the recidivist but the *business man gone wrong*.[10] (emphasis added)

Had this perception endured, its application to the situation in post-Soviet Russia would have had far greater currency and arguably provoked a more intelligent and effective response to the chaos of the 1990s, providing a broader framework for understanding the economic problems – both criminal *and* legal – that were tearing the country apart. The Wickersham Commission's findings largely fell on deaf ears. The change of administration in 1932 and the abrogation of the Volstead Act a year later brought with it a different ethos and a public moral cohesion that focused on the dichotomy rather than similarity between criminal and legitimate business. Less than 20 years later, this split was given even greater emphasis as ethnicity was brought centre stage in the presiding narrative on organised crime.

The Kefauver Committee of 1951–52, set up to investigate interstate gambling, brought into the criminal lexicon the term 'mafia', and with it a whole series of assumptions about the nature of illegal business. Tapping into the prevailing mood of xenophobia during the early Cold War years of the post-war period,[11] the Committee's report identified the existence of 'a shadowy, international criminal organization known as the "Mafia"' which acted as an arbiter for 'the local mobs which make up the national crime syndicate … milking and perverting society for their own gains'.[12] The significance of these conclusions was strengthened by the fact that the hearings were transmitted to the nation through the popular new medium of television, thus familiarising a huge audience with the concept of the dangerous criminal 'other'. Introducing the ethnic card also served to further disengage criminal business from its legal counterpart and obfuscate the common interface between the two. 'Who' rather than 'what' became the defining factor of risk and the focus of law enforcement; in this case, American-*Italian* criminals. It was a concept easily transferred to other minority communities in the country. Not surprisingly, in its recommendations, the Committee urged the government to toughen up immigration policies and bring more efficiency into the deportation of foreign criminals 'who make a mockery of the laws of the land'.[13]

These ethnic designations have continued to dominate official discourse, as in the reference to Colombian cartels, Chinese Triads, Jamaican Yardies, Japanese Yakuza, Russian, Albanian and Bulgarian Mafias. Clearly ethnicity *does* play a role in criminal enterprise. Daniel Bell's famous study into organised crime showed how ethnic crime acts as part of the process of assimilation by those members of immigrant groups for whom the legitimate means of material success are unobtainable, what he refers to as a 'queer ladder of social mobility'.[14] Others have pointed to the manipulation of ethnic stereotyping by crime groups themselves as a means of advancing business and status: 'at one extreme of the spectrum individual gangsters use their ethnic reputation to their own advantage; and at the other extreme, entire crime syndicates use ethnicity for political mobilization'.[15] There is a clear logic behind ethnic affiliations as communication and trust are often made possible through a common language and a shared understanding of customs and traditions (although in many instances, these commonalities can cross ethnic identity into other shared attributes). But official narratives of 'alien conspiracy' concentrate less on the business logic behind these relationships and more on the threat they assume to be intrinsic to the 'otherness' of ethnicity. It is this latter aspect which has informed debates and understanding of collaborative criminal enterprise, and imbued the concept of organised crime with a dangerousness built on difference.

The Kefauver Committee's assignation of criminal threat as the ethnic 'other' continues to resonate within official circles, and has become even more potent in the global context. The collapse of communism heralded the notion of a *Pax mafiosa*, a worldwide collaboration between various ethnic and national crime groups.[16] This presupposes vast and complex levels of organisation, a centralised administration and the ability to access from a distance local operators who have the knowledge of markets and distribution within their own jurisdictions. Alan Wright cautions against accepting a rational integration of criminal enterprise on a global scale:

> Here again, we have to take care not to over-rationalise the organisational structures of these groups. Although they may be proliferating and may cooperate in some arenas, this does not mean that an international organisation structure enables them to do so. Given the extent to which these groups continue to work independently in many cases, we are entitled to remain sceptical as to whether the *pax mafiosa* or 'merger' theses represents the reality of international organised crime at the turn of the century.[17]

There is little evidence to support the idea of global organised criminal business, and yet alien conspiracy theory has retained its hold on the official and public consciousness, given a boost by the events of 9/11. Attention is now focused not only on organised crime as a global threat but on terrorism, this latest version also resplendent with ethnic, religious and ideological labels of 'otherness'. The worst possible scenario for alien conspiracy theorists is an organised crime–terrorist nexus. In 2005 Louise Shelley presented this double-evil setting to the US authorities, warning that 'criminal groups in the former Soviet Union are not averse to working with terrorists, and often the two groups feel that they have common enemies'.[18] That this pairing is possible is not in dispute. What is debatable, however, is the implied scale of danger to the international community, as opposed to the very real threat of these liaisons to local communities. Hence Western-centric narratives of alien threat and danger which dominate the discourse on entrepreneurial crime (and terrorism) displace concerns and resources away from the areas they would best be deployed – the tangible and local – towards an intangible space, holding to account an easily 'readable' but amorphously constructed group or community. Ironically, in doing this, they intensify the very problems they purport to identify and aim to eradicate, not for themselves but for those most likely to suffer the consequences of these collaborations.

Why, we might ask, has alien conspiracy theory found such fertile ground in American politics and culture, and in doing so, been transmitted globally as one of the dominant narratives of organised crime? And what bearing does this have on the importation of these discourses to the Russian context? In his essay 'The Paranoid Style in American Politics', Richard Hofstadter charts the predilection towards the 'heated exaggeration, suspiciousness and conspiratorial fantasy'[19] of a nation which constantly defines itself according to a Manichean world of good and evil, seeing itself as 'the brightest beacon for freedom and opportunity in the world'.[20] It is this 'American mythic vision' which, according to Hofstadter and others, has largely defined the country's identity and its role as military leader in world affairs and global policeman in the fight against crime. According to Sardar and Davies, the vision comprises 'morality tales in which the idea of America is pure and perfect, and the American self is innocent and good'.[21] This notion is exported not only through foreign policy but through media imagery, both fact and fictional, often framed in simplistic binaries, such as those of the 'good' and 'bad' guys in genres such as the western. The discourse of war is especially apt at creating this neat dichotomy. Declarations of 'war', against organised crime, terrorism, drugs (even poverty), dress up the underlying and more complex aetiologies behind these issues as simplistic choices between 'us' and 'them', the innocent and the blameworthy framing the divide according to geography, culture, ethnicity, religion, ideology, and so on. Any identification with the hostile 'other' thus becomes a betrayal of the declared values asserted by those who create the divide, the narrators of this Manichean world. Or, to put it another way, 'You're either with us, or against us.'

Subsequent Presidential commissions on organised crime have reiterated this paradigm of the 'other' and, in the last couple of decades of the twentieth century, extended it to the international arena. Prior to the events of 9/11, the Bush administration declared that 'combating transnational crime is one of the newest and most important diplomatic interests of the United States',[22] once again appealing to the mythic vision of American goodness and innocence under attack. Alongside terrorism, *transnational* organised crime (TOC) now identifies the great danger from 'without', a convenient replacement for the communist threat. In doing so it has provided a legitimacy to policing as well as military incursions into other states by powerful nations as a means of securing control over crime-fighting strategies at local as well as international levels.[23] So too has the climate of fear nurtured by narratives of TOC given greater legitimacy to a range of immigration policies, including those which facilitate deportation. While immigration continues to be aligned with organised crime, the focus has moved away from the American-Italian gangster onto other ethnic groups as presenting the clear and present danger to US security. Russian-speaking criminals (sometimes collectively referred to as 'Eurasian organised crime', a regionally broad term encompassing crime groups from Eastern Europe, Russia and Central Asia) continue to be regarded by the Federal Bureau of Investigation as a destabilising force, despite the fact that the sobering conclusions of studies such as Finckenauer and Waring's show that 'the facts do not support the proposition that Soviet émigrés currently constitute an organized crime threat to the United States'.[24]

Mythic visions of self and paranoia are not confined to America. Alien conspiracy narratives of organised crime sit comfortably in Russia's culture too. Its sense of a unique Slavonic destiny and the unfortunate xenophobic traditions that have often accompanied this self-perception, play into the hostile binaries central to this particular narrative. Russia, as victim of the ethnic card in other states, has used it domestically and in more brutal ways, against its own ethnic minorities (see Chapter 5). Once admitted into the official lexicon, organised crime became politicised, and, as in the

US, was employed as a rhetorical device in the numerous power struggles within the higher echelons. In the early post-Soviet years, its usage by both erstwhile superpower enemies amounted to little more than hyperbolic excuses for the disastrous unfolding of shock therapy or ambiguously grand promises to tackle the crime problem, garnering support for further funding of agencies either too corrupt or incapable of tackling what was actually a crisis *within* rather than outside the legal economy. The nature and extent of this crisis was further concealed behind the other popular narrative of organised crime as 'dangerous business'.

BUSINESS MATTERS

Michael Levi's description of organised crime as 'a set of people whom the police and other agencies of the State, regard or wish us to regard as "really dangerous" to its essential integrity'[25] captures the essence of the perceived disengagement between legal and illegal business. Danger invariably lies 'out there', away from the familiar and banal. In reality, the legal business/organised crime divide is often a whispered form of alien conspiracy, one that finds itself rooted in the binaries of legality rather than identity, though the latter still plays an important part. 'Their' business is not 'ours'. It remains distinct from legal business by virtue of the mode of its execution rather than the motivation behind it. The Council of Europe, in what is a standardised understanding, defines organised crime as:

> ... the illegal activities carried out by structured groups of three or more persons existing for a prolonged period of time and having the aim of committing serious crimes through concerted action by using intimidation, violence, corruption or other means in order to obtain, directly or indirectly, a financial or other material benefit.[26]

This emphasis on wealth acquisition moves away from alien conspiracy emphasising the 'what' over the 'who'. Nonetheless, there still exists a strongly emphatic moral dissonance between legal and illegal business through the use of descriptors such as 'intimidation', 'violence' and 'corruption'. It is assumed that criminal business employs these techniques almost as a matter of course, although the actual use of violence is frequently avoided as it can attract unwanted attention.[27] Nonetheless, the possibility of arbitrary forms of violence as a substitute for regulated forms of violence remains implicit in asserting control by those operating outside the boundaries of the state. Presented as the defining characteristics of the behaviour of organised crime groups, the inference is that they are absent in legal business conduct. And in those instances when respectable businesses are found guilty of employing similar techniques (there is no shortage of examples[28]), their activities are described as 'corporate' crimes rather than organised crime, even if they tick all the required boxes for defining organised crime. The disassociation is then completed by the reference to the guilty as 'bad apples' in an otherwise sound barrel, thus preserving the moral status of their inhabited legal world. In reality, the modern economy, however, does not encourage disassociation. Its labyrinthine networks and complex system of division of labour confound the notion that an 'overworld' and underworld exist in parallel. While the former can operate autonomously, the latter is inescapably hooked into the legal economy for the opportunities it creates (or denies) to the criminal entrepreneur. Indeed, for criminal business to expand its profits and influence it must be able to move in and out of the legal sector, traversing myriad boundaries in equally diverse situations inhabited by residents of eclectic backgrounds. In this context criminal entrepreneurs are no more invasive than any other business types trying the hard sell, no different in their aspirations to the multinationals, medium and small businesses with whom the consuming public interact daily.

Closer inspection of the consumer's behaviour also refutes the notion that there exist emphatic differences between legal and illegal economies. The proliferating trade in pirated entertainment, such as DVDs, depends on a consuming public willing to purchase from illegal traders and law enforcement and regulation agencies prepared to turn a blind eye. The purchase of counterfeit goods is especially attractive to the regular client in a market society, following, as it does, the capitalist ethos of endless consuming which involves, for the most part, buying as cheaply as one can, hence the mantras that constantly urge us to 'save 50 per cent' or 'buy one, get one free'. Illicit business depends on this large degree of willing, albeit tacit, cooperation across the legal divide. Part of this arrangement involves making invisible the brutalities upon which some of the trades are based so that the 'respectable' consumer can purchase with a relatively clear conscience (even if he or she is vaguely aware of the possibility of violence). Stag-night celebrations in a brothel in Prague would clearly be ruined by the bruised bodies of women beaten and raped into submission.[29] The 'goods', as in any sales transaction, need to be attractive and pleasing to the consumer.

A further message implicit in the legal/illegal business divide presumes not only an exclusivity of bad behaviour by criminal entrepreneurs, as, for example, their corrupting influence on the powerful in legitimate society, but that this type of conduct generally works one way. Innocence becomes an assumed attribute of the legal. However, as Lupsha points out, the divide is a lot less clear once greed is factored in: 'transnational organized criminals do not have to be geniuses, for smart, supposedly legitimate businessmen and entrepreneurs beat a path to their door with new ideas, technologies, techniques and investment opportunities to enrich themselves while furthering the business of transnational organized crime'.[30] Indeed, there is, according to Ruggiero, a continuous movement across the legal divide as mutual interests are served through the transmission of a number of capabilities held by different entre-preneurial populations: 'learning processes appear to cross the boundaries of social groups, as criminal know-how is transmitted to a variety of actors. In other words, techniques are exchanged and skills enhanced within an economic arena inhabited by legal, semi-legal and illegal businesses'.[31] These boundaries are further blurred in the transnational context of criminal enterprise. Despite the attempts to standardise understandings and approaches, as in the United Nations Convention Against Transnational Organized Crime 2000,[32] there remain jurisdictional disparities and cultural idiosyncrasies which help facilitate these reciprocal arrangements across the legal and illegal divide, arrangements that are clearly exploited by *both* sides.

The greatest incidence of these liaisons is obviously more evident in endemically corrupt or 'weak' states such as Russia and African countries where the rule of law has been jettisoned, if it ever existed. When the state loses control over the monopoly of violence, this can lead *inter alia* to an economic free-for-all, entailing the indiscriminate use of coercion and violent behaviour in property accumulation, leaving the country and its inhabitants vulnerable to physical harm and financial ruin. Gambetta's study of illegal private protection in Sicily demonstrates that in the absence of effective protection of commercial property rights and a breakdown of trust in the state, the Mafia assumed a monopoly of illegitimate violence in the region. It was able to guarantee its service not only through the use of violence but by the reputation it built on having access to and the ability of this provision.[33] A similar scenario can be found in countries such as Colombia and Afghanistan, two of the largest producers of cocaine and opium respectively. But the perception of what are termed 'weak' or 'failed' states[34] (now listed according to an annual index of Failed States[35]) can distract attention away from relationships that link criminal states to respectable business and politics in enduring states such as Britain, France, and the US. The reality is that many of these failed states are often sustained in their failure by the very countries that brand them thus. Examples of intimate liaisons involving the economically great and politically good with the bad and ugly underworld in democratic states have been uncovered by serious journalism and discussed by a number, albeit relatively small, of academic studies.[36] The arms trade is a typical example of these *liaisons dangereuses*. Naylor's study of the black market in arms dealing provides an uncomfortable insight into the fusion between legal and illegal actors and associations, where the law (domestic or international) is routinely circumvented by the guardians of a state's national security, with the tacit approval of the political leadership:

> Covert arms deals were (and are) an essential part of the art of clandestine statecraft at times when the formal government apparatus must have deniability. For example, when the world shook its public head in horror at atrocities in the Balkans and slapped on a general arms embargo, German intelligence sold arms out of old East German army stockpiles to gunrunners acting for the Croatian secret service while the CIA kept watch.[37]

In the complex international world of economics and politics, it is easier to hide the less than savoury activities of legitimate bodies than it is within a single jurisdiction.

Geographical distance, convoluted business links and the inaccessibility to reliable sources of data information, especially in failed states run by authoritarian regimes, can provide a convenient cover for the murky fusion of licit and illicit. Nor is this confined to the more obvious trade in arms. Drug smuggling, human trafficking, money-laundering and other illegal activities frequently involve similar actors operating across familiar routes and within the same networks as those in the arms business. These also interface with the interests and representatives of corporate business and government when expedient to do so, and not only in the occasional 'bad apple' way. Hence foreign policy can involve the manipulation of criminal groups by interference in external states. First world interests often lie in the destabilisation or maintenance of domestic factions sympathetic to their economic and political agendas, by supplying arms to the 'favoured' rebels or dictatorships, or covertly financing or turning a blind eye to the narcotics trade whose profits support the preferred faction. 'Thus, the essence of a black market transaction', as Naylor succinctly writes in relation to the arms industry (but equally applicable to other business), 'is summed up by the fact that black is not a color; it is the absence of light.'[38]

The narratives implicit in the legal/illegal business divide as currently constructed can also disguise the functional role criminal enterprise plays in rule of law states when sections of society are marginalised or excluded by the dominant economy from essential services and opportunities. For example, denied access to the legitimate provision of loans by banks and other high street lenders, especially in times of acute economic hardship, society's most vulnerable often turn to loan sharks. Despite the crippling charges on the loans, many of their clients/victims regard them positively, and have refused to report them to the authorities for fear of losing the only source of credit available to them.[39] Hence the role of the loan shark in terms of the *services* offered is that of banker. Objections to a direct comparison between legal and criminal business are usually based on the level of harm inflicted by the latter and, in the absence of any regulatory bodies to which such business is accountable, the fact that illegal businesses can and do act with impunity. It goes without question that loan sharking is an especially pernicious and exploitative business, employing intimidation and violence as a means of extracting debts from the desperate. But harm in an economic context is difficult to ringfence. Its origins, as in this case, can be traced back to the legal sector – the harm of exclusion based on the interests not of the vulnerable individual, but of the strong. The relationship between the legal and illegal here is less proactive than that described in the arms trade but exists nonetheless, insofar as one side sustains the other through its actions. When an economic system inflicts harm, especially on its most vulnerable, it is clearly failing. In this sense, all that separates the failed from the enduring state in terms of criminality is a question of degree, the extent to which the dominant system provides opportunities for criminal enterprise and has control over this provision.

The assumptions underlying what we regard as legal and illegal economy are based on the extent to which economic behaviour is regarded as socially advantageous or harmful. The question, however, is, for whom? The implicit tenor of legality is that those acts designated illegal are more harmful than those that are not. But as the Soviet experiment with communism has shown and the current crisis of free market capitalism makes clear, harm is not necessarily a yardstick for proscription. Instead, what we have is a moral rupture between legality and outcomes, a rupture that is concealed by the narratives that distance legal and illegal economic behaviour, narratives that sustain their message through labels such as 'organised crime' and 'mafia', by drawing attention away from *outcomes*. It is to the concept of harm and its role in understanding the stories we tell about the modern economy that we now turn.

IN HARM'S WAY

Unrestrained by social constructions of crime, theories of harm focus on the injurious outcomes of certain actions irrespective of their legal designations and the status of those who have perpetrated the acts. If the aim of criminal justice is to protect the public within its respective jurisdictions, the harm paradigm makes it clear that proscribed acts and punishments meted out for legal violations are highly subjective and often unrepresentative of the level of damage inflicted on individuals and their environment. Paddy Hillyard et al. argue convincingly in favour of incorporating harm into criminological debates which, for the main part, blatantly fail to tackle a whole series of activities that create the instability, insecurity and fear generally attributed to 'crime'. For, as Hillyard states, 'it is not simply that a focus on crime *deflects* attention from other more socially pressing, harms – in many respects, it positively *excludes* them'.[40]

In an economic environment this observation invites us to consider the impact of business, consumers, producers and other actors involved in the complex division of labour determining the modern economy. It is not just a question of considering the harms caused by what we refer to as organised, corporate or white-collar *crimes,* but those inflicted as a consequence of *legal* economic interactions. We need to expand the discussion beyond that of cocaine users in the city, the growing demand for pornography and prostitutes, slave labour and those other services and commodities the state might choose not to legislate in favour of, to the consequences of legal demands and provision resulting in harm to others. This moves the debate into the contentious area of morality, those 'intrinsic questions of right and wrong, the good and the bad, obligation and duty, consequences and intentions'.[41] It is a world criminologists usually prefer not to inhabit, messy and riddled with subjectivity and inexactitude as it is. But in an environment as changeable as Russia's, where entrepreneurship was illegal one minute, even punishable by death, and legal the next and where in the 'new Russia' state policies on economic development, many of them endorsed (and even encouraged) by Western advisers and governments, have been responsible for more injustice and suffering than any amount of illegal business, the inclusion of harm and its uncomfortable moral discourse is not only desirable but essential. In this way the acts themselves are the central feature; the entrepreneurial rather than the illegal becomes the focal point.

One of the major objections to this approach rests on the concept of *mens rea*. The prosecution in a criminal case must prove that an individual had the *intention* (guilty mind) and *knowledge* of the offence being committed. The absence of intention has long been a mitigating claim by corporate bodies when hauled up in court after a 'disaster' or 'accident' in which lives were lost. For Reiman, however, the emphasis on intention, which presumes a known or understood target or victim, is morally unsustainable. In his example of the 'mine executive who cuts safety corners', and who 'wanted to harm no-one in particular', Reiman argues that in failing to ensure total compliance with safety regulations, 'he *knew his acts were likely to harm someone* – and once someone is harmed, the victim is someone in particular'.[42] In the knowledge of *possible* harm and the failure to prevent it, the executive displayed a general disdain towards any number of anonymous others, those with whom he had no contact or knowledge, making his omission even more inexcusable. This point is further emphasised by the fact that each year more people are killed or seriously injured through this type of negligence, or omission, than by homicide.[43] (Italian corporate law, which deals with 'imagined consequences',[44] comes close to instigating the type of responsibility Reiman implies, though the absence of any notably successful prosecution under this Act, ratified over five years ago, underlines the reluctance to go down this particular path.) Where harmful acts on a scale and magnitude of the Bhopal disaster, in which approximately 15–20,000 people died as a direct result of a toxic gas leak from the Union Carbide factory, can evade criminal prosecution,[45] conversely, those labelled 'organised criminals', some of whose acts have beneficial consequences, such as the use of 'dirty money' to build schools and hospitals in the poorer quarters of

Colombia,[46] do not find official punitive responses mitigated by these acts.

The inability to successfully prosecute corporate business for the harmful consequences of its activities is, in large measure, down to the emphasis on individual agency as a central concept of liberal criminal justice. But the allocation of responsibility is blatantly inequitably applied within the criminal justice system. In some jurisdictions legal violations by individuals acting collaboratively as part of a criminal group incur sanctions more severe than for individuals who commit the same act but operate solo. Recent moves in UK law to tighten up the criteria for 'conspiracy' suggest that if a person agrees to commit an offence even where he or she 'suspects' but does not 'know' or 'intend' it to be part of collaborative criminal conduct, as with the laundering of money, then he or she should be regarded as guilty of conspiracy.[47] Responsibility thus falls on the individual *and* his collective persona. On the other hand, with corporate offences 'the difficulty in defining "the mind and the will" of the corporation ... and who can held to be the "embodiment" of the company'[48] can let off those whose company could be 'responsible' for the deaths and injuries of hundreds or thousands. Despite the introduction in the UK of the Corporate Manslaughter and Corporate Homicide Act, which places greater responsibility for deaths related to activities by legal corporations on senior management, the relatively mild punitive forms of sanctions and the absence of appropriately severe powers to be granted to regulatory bodies have removed many teeth from the Act.[49] In contrast, the passing of the Serious Organised Crime and Police Act in 2005, tasked to counter the growing threat of criminal business, set up the Serious and Organised Crime Agency with powers that go beyond those of accountable agencies such as the police. The Agency's ability to access legislation, such as the Proceeds of Crime Act, in the fight against serious and organised crime, according to one Law Lord, in the absence of judicial oversight has turned it into a 'truly frightening and draconian piece of legislation where the rights of the individual come a distant second to those of the state'.[50]

This unbalanced response to the harmful consequences of acts, some which clearly impact on greater numbers and with greater severity than others but are dealt with according to legally defined and morally limited criteria, lies at the heart of Hillyard et al.'s thesis. The point made over and over again is that *harmful outcomes* must be given greater significance in criminological discourse. In the organised crime debate, in particular, the arbitrary nature of the criminal classification of business, and an obsession with the status of the actor rather than the act, requires this inclusion of harm. Once the debate moves away from personality, from ideology, ethnicity (or religion) as significant determinants in criminal behaviour, and begins to include the broader and messier moral question of outcomes, the dividing line between the 'businessman gone wrong' and the gangster is less clear. As Smith observes, 'if businessmen and gangsters behave like each other, what is the sense in having two categories that, by definition, are not mutually exclusive?'[51] Hence, in understanding the significance of narratives of organised crime and the attendant ambiguities which emerge from its various cultural and historical settings, this broader framework is crucial. Not only does it ask us to deconstruct the meaning of the term 'organised crime', it also helps to explain the context of its usage and provide a more self-critical approach to agendas behind these narratives.

RESPONSIBILITY AND THE INDIVIDUAL

The harm paradigm, as expressed above, is often sited within the Marxist critique of capitalism, for obvious reasons. Many of the abuses referred to are the result of neo-liberalist driven policies, which continue to perpetrate and endorse a range of harmful and violent acts against increasingly vulnerable populations. Poverty, disenfranchisement and crime have become inevitable by-products of an economic model, which demands servitude to free market principles and has no scruples about punishing resistance. However, while much of this discourse is placed in an ideological context, to limit the understanding of this paradigm to such a context can short-change its valuable contribution to the debates on crime and harm. Clearly there are significant structural factors – political, economic, ideological, religious, and so on – which shape conditions beneficial or inimical to individual moral agency, and it is crucial to understand the conditions under which each harmful act or collusion with such an act prevails. Nevertheless, in critiquing mainstream accounts of crime from the stance of social harm, especially as regards the economy, it is equally important to place the individual centre stage as the agent of moral action from which an understanding of the particular external conditions on agency can be assessed. In this, the book follows Bauman's assertion that 'the autonomy of moral behaviour is *final and irreducible*' (emphasis added).[52] Social organisation might indeed produce conditions conducive or not to the display of moral autonomy, but it is not the *source* of moral deliberation and subsequent conduct; that, and the subsequent accountability for the consequences of one's conduct, lies in the domain of the individual. In his study of the Holocaust, in all its unimaginable horror and the daily challenges to humanity at its most basic, Bauman considers how the unbearable moral choices facing ordinary people under the Third Reich – Jews as well as Germans – not only elicited what might be regarded as a rational response towards self-survival, even if this meant the betrayal of one's family and friends, but, flying in the face of an apparent deterministic drive towards these principles of self-preservation, drew out of some the ultimate sacrifice:

> putting self-preservation above moral duty is in no way predetermined, inevitable or inescapable. One can be pressed to do it, but one cannot be forced to do it, and thus one cannot really shift the responsibility for doing it on those who exerted the pressure. *It does not matter how many people chose moral duty over the rationality of self-preservation – what does matter is that some did.*[53]

In other words, in extreme situations such as the Holocaust, the ability of those few to choose 'moral duty over the rationality of self-preservation' indicates an inherent capacity for free, morally inspired action; that is, the ability for each individual irrespective of external conditions to place the 'other' above one's self, and in doing so to ultimately take full responsibility for the consequences of one's actions. This is in no way meant as a denial of the influences that obstruct the propensity for free moral action nor to demean the impact that fear can have on the human condition. Clearly there are gradations of autonomy. An academic living in a democratic system has more freedom to act according to his or her conscience and avoid acts that produce harmful outcomes than those caught up in a war zone or struggling in poverty. Yet, as Bauman points out, while external factors are significant, we cannot abandon the moral impulse to absolute determinism.

While liberal legal systems operate on this very principle of free choice and hence individual responsibility, when related to certain forms of economic behaviour and legislation they are hardly consistent in this view. The disposition of the law and society is distinctly irrational in its contradictory application to crimes committed by respectable actors working in the legal economic sector and those operating outside it, irrespective of the extent of the harmful outcomes. In the majority of criminal cases, despite the centrality of individual responsibility, mitigating circumstances are taken into account when determining the level of responsibility that can be reasonably expected of the defendant at the time of an alleged violation. Crucially, this is reflected in sentencing decisions. However, the attitudes to so-called white-collar and corporate crimes and those designated organised crime by the criminal justice system, as discussed above, reflect the arbitrary interpretation of mitigation and responsibility. The corporate executive, the company lawyer, foreman or shopfloor worker arguably has more freedom, relative to his or her status, to 'choose moral duty' over self-interest than his or her illegal counterparts. Even those at the bottom rung of the corporate ladder, in a half-way functioning democracy, have access to some form of support system, whether trade unions or similar bodies, that allows them a degree of freedom to act with some level of accountability or seek redress if they are thwarted in this. And yet, when a corporate business is responsible for injury or even death, the law often defers to a diffusion of responsibility, folding in on itself because intention cannot be proven satisfactorily.[54] On the other hand, many (but by no means all) of those who participate in illegal business do so only as a last resort, in the absence of legal employment opportunities or as a means of escaping a vicious cycle of poverty.[55] The illicit nature of the group allows more authoritarian forms of management that cannot be offset by recourse to a union-like support system, leaving the less powerful in the group susceptible to constraints in their moral choices. For many of those involved in illegal business, especially in small geographical areas known to the more powerful operators, freedom to act according to one's conscience is further challenged by the potential harm that can be done to relatives or friends of the minor players.

The broad sweep of the UK conspiracy law, and the tendency for sentences across a number of jurisdictions to be more severe for crimes committed by those within or attached to an illegal organisation in contrast to the dilution of punitive responses to those involved in crimes committed by a legal economic organisation, reiterate the message of official narratives of organised crime. Constructed identity rather than tangible reality determines the nature of the law and its implementation in the economic realm. Responsibility is arbitrarily defined and often bears no relation to harmful outcomes. But this is nothing new to the Russian people.

MORALITY, ECONOMY AND CRIME

On the face of it, issues of individual accountability, crime and economy seem incongruous in a country such as Russia, dominated as it has been for centuries, and now gradually returning to, authoritarian rule. Yet it is in Russia that the orthodox narratives of organised crime, so readily transported from the West as a mode of explanation for or comparison with indigenous criminality, have met their most critical test. Ironically, it is because authoritarianism has been a consistent part of its social and cultural landscape, and that the concept of the individual as a rights bearing, morally autonomous entity has been largely absent in its history, that makes Russia an important case study in how we understand and read the narratives of organised crime and the broader meanings they hold in relation to modern legal economy. In other words, Russia as the site of two economic experiments – communism and capitalism – in which individual accountability has been glaringly absent, provides us with an insight into the possible consequences of economies without morality; that is, when responsibility is structurally determined or so diffused within the system that it becomes, in Bauman's terms, 'free floating'.

The analogy with the Holocaust and the negative impact of the modern economy is not as far-fetched as it might initially seem. Similar circumstances to those that facilitated the mass execution of the Jewish people – division of labour, rational determinism and the consequences of these phenomena on the human condition; that is, the propensity for 'free floating' responsibility – endure within modern economy. Millions have died as a consequence of the pursuit of economic ideals, and while not as clinically and directly intentional as the extermination of an entire population, these deaths have been probabilities, even inevitabilities, packaged as 'collateral damage' that results from self-interest and indifference. The economy as the material manifestation of human existence, of our fundamental needs and subsequent desires which in 'normal' circumstances are individualised according to taste (what we consume) and capability (how we produce), can in the modern economy only be realised within an economic community. It is therefore incumbent upon the individual as a member of this community to hold some form of responsibility as to the outcomes of these needs and, most certainly, desires on fellow members. In fact, the opposite has been the case in both communism and capitalism, as each has subjugated individual accountability to the deterministic structures of their respective systems.

In Russia, this situation has been especially acute. The absence of individual accountability and hence moral autonomy provided fertile soil for untold abuses driven by economic and political ideals that bore little relation to the reality they were creating. Lenin made it quite clear where the source of morality should lie in Soviet communism:

> We reject any morality based on extra-human and extra-class concepts. We say that this is deception, dupery, stultification of the workers and peasants in the interests of the landowners and capitalists ... Our morality stems from the interests of the class struggle of the proletariat ... That is why we say that to us there is no such thing as a morality that stands outside human society; that is a fraud.[56]

But in the absence of a counterbalance of individual conscience and resistance, acts and outcomes are read in terms of their usefulness to an amorphous collective, to everyone and therefore to no *one* individual. In this mass of unidentifiable persons (of which we are all one), harm becomes relative. Ends justify an array of destructive means. In economic life, the negative consequences of our actions are thus diffused into a space of collective culpability in which we are forever seeking an 'other' to blame, where the 'other' can never be each and every one of us.[57] Scapegoats are readily available, and indeed encouraged, in a system that lacks accountability of the self. The narratives of organised crime create the ideal scapegoat.

Organised crime as a concept is the antithesis of responsibility and moral concern over the well-being of others. The narratives we construct around it serve to distance the horrors of starvation, poverty, violence and human degradation from the banally respectable existence of our everyday economic life, horrors that must ultimately find their origin in legal economic activity. It acts as the doppelganger of the individual self and our organisational structures in economic life. Yet behind the tales we tell of organised crime as the economically depraved 'other' is a bigger story and one that Russia has been telling us for decades, although even the Russians themselves (or many of them) have failed to read it clearly. The presence and growth of the illegal economy, of its myriad inhabitants – consumers, producers, managers, facilitators of all descriptions – is clearly a problem, but not a threat in the traditional sense, as revealed in the narratives of organised crime. Irrespective of whether solo operators or collaborative groups or networks drive it, criminal enterprise tells the tale, or indeed a number of tales, about its legal counterpart, of its healthy or pathological state. The actual threat comes from within, from the occupants within the system that generates the illegal economy.

Organised crime, better explained as criminal enterprise, is a very real phenomenon, one that does indeed show us the underbelly of human activity. But it is of our own making and it is we who sustain its activities. The Russians know this well enough, through difficult and often tragic experience. When they imported the discourses and definitions 'from the overheated world of criminal exotica in which organized crimes are typically explained by some form or other of "mafiology"',[58] they were simply reconfiguring the distracting narratives of their Western counterparts into their own situation. Selectively chosen characters and activities became tarred with the label 'organised crime', immoral economic actors. Many of them were. However, in the rapid implosion of Soviet communism and the violent emergence of capitalism, these narratives were loudly related by conflicting voices *simultaneously*. Supporters and critics of both capitalism and communism saw, in the dying days of one system and the birth of another, the pathologies of each, fully blown in a chaotic society whose transition consisted of movement from one state of economic irresponsibility and catastrophe to another. This clash of narrations provided one moment of truth in the cacophony of these contradictory explanations, one that told the story of the two ideological streams of the modern economy, in its deterministic essence, as ultimately destructive. The corrupting forces of the denied 'self' nurtured the illegal economy as a breeding ground for 'organised crime' under communism; the 'self' inflated in pursuit of its own interest nurtured the illegal economy as a breeding ground for 'organised crime' within capitalism. Both narratives were right.

3
From Bandits to Bolsheviks
to Brezhnev[1]

'Twelve voices were shouting in anger, and they were all alike. No question, now, what had happened to the faces of the pigs. The creatures outside looked from pig to man, and from man to pig, and from pig to man again; but already it was impossible to say which was which.'

(G. Orwell, 1989)[2]

If, as Dolgova wrote, organised crime is a product of society, and, as our meta narrative claims, is a reflection of the underlying pathological state of its indigenous society, we clearly need to understand the social and political, as well as economic contexts which breed conditions conducive to illegal economic activity. The history of Russia's underworld or criminal outcasts is colourful, often violent and complex. It encompasses political banditry, revolutionary terrorism, ruthless profiteering and an all too unholy alliance between the criminal world and the powerful elite. The dramatic nature of much of Russia's history, its political twists and turns, has also radically influenced the definitions and referents of what might generally be termed 'criminal collabora-tions'.[3] Underlying these changes, however, has been an enduring domination of authoritarian-style governance, impacting on every aspect of society and shaping its perceptions and relationships with the criminal and the deviant.

AUTOCRACY AND ARTIFICE

Our customs are cruel, but they are cruel both at the top and at the bottom. We reap in cruelty what we have diligently sown ourselves.

(S. Kucherov, 1953)[4]

In 1941, the year that the USSR was dragged into the Great Patriotic War,[5] Sergey Eisenstein, one of the country's most famous directors, was commissioned by the Soviet Chief of Ideology to make his epic film *Ivan the Terrible*.[6] Stalin intended to use the film to tap into the traditional political psyche of his people, their desire for a firm hand in trying times. As the writer Pasternak wrote of him:

> Our benefactor thinks we have been too sentimental. Peter the Great is no longer an appropriate model. The new passion, openly confessed, is for Ivan the Terrible, the *oprichina* [Tsarist secret police], and cruelty. This is the subject for new operas, plays and films.[7]

The conditions that bred the cruelties of Soviet communism were intrinsic to centuries of autocratic rule, manifesting as arbitrary forms of justice, endemic corruption, political sycophancy and vicious forms of self-protection against the capricious nature of its political leaders. It was the environment responsible for sending the young writer Feodor Dostoevsky into exile, into a world of violent criminals, which provided him with a topic and subjects that would generate some of the greatest novels on crime, morality and the human condition. But not all outcomes of this ubiquitous brutality ended up as classical works of literature set to inspire generations to come.

Surviving these conditions, under Tsarism as well as communism, necessarily entailed sacrificing conscience to pragmatism often devoid of morality. Corruption, a condition 'from which my country groans',[8] as Prince Shcherbatov opined, was an inevitable consequence of the expediency of survival, especially amongst the numerous bureaucrats whose livelihoods rested on maintaining the right connections in powerful quarters. Russia's vast geographical expanse was especially conducive to corrupt behaviour, allowing bureaucrats to run their provincial territories as little fiefdoms, thousands of miles away from the eyes of the Tsar and his court. Gogol's nineteenth-century satirical drama *The Government Inspector* exposed, with his typical wry wit and sharp observation, the machinations of local dignitaries and opportunists. 'If your face is crooked, do not blame the mirror', runs the epigraph of the play, as a damning critique of the state of his country. Fear, greed and the capricious nature of law and justice distorted the relationships at court, in the palaces, in the fields and in between.

To be cunning meant to survive. To be corrupt helped one get on in life. Naïve duplicity became a trademark of the peasantry, while the bureaucrats and courtiers fell upon the art of imaginative thinking to remain in favour with the Tsar and those upon whom their uncertain futures rested. A vocabulary emerged to express the idiosyncratic behaviour of a society trapped in the brutality and arbitrariness of autocracy. *Pokazhuka*, or 'deception', is also known as the 'Potemkin effect', named after the eighteenth-century noble Count Potemkin who found himself having to dream up a particularly elaborate form of window dressing. The Count had been entrusted with the development of a number of townships along the River Volga by Empress Catherine the Great, a task he clearly felt unnecessary. When the short-sighted Empress declared her desire to inspect the progress of the project, the terrified Potemkin ordered that frontispieces be erected where the townships should be standing. As the Empress sailed along the Volga, the ersatz villages were quickly assembled before she arrived and taken down on her departure to be reassembled further down the river. Catherine was not the only leader to find herself victim of such elaborate conniving. A couple of centuries later, Mikhail Gorbachev as General Secretary of the Communist Party was to have first-hand experience of an attempt at high-level duping which lost none of its imaginative qualities. This time, however, the leader was less naïve and the ruse angrily discovered.[9]

Duplicity became embedded in all parts of society. The peasantry, in particular, having little or no recourse to legal protection in their status as *personae non grata* until the 1860s, developed such characteristics that enabled them to avoid, as best they could, the arbitrary cruelties of their masters. As the Marquis de Custine observed, they must 'compensate themselves by artifice what they suffer through injustice'.[10] Despite a number of reforms to the legal system in the nineteenth century intending to introduce a more fair and transparent system,[11] in practice the law remained open to gross manipulation by the powerful. As late as 1905, the defence lawyer, V. A. Maklakov watched as the case against the peasants for whom he was acting descended into farce, prompting his frustration that 'the law is not honoured in Russia! Before the eyes of everyone, openly, the law is violated, lawlessness flourishes, and this embarrasses nobody, no-one thinks about it.'[12] His words still resonate with glaring accuracy in the twenty-first century.

In a society infected with endemic corruption, relationships between the criminal world and those tasked with maintaining law and order were common. The life of Vanka Kain, a famous thief in Moscow's eighteenth-century underworld, serves as a typical example of the symbiotic relationship between the authorities and the pre-revolutionary criminal fraternity, a relationship that would continue to proliferate in the days of communism.

Kain's most successful trade was as a racketeer, which made him, according to Dixelius and Konstantinov, 'one of the predecessors of contemporary extortionists and bandits'.[13] His long criminal career began in childhood as Ivan Osipov, his real name. Showing an aptitude for law-breaking, Kain progressed in his craft sufficiently to be inaugurated into Moscow's criminal fraternity. The story tells (no doubt with much embellishment) that he was required to pay a subscription (*paya*), and give an inaugural address using criminal argot, as part of the initiation rites demonstrating loyalty to the underworld. (The same traditions were said to operate in the so-called world of the *vory v zakone* (thieves in law), an overused and often mythically represented understanding of professional criminals in twentieth-century Russia.) Kain was arrested during one of his thieving excursions but managed to escape from prison, ending up working for the local regular police (*militsiya*) as an informer (*donoschik*). During the first night of his employment he is said to have been responsible for the arrest of 32 criminals. Kain allegedly received no payment for this work but was allowed to regularly extort money from erstwhile colleagues and the local merchants, having the protection or *krysha* of the local constabulary. He too, however, found himself victim of the unpredictable nature of Tsarist policing. When a new police chief replaced Kain's protector, he regarded the informer to be more of an embarrassment than help. Not long after his appointment in 1741, he had Kain arrested and thrown into prison.

Outside the towns and cities marauding hordes regularly ambushed and stole from the rural and travelling population. They were hardly the romantic bands of merry men led by legendary heroes of the poor against the rich. It was their brutality that was legendary. One bandit, according to Chalidze, had a penchant for hacking unborn children out of their dying mothers' wombs.[14] However, like Kain and his ilk, and despite the heinous nature of their crimes, they were not classed as the most dangerous of the criminal classes. Autocratic regimes fear most of all the very thing they are likely to provoke: organised political resistance. Two large-scale rebellions in the seventeenth and eighteenth centuries raised to celebrated status their respective leaders, two bandits who led the masses, albeit unsuccessfully, against the tyranny of the powerful boyars or barons. The historian Eric Hobsbawn classifies neither as revolutionaries, preferring the label 'social bandits' because they were driven by 'the defence or restoration of the traditional order of things "as it should be"'.[15] Immortalised in folk song and literature, these most famous *razboiniki*, or bandit leaders, Stenka Razin and Emelyan Pugachev, led their respective rebellions amongst the Don Cossacks in protest against the cruelties inflicted on their people. Neither wanted structural regime change (although Pugachev had designs on the imperial throne) and managed to garner widespread support not only from the peasantry but even from the more sympathetic amongst the nobility. Both were defeated and executed. Despite their support for the political status quo, Razin, and Pugachev in particular, would become heroes for the genuine revolutionary movements that would eventually lead to the events of 1917.

It was in the nineteenth century that Russia found itself in the grip of fierce political resistance as the Tsars and their governments continuously blocked attempts to engage with the ideas of democracy that were emerging from the enlightenment in Western Europe. The first real attempt at radical reform came from within the establishment, an attempted *coup d'état* led by a group of disaffected members of the aristocracy known as the Decembrists. Their intention to establish a democratic government by turning the country into a constitutional monarchy was discovered by the Tsar and they were sent into exile with their families. Despite this defeat, the scene was set for a century of political unrest. The anarchist movement, led by Bakunin, believed in the bandit as the genuine revolutionary. An inspiration to younger radicals from the intelligentsia, Bakunin's ideas were taken up by the Narodniki (literally, 'of the people') who believed that revolution in Russia could only come from below, from the peasantry. They formed an idealised view of the peasant, misinterpreting his or her love of the commune, shared ownership of village property, as a socialist aspiration. The reality could not have been more different. As they went out amongst the peasantry to gather support for their cause, the Narodniki were given an uncomprehending and hostile reception. Frustrated by the failure to garner resistance to Tsarist oppression, one faction split off to become the inaptly named *Narodnaya Volya* (People's Will). Their violent revolutionary tactics culminated in the assassination of Tsar Alexander II in 1881. The backlash that followed this and previous revolutionary terrorist attacks was draconian and served only to intensify political rebellion, driving it underground or abroad. It was this unbending response, according to Richard Pipes, that created the structures that would enable Lenin, followed by Stalin, to eradicate opposition to Bolshevism and collectivisation:

In its eagerness to meet the threat posed by terrorism, the imperial government greatly over-reacted. It began to set in motion, sometimes overtly, sometimes secretly, all kinds of countermeasures, which in their totality strikingly anticipated the modern police state and even contained some seeds of totalitarianism. Between 1878 and 1881 in Russia the legal and institutional legal bases were laid for a bureaucratic-police regime with totalitarian overtones that have not been dismantled since.[16]

In 1887 an abortive attempt on the life of Alexander III saw the execution of Alexander Ulyanov, one of the plotters, and brother of Lenin. Ulyanov's death made a deep impression on his brother, but did not endear Lenin to terrorist banditry. He had little time for Bakunin's romantic coupling of the revolutionary with the traditional brigand. Trotsky, too, rejected terrorist tactics as an effective form of anarchic opposition, seeing them as no more than an act of desperation, *ad hoc* attacks on individuals, which bruised but hardly destroyed the existing regime.[17] Further, it would become impossible to afford bandit groups such idealistic status as 'fighters against oppression' when in the aftermath of the October Revolution so many groups of organised resistance sprang up in defiance of the new regime. While banditry was to become instrumental to the Bolshevik cause, in both its political and its economic forms, its presence and the responses to it in Soviet Russia would reflect the amorphous nature of 'organised' and the vagaries of the socially constructed notion of 'crime', all played out against competing and contradictory textures and tensions of ideology and pragmatism.

PATRIARCHY AND PROPERTY

Attitudes to authority and property have a direct bearing on what is regarded as criminal, on the types of crime deemed 'serious' and/or the punitive measures used against offenders. A tolerance of, or even need for, strong authority as an external entity brings with it a host of dangerous possibilities, not least the ability to carry out orders of the most inhumane nature and regard them as legitimate. So too do attitudes towards property often determine the type of acts people are prepared to engage in driven by the level of respect or contempt held towards the owner or user.

One of the important errors of the revolutionary movements such as the Narodniki was to underestimate the peasants' love of authority, that is, the love of the Tsar. For a people gripped by religion and superstition, the Tsar as God's representative on earth – temporal ruler of the Church and secular head of the empire – was irreproachable. Even during times of rebellious ferment, the status of *Batyushka*, or 'Little Father', went unchallenged, for the peasant 'could conceive of no source of worldly authority other than that emanating from the tsar'.[18] Anger and hostility for the wretched conditions the people were forced to endure were directed at the aristocracy and bureaucrats, servants of the ruler who clearly abused the power given to them to care for the 'children' of the Tsar. There was never any doubt from the peasants that it was they, rather than the Tsar, who were responsible for their trials and hardships, unless inflicted by natural causes. The peasant 'rarely credited any event, especially a misfortune, to his own volition. It was "God's will", even where responsibility could clearly be laid at his own doorstep, e.g. when carelessness caused a fire or the death of an animal.'[19] Naïve and, by the end of the nineteenth century, dangerously anachronistic, this dependence on political authority provided the justification for the Bolsheviks as a vanguard party that would energise the peasants and urban labourers into a genuinely proletarian revolution (rather than revolution emerging naturally from the proletariat's developed consciousness and dissatisfaction with their working conditions, as Marx had predicted).[20] Lenin and the Party exploited this deference to authority as a means of violently subjugating opposition to the revolution. Orders given from above were rarely questioned, despite their brutal nature. So too was the underdeveloped sense of the individual a key component in the attempt to create 'Soviet man'. Indeed, the Russian character was ideal for social engineering on this huge scale, for here was a people whose language has within its grammatical structure a constant avoidance of the individual as subject, where, in the most fundamental assertions of individual identity, the naming of the 'self' as in 'I am called' is constructed as 'they call me'.[21]

The priority of the collective in the consciousness of the peasant manifested most tangibly in his relationship to property. As various forms of ownership rights emerged in other parts of Europe and the United States, much of the Russian peasantry remained tied to the land in bonded labour. Serfdom, which included over one third of the population in the nineteenth century, was only abolished in 1861, but many of those liberated from slavery were left without the modicum of security they had enjoyed as serfs. Despite the harsh conditions of their bondage, they could at least eke out some kind of existence once they had submitted the required quota of produce to the landowner. Once freed, however, and subject to land tax and corrupt bureaucratic procedures, those that could afford to purchase land often found they were able to buy only small hectares of poor-quality land which could barely feed their families. Many subsequently made their way to the cities in search of employment when Russia embarked on its first wave of industrialisation during the 1880s and 1890s.

Prior to and after the Emancipation decree, rural life continued according to the principles of the village *mir*, or commune. Traditional patriarchal family hierarchies were overseen by a group of elders who were responsible for the secular concerns of the community.[22] Central to this arrangement was the management of land, most often, though not always, through the commune. It was a highly practical arrangement, and certainly not one that fitted with the romantic notions of bucolic altruism ascribed it by some of the Russian intelligentsia. The *mir* as a symbol of economic fraternity remained for others an incomprehensible 'predisposition of our simple people toward communal ownership'.[23] For the revolutionary factions, however, the small shift in ownership demographics towards those peasants who were able to successfully acquire and work with the land rang alarm bells as they watched the emergence of a bourgeoisie of shrewd and wealth-loving workers.[24] By the beginning of the twentieth century the appeal of landownership was starting to break up conventional family structures as the younger generation sought to extricate themselves from the traditional patriarchal arrangement that burdened them with responsibility for the upkeep of the land while maintaining their deference to the authority of the elders. Those who could, purchased small tracts of land to be worked independently; others migrated to the town or city in search of work.

This relationship to the land formed the basis of the Bolshevik drive towards collectivisation, but it did not accord entirely with the expectations of the peasantry and urban workers. The stirrings of property acquisitiveness within the Russian people were being realised in the growth of the *kulaks* (rich peasants), encouraged by the post-1905 government, which attempted to break up the commune.[25] As the country lurched closer towards anarchy and economic desolation, the call to revolution and its promise of a new egalitarian society were taken by many to mean that property would be seized from the aristocracy, the small industrial middle class and the *kulaks* to be distributed amongst the peasants. Their understanding of revolution was more connected to the politics of envy, as an attack on avarice and privilege. As Figes observes, 'the practical ideology of the Russian Revolution owed less to Marx – whose works were hardly known by the semi-literate masses – than to the egalitarian customs and utopian yearnings of the peasantry'.[26] These utopian yearnings were fuelled by a desire for betterment, but not in the competitive sense as in capitalist states, what in English parlance is known as 'keeping up with the Joneses'. Egalitarianism was understood as a levelling down, as revenge against those who had more. A well-known Russian anecdote sums up this attitude. Ivan the peasant, having finished a hard day gathering in the harvest, offers up his share to the Lord. Pleased with the peasant's action, the Almighty sends down an angel to grant Ivan one wish. As he ruminates on what to ask for – a beautiful young wife, more land, cattle – Ivan is interrupted by the angel. 'Oh, I forgot to mention, whatever you ask for, the Lord will grant your neighbour twice over.' Without a moment's hesitation, Ivan answers: 'Tell him to make me blind in one eye.'

Property as an extension or realisation of the individual, requiring the acknowledgement of rights and property (as understood by the British philosopher John Locke) had not been established in Russia to any realisable degree even during the surge of industrialisation. It was in part this underdeveloped sense of a 'self' as an economic and political entity that allowed the Russian people to be more easily led to revolution than their European neighbours. While Lenin's vanguard thesis was typically suited to the conditions of Russian society, it failed to anticipate the strength of those nascent shoots of economic individualism. Although a collective consciousness continued to dominate, it was not, as Figes noted, an ideological aspiration, but more a pragmatic response to the peculiar characteristics of Russia's climate and land, the distribution of risk in a country subject to the extremes of nature and politics.[27] The emerging entrepreneurial spirit, which would be brutally eradicated, was to find eventual expression as a deviant form of economy, combining the worst aspects of the Russian character – a disregard for the law and justice with a vicious politics of envy. Further, as the vanguard-patriarchy of Marxist-Leninism turned into despotism, the 'self' as an economic actor, bearing responsibility for the 'other', the aspirations of a genuine economic fraternity, was crushed under the brutal heel of a forced and mechanical 'socialism'.

THE EDGE OF DARKNESS

Industrialisation in Tsarist Russia was too little too late. What did emerge as some form of market economy worked against, rather than for, its successful development. As a hybrid form of capitalism the merchant class remained dependent on the Tsar for the preservation of high tariffs in an especially acute form of protectionism. This patronage further discouraged Russian entrepreneurs from keeping abreast of developments in the market, such as the creation of stock holdings. This tentative approach to free enterprise left the economy dependent on foreign investment, much of it from Germany, which in 1914 accounted for approximately 33 per cent of capital in private companies.[28] It came as no surprise therefore when, at the beginning of the First World War, much of the capital was subsequently withdrawn by the now hostile German government. As the impact of a series of failed harvests drove masses into the cities and towns, the growing food crisis was further exacerbated by Russia's ill-advised entry into the war. The desperate need for army recruits (Russia's casualty rates were amongst the highest in Europe) bled rural areas of much-needed labour to harvest what was available from the blighted crops.

This unprecedented explosion of the urban population brought with it poverty, unemployment and a surge in crime. In the new industrial climate, pickpockets, swindlers, robbers and forgers were attracted to both the new rich and the growing vulnerable poor. More organised forms of criminal activity began to evolve in the heavily populated areas. At the turn of the twentieth century, criminal *artels*[29] known as the *Khory*, or 'Choirs', appeared in St Petersburg. These were loose criminal associations, run by astute business minds which would meet to discuss how best to promote criminal enterprise, including how to nurture mutually beneficial relations with the authorities. Other, less sophisticated groups roamed the increasingly chaotic streets of Moscow. Sporting names from the dramatic to the ludicrous, such as the Black Mask Gang (*Shaika Chornoy Masky*) or Your Money will be Ours (*Den'gy Vashy, budat Nashy*), they carried out armed robberies against rich individuals and businesses.[30]

Despite his disdain for the 'social bandit' Lenin did lend his support, while in exile, to organised armed robberies targeting banks, post offices and mail trains, or 'exes' (expropriations), as they were termed. This was not the bandit as revolutionary, but the revolutionary employing bandit tactics to support the cause. So long as collaboration with the more orthodox criminal underworld was driven by ideological motives then banditry had legitimacy. It was this rationale, no doubt, which inspired Stalin's participation in these exes. Operating under the alias 'Koba', he was alleged to be one of the masterminds behind the Tiflis post office robbery, which netted the cause well over 200,000 roubles,[31] a moment of *razboinik* 'glory' the Soviet history books failed to mention. One of the first acts of the new revolutionary government was to free those criminals imprisoned by the Tsarist regime, on the premise that anyone who had committed crimes against the Tsarist regime must be regarded as an ally (if you're against them, you're with us). According to one senior member of the Ministry of the Interior (MVD), the alliance between the Bolsheviks and the underworld was so strong that his father, a Bolshevik supporter, claimed to have worked with a former brigand leader, Papanin. The latter's support for the Bolsheviks was rewarded with promotion to the head of the dreaded Cheka[32] (the Extraordinary Commission for Combating Counter-revolution and Sabotage).[33] Others also released from the cities' prisons were to find employment 'policing' the ensuing unrest, as the nightmare of civil war and famine drove the country into anarchy. According to Vladimir Orlov's 'Secret Dossier', the Bolsheviks were not averse to exploiting other criminal capabilities. The Tofbin brothers, professional criminals from Odessa, were alleged to have forged money and shares for the Party which were sent abroad to more stable financial systems, as in Paris.[34]

Despite the propaganda of Soviet history, the revolution was not welcomed with open arms by many of the peasants and urban workers. The events of 1917 were as much a convergence of apostasies as the emergence of revolutionary ideals. The backlash against Tsar Nicholas II was less connected with a desire for genuine regime change than his inability to provide the firmness and stability that his people sought and expected from their leaders. Nor could the new government, faced as it was with civil war and an ensuing famine, reinstate quickly enough food and security the people yearned for. So too were the brutal tactics used to quell opposition deeply unpopular amongst many of the workers. A wave of anti-revolutionary banditry spread across Soviet Russia, threatening to wreak the very havoc the Bolsheviks themselves had participated in to a few years previously. Organised groups comprised of dispossessed factory owners and/or White sympathisers[35] sprang up across the country, adopting names such as 'Hurricane', 'Avant-garde' or the 'Commune of Moroz', bombing factories and carrying out armed raids on appropriated property. The official line described them as 'anarchist groups [which] attracted criminal elements and under the flag of anarchism began to rob stalls, depots, shops and private flats'.[36] Most politically embarrassing was the formation of the

'Petrograd Militant Organisation', initially comprised of sailors from the port of Kronstadt, who were the most active supporters of the revolution in its early days. Disillusioned with the tactics of the new regime and the perceived betrayal of revolutionary ideals, the sailors mutinied and, after their defeat, formed their underground association which eventually attracted former White Army officers, members of the aristocracy and intellectuals opposed to the revolution. Its members were accused of colluding with foreign bodies and of conducting operations from Paris – a dark reminder for Lenin that history has a habit of repeating itself.

It took little time for the new government to abandon its initial pledge that 'We shall not allow the police to be re-established!'[37] Unleashing the bloody might of the Cheka against the families of members of the organised resistance, or *zhigany*, as they were known, summary justice was meted out in the maintenance of uncompromising directives such as the following:

> A family that has concealed a bandit is to be arrested and exiled from the province. Its property is to be confiscated, and its oldest member shot on the spot without a trial.

> A family that gives shelter to members of a bandit's family or hides the property of bandits is to be treated as bandits ... This order will be carried out strictly and mercilessly.[38]

Brutal force helped bring the civil war to an end in 1921 but it could not feed a starving population. Nor could the appropriated industries or the devastated rural economy provide anywhere near the bare minimum for the desperate and hungry millions. Lenin had compromised on his pledge to abandon the repressive organs of law enforcement. He was now forced to compromise on his economic ideals. War communism, the aggressive appropriation of private property, was suspended, to be replaced by a short-term revival of capitalism known as the New Economic Policy (NEP). It was explained as a 'tax in kind', in which the producer was allowed to sell any surpluses over the designated amount of tax. This was no retreat, the Party claimed, but 'a striking instance of the wisdom and far-sightedness of Lenin's policy'.[39]

Out of this 'far-sighted' policy came the NEPmen, businessmen or profiteers, whose role as a temporary fix to the economic problems of the young communist state made them reviled by Party purists. In defence of this ideological volte-face, Trotsky offered assurances that their activities were not only of a temporary nature, but would also be curtailed: 'we can allow the speculator in the economy, but we do not allow him in the political realm'.[40] (In many ways there was as little comfort drawn from these reassurances as the partial nationalisation of banks has been in free market societies confronted by economic crisis.) The Soviet criminologist Lev Sheinin saw them as little more than hedonistic exploiters, 'aiming to corrupt the Soviet workers they met'. They were 'kings' who sat around in the most expensive restaurants and 'made deals involving millions; they haggled, formed commercial alliances, drew up agreements, and in great detail discussed the "general situation", which they considered tense and unpromising in 1928'.[41] The parallels with Russia's other great transition – perestroika (political and economic restructuring) and the inception of the free market – are obvious with one clear exception; unlike their latterday counterparts, however, these 'kings' were on the verge of being ruthlessly dethroned.

The apprehension they allegedly expressed at the 'general situation' was justified. Stalin, having consolidated his position as the Soviet Union's most powerful individual in the late 1920s, set about dismantling Lenin's far-sighted solution and imposed a series of draconian policies, including collectivisation,[42] which heralded a decisive and brutal break from the more temperate era of the NEP. In the rapid move towards complete centralisation of the economy, realised with the first Five Year Plan of 1928, private enterprise was stamped out. Speculation became a criminal offence, carrying a penalty of up to ten years in a labour camp. That same year Soviet Russia ratified its first Criminal Code. Under the section headed 'state crimes' Article 77 defined '*Banditism*' as 'the organisation of armed gangs having the intention to attack government or public enterprises, institutions, organisations or private individuals, and in the like manner, the participation in such gangs and the carrying out of such attacks'.[43] The statute was sufficiently broad to encompass a whole raft of illegal group activities, but it was not until the Resolution of May 1990 'On the creation of inter-regional sub-divisions of the Ministry of the Interior of the USSR in the fight against organized crime'[44] that it became ringfenced as an economic offence.

The economic problems facing the Soviet Union and the leadership's response to them were, as Peter Juviler notes, moulded by 'trends in crime and prevention after NEP' than by any other factors. The notorious Article 58, a catch-all for a host of activities listed as 'counterrevolutionary', together with the laws on, for example, 'hooliganism', 'grain hoarding', and legislation directed specifically towards economic crimes such as speculation and theft, threw together an eclectic mix of offenders (and non-offenders) as 'class enemies'. Crime in almost all its forms was thus politicised. Causation was located in the 'lag of consciousness' of those who remained tied to bourgeois ideals and whose sole motivation was to destroy the Soviet Union as it embarked on the most bold and rapid economic development of modern times. 'Enemies of the people' and industrial 'wreckers' became prime targets for the state organs of power, but these were ambiguous labels aimed at arbitrary targets, from the genuine counterrevolutionary to the unfortunate who happened to be in the wrong place at the wrong time. Narratives of the dangerous other or 'old theological devil theories', framed in the tension between crime and class struggle 'cleared him [Stalin] and the Party of responsibility for disruption and disorder. The economic disruptions could be blamed on criminal disorder, and the criminal disorder, on survivals of the past and "intensification of the class struggle."'[45] These were classic alien conspiracy and disassociation narratives, an unwieldy and especially violent attempt to support an economic model whose indisputable advances required unspeakably high levels of human sacrifice, and one which eventually collapsed in on its own corruption and criminality.

GULAGS AND GANGS

The surge of witch hunts and random arrests created an unprecedented surplus of labour as millions were incarcerated in the gulags or labour camps. Driven by quota rather than offence in the early days, the gulags held an eclectic mix of inmates. They included the NEPmen, now classed as 'enemies of the people' who continued to wheel and deal on the black market, a growing number of juveniles orphaned during the civil war and years of famine and for whom crime was the only means of survival, and an array of corrupt officials, some of whom turned their hand to the very activities they had been tasked to eradicate:

the Moscow police force was deployed to try and stamp out this dark reign of terror. It was months before the thugs were captured, and no wonder. One of the ringleaders was caught in a round up one night and when he arrived at the police station he was found to be Captain Antonov, a Moscow police chief.[46]

They were joined in the camps by the swelling number of prisoners known as 'politicals', victims of Article 58, as diverse as the Soviet population itself and in most cases innocent of their alleged crimes. The incarcerated population, as Piacentini wrote, was actually 'an exaggerated microcosm of the bureaucracy and social control of the Soviet regime',[47] and no more so than in the relationship between the authorities and select sectors of the criminal world.

The relentless flow of human fodder into the mouth of the prison system presented the authorities with a problem of control. Faced with ungovernable numbers of inmates, prison staff came to rely on some of the prisoners themselves to help maintain order, a type of informal subcontracting. They recruited from the apex of the hierarchical structures which emerged in the camps, the *vory v zakone*, or 'thieves in law'. These were professional criminals, recidivists of the 'highest order' who purported to live by a code of honour. Respected and feared amongst the *urki* or common criminals, they established their exclusive status through a series of initiation ceremonies and traditions (similar to those Vanka Kain had engaged in), all of which supposedly demanded strict observation. They included the requirement to reject family life for that of the criminal 'family', a compulsory contribution to a support fund, or *obshak*, for times of need, the usage of an arcane and rich criminal argot, known as *feni*, or *blatnaya musica*. The *vory* were also responsible for the maintenance of order in the underworld, dealing with transgressions through a special 'court', *sud*.[48] It was this latter characteristic the prison authorities were keen to exploit. In recent years, the *vory v zakone* have acquired an almost mythical status. On the one side they claim a heritage from the golden years of Russia's underworld, of honour among thieves and a rejection of the political influences and corrupting relationships outside it. On the other, they have become a symbol of power and influence in post-Soviet society, an elite of skilled and well connected ruthless businessmen able to call on criminal fraternities across the globe in their shared pursuit of profit and power.[49] Both scenarios are questionable. Within the camps the legendary tales of resistance to the Soviet authorities relate to but a few. For the most part the *vory* were more than prepared to collaborate in return for better conditions of servitude. The order they maintained in the camps was delivered via the most brutal means, directed mainly against the politicals. Alexander Solzhenitsyn, a political prisoner for eight years, who witnessed first-hand their treatment of other inmates, wrote scathingly of them in *The Gulag Archipelago*: 'All their "romantic bravado" is the bravado of vampires.'[50]

The structure of this interred microcosmic population of Soviet society, however idealistically understood, changed with the onset of the Great Patriotic War in 1941. As high casualty rates of the war rapidly depleted the number of recruits from the population outside the camps, the leadership turned to its vast prison population.[51] Inmates who signed up (politicals were excluded, considered too high a risk) were promised an amnesty after the war had finished. Many accepted, the less naïve understanding it to be a choice between an ignominious death in the camps or a more glorious end at the front. In 1945 the government, true to form, sent the survivors back to the camps. It turned out to be a death sentence for many of them. Those who refused to fight, the so-called loyal *zakony*, branded the returning collaborators *suki* or bitches. Conflicts broke out across the camps, known collectively as the 'War of the Bitches', passively observed by the authorities who did little to obstruct the bloody depletion of the old guard.[52] Meanwhile, the vacancies were rapidly filled by a new younger criminal, once again many of them orphaned and homeless because of war and its economic aftermath. These new inmates had little time for the traditional codes. They challenged the authority of the older *vory* and with it the myths of solidarity and detachment from the overworld. By the beginning of the 1960s the reign of the traditional criminal elite was all but over,[53] the new leaders enticed more by roubles than rules.

The gulf between the legitimate and illegitimate began to disappear as new aims and relationships brought the politically powerful and the criminal elite into closer proximity. Further, as the economy continuously failed to deliver to its targets, the criminals honed their skills to emerging entrepreneurial opportunities.

NEW ECONOMIC PROBLEMS

Our revolution is the only one which not only smashed the fetters of capitalism and brought the people freedom, but also succeeded in creating the material conditions for a prosperous life for the people. Therein lies the strength and invincibility of our revolution.

(Commission of the Central Committee (CC)
of the Communist Party of the Soviet Union (CPSU), 1939)[54]

Stalin's confidence in the performance of the economy was not shared by everyone. Even in the early 1950s, before his death in 1953, it was evident that Soviet industry, the flagship of Stalinist achievement, was running into difficulties. A study published by Joseph Berliner on the informal organisation of Soviet firms, based on a survey taken from the first wave of post-war immigrants from the USSR, pointed to the existence of a penumbral world of facilitators and alliances upon which the efficient running of the economy rested.[55] A whole vocabulary to describe these informal practices had made its way into unofficial common usage: *blat*, having the 'right connections'; *ochkovtiratel'stvo*, 'pulling the wool over someone's eyes' (as in Potemkinisation); *krugovaya poruka*, mutual support between officials in such activities as fiddling accounts, pocketing payoffs and illegally gained 'extras'. In addition, a penumbral workforce emerged, the most effective member being the *tolkach* or 'fixer', a wheeler and dealer who negotiated the exchange of necessary goods or equipment which would enable firms to meet their official quotas. Centralised planning, the cornerstone of the Soviet experiment, was malfunctioning. To admit as much was ideological suicide and so the great deception, the building of propagandist frontispieces to hide economic inadequacies, became a full-time task for many of the bureaucrats and workers. It also exacerbated the continuous problems of shortages and poor-quality products.

Cheating the system was an important aspect of survival in the Soviet Union. While burglary and personal theft were rare (ethical issues aside, there was little to steal from one another), millions of workers regularly pilfered from their place of work. They operated on the perverse logic that as the people are the state, state-owned property belongs to the people, therefore how can a person steal from him- or herself? The empty shelf, full fridge syndrome, a mystery to the foreign guest in the Soviet household, was explained by the industrious exchange of goods 'removed' from work. An employee in a dairy factory might provide products in short supply (sometimes exacerbated by theft at work) to a friend or neighbour in the knowledge that the favour would be repaid in kind. Goods 'obtained'[56] in this way also had a special status, as one of the respondents of Ledeneva's study explained: 'You wouldn't treat a guest with what was bought in a shop (*kupit*), it had to be something obtained (*dostat*). When you visited someone and got treated with something special, you did not ask where he obtained this.'[57]

As demand continued to outweigh supply, the population had recourse to another source: the black market. The burgeoning unofficial economy employed hundreds of individuals working in a variety of jobs such as *speculyanty* or profiteers, *fartsovshchiki* or foreign currency dealers, and *putanki* – hard currency prostitutes, the foreign (male) visitors foray into the hedonistic services of the black market. An increasingly important section of the shadow economy were the *tsekhoviki*, underground entrepreneurs who ran small and even large illegal factories producing a range of goods including jeans, bags, knitwear, leather jackets and toiletries. It was not only shortages that drove the trade in illegally produced goods but also the substandard and unimaginative quality of state output. And while the goods produced by the *tsekhoviki* were not always of higher quality, the range they offered often emulated Western styles which immediately made them a premium buy. The larger operations worked alongside official ones, sometimes using the same equipment and workforce but producing goods from materials purchased on the black market, usually siphoned off from the legal economy. Avoiding detection and prosecution naturally entailed paying off the right people – law enforcement, factory managers and local Party officials. Political patronage was essential for continuing business undisturbed. The higher the patron's status, the less likely the entrepreneur would meet with any trouble. A telephone call was often enough to terminate an investigation or lessen the punitive level of the sentence. However, patronage did not always guarantee long-term protection. The ever-present Machiavellian intrigues within the Party assured no one of a tenured post, leaving the *tsekhoviki* vulnerable to the vagaries of Kremlin and republic level politics.

The *tsekhoviki*, according to Konstantin Simis, comprised myriad characters with equally diverse motivations. They covered a spectrum of roles and activities, from the vocational capitalist for whom doing business was an end in itself, a means of achieving creative satisfaction, to the ruthless entrepreneur driven by self-interest and greed. As a defence lawyer, Simis came across a number of these underground entrepreneurs when patronage and bribe-giving failed. One such client left a particularly memorable impression:

> As I came to know him better I began to appreciate the native wit and worldly wisdom which had allowed this scarcely literate Jew to become a millionaire and to win respect in his world of business. Once, when we were sitting in the office sorting through the expert accountant's labyrinthine opinion, I said to him, 'Tell me, Abram Isaakovich: why didn't you retire ten years ago? Why did you continue to do business, to take risks? You knew very well that even if you and your children lived a hundred years you

could never spend even half of what you had saved.' And this man, threatened by many years in prison, even by death, replied with surprise, and even with reproach: 'Don't you understand? Do you really think I need the money? I need my life! And my life is my business.'[58]

Abram Isaakovich, as with the old-school tradesmen of developed capitalist states, was destined to become an extinct breed. Many of the underground businessmen, whose hidden assets, like his, came to millions of roubles, became a target for criminal groups, a large number of whom had served time in the prisons and camps, and built their careers on running gambling dens, prostitution rings, narcotics and contraband. Large sums of money were extorted from the *tsekhoviki*. They could be subject to physical intimidation, threats or the kidnapping of relatives, especially children.[59] But money was not the only demand. The more sophisticated criminal offered bodyguards to the *tsekhoviki* as protection against other groups (Russia's illegal protection industry was no new phenomenon in the 1990s) in return for 'shares' in the business and a seat on the 'board of directors'. As the *tsekhoviki* were unable to go to the authorities for judicial redress, those of Abram Isaakovich's mindset were gradually squeezed out of business to be replaced by a more ruthless breed of entrepreneur. The development of the Soviet black economy was emulating its capitalist counterpart. Survival depended more and more on a hard-nosed attitude to business, and being the fittest meant not only having the right political connections but being able to exploit them as much as they, too, exploited their criminal associates. Russia's illegal economy, marching its way towards eventual legitimacy, was acquiring a distinctly Darwinian feel. Those in the vanguard were increasingly in collusion with their political masters, who also detected the prevailing wind of economic change.

COMMUNISTS AND CRIMINALS

In a country run by a single political group and its economy, in theory, totally in the hands of the state, the black economy could only function successfully with the complicity, tacit or otherwise, of the state structures. Corruption in the organs of power was crucial to its continuing proliferation. The Brezhnev-led government (1964–82) is remembered as a period of political profligacy unparalleled in the Soviet Union's 74-year lifespan. Corruption ran right to the top, and nor was it always a hidden affair. Brezhnev's daughter, Galina, openly flaunted her relationship with a known speculator and smuggler in icons and diamonds, 'Boris the gypsy', the latter for a long time protected in his dealings by the family name.[60] It was a perfect example of the relationship between officialdom and the underworld – the former screwed the latter, until the time came to expediently discard the criminal connections once they became too much of a risk. The Brezhnev clan were eventually targeted by the KGB, whose head, Yuri Andropov, was set to assume the role of General Secretary after the death of Brezhnev. The investigations instigated by Andropov, and continued by his protégé, Gorbachev, in 1985, shocked even the most hardened cynic. Corruption had eaten into the very fabric of the Communist Party. Worse still, it was not just corruption that they uncovered, but criminality of an altogether more devastating nature.

The scandals that broke were numerous, one of the most notorious being that involving the so-called 'Cotton Clans' of Uzbekistan. Away from the eyes of the Kremlin, which had knowledge of the massive criminal undertakings but were silenced in their opposition by the extent of the largesse offered by the Uzbek Party leaders, this central Asian republic was run as a fiefdom. The criminal justice system and local KGB were subjugated to the will of the First Secretary and his cronies who ordered the murder of opponents or suspected informants of the multi-million rouble scams that claimed government payment for the cotton production that never was. Manipulating the peculiar method of Soviet book-keeping, the Uzbek Party elite stole not only from Moscow but from the local population, driving them into poverty as the embezzled funds were used for the hedonistic pleasures of the people's vanguard.[61] Other more localised outrages were endemic across the USSR. The Okean affair, named after the chain of state shops embroiled in the scandal, operated from the very centre of the Moscow government and typified how the hierarchy of corruption worked:

> ... top officials in the ministry [of Fisheries] would reach an agreement (naturally, for a consideration) to open a branch of Okean in some town or other. Local officials would appoint (naturally, for a consideration) people to run it. The ministry officials would fulfil an order (naturally, for a consideration) from the local officials for a supply to their Okean shop of additional quantities of caviar, crab and other special seafood. These supplies, it goes without saying, would never appear on the counter.

Apart from a tiny quantity, they would all be swallowed up by underground dealers at five or six times the official price. Roughly a third of the money would be appropriated by those immediately involved in the operation; the rest would go in bribes to those capable of guaranteeing complete protection of the criminals – not only their job security but also their future careers.[62]

The rot had begun early on with Stalin's creation of the *nomenklatura*, a list of administrative posts designated for Party nominees who were effectively 'loyal henchmen'.[63] The posts brought with them a scale of privileges including access to special rations or *payok*. Stalin's purges had effectively eradicated any remaining genuine revolutionaries, replacing them with careerists. This then was his legacy, a system of patronage, which could be bought and sold. A 'shopping list' for senior positions in 1969 read: 'Public Prosecutor, 30,000 roubles, First Secretary of the district Party, 200,000 roubles and for the artistically inclined, theatre manager 10,000–30,000 roubles'.[64] Unlike many of the *tsekhoviki* who had to hide their excess wealth, the *nomenklatura* sought means of enjoying at least some of their illegal wealth, provided for by the underworld and other illegal sectors.

There are numerous accounts of political corruption in Soviet Russia, with myriad examples to illustrate its depth and breadth.[65] Indeed, we can go as far back as the Civil War (1918–21) to find accounts that point to its endemic presence.[66] Given the picture of corruption in the Tsarist bureaucracies this is hardly surprising. But what was being described above was not the corruption Prince Shcherbatov complained of 200 years previously. Nor was it the corruption employed by the average Soviet citizen as a means of basic survival, the need to pay for education and the 'right' exam results, for decent treatment in the health system or for the judiciary to carry out (or usually fail to carry out) its appointed task. Zinoviev proclaimed to Western readers in defence of his countrymen: 'It is easy to be moral if you live in conditions which do not force you into morally reprehensible actions.'[67]

This was not the case for the political elite. Theirs was an act of total betrayal, an abuse not only of power but of the trust and dependency which had been nurtured in the psyche of the Russian people and then used as a tool of ideological repression. As with any abuse of this nature, it served to eradicate the foundation upon which moral perceptions and actions can be constructed, and in its place erected a new reality with conflicting messages that demanded conscience defer to collusion. In doing so, it not only permitted but positively encouraged the acceptance of deviant and criminal behaviour.

COLLUSION AND DELUSION

One of the acts deemed most heinous in any civilised society is abuse within families. It can take on a number of forms – physical, sexual, psychological, emotional – but ultimately, it boils down to mistreatment of the weak by the strong through the abusive use of an environment in which trust and dependency are deemed central to relationships. In such an environment, control by the powerful is exerted by manipulating loyalty through the collusive forms of denial in which occurs such abuse. Cohen describes how this works: 'There is a subterranean level at which everyone knows what is happening, but the surface is a permanent "as if" discourse. The family's distinctive self-image determines which aspects of shared experience can be openly acknowledged and which must remain closed and denied.'[68] The whole family, the abused and abuser(s), are thus drawn together in a web of deceit, further extending the abusive process. Responsibility for the unhealthy environment is diffused amongst the family members, not as individuals but as a collective. In this way the weak are further undermined by their collusion, their responsibility inferred but in reality having no actual substance. In contrast, the powerful are able to shrug off the responsibility they carry for the harmful effect of their acts thereby ensuring a form of legitimacy for further abuse.

The Soviet 'family' operated according to these pathologies. The factory worker, schoolteacher, low-level civil servant, underground entrepreneur, crime-gang member, were all enmeshed in collusion, firstly as part of the collective denial of the economic problems of the system, which entailed refuting publicly the presence of its shadow counterpart, and secondly because of the almost compulsory participation in the very thing they had to deny existed. Hence they assumed the roles of abuser and abused, a position the political elite was able to fully exploit to its advantage. What made the situation so devastating in Soviet Russia was the nature of the system, which had placed its legitimacy on the successful delivery of a socialist model of economy, one that, contrary to more orthodox versions, would be constructed and implemented from above. This in effect intensified the parent–child relationship between the rulers and the people. Unlike Tsarist patriarchy, where dependency rested on deference to the amorphous spiritual and traditional nature of the Tsar's authority, the patriarchal relationship between the Party elite and the people had a more tangible, material form. It defined this relationship in terms of building communism according to a number of scientific measures which were intended to inspire and realise levels of production for achieving the promised prosperity. Situated in a heavily positivistic frame, such as Stalin's system of Five Year Planning and Khrushchev's famous 20-year goal of surpassing capitalist levels of wealth,[69] promises were made and broken, reconstructed and propagandised way beyond economic reality. Hence those economic relationships which delivered the people's material needs, which became the *actual* basis of relations between the people and the state, were founded on deviancy and criminality and their simultaneous denial. Nor was it just fear that nurtured this denial. The dependency hook, as in family dynamics, meant that exposure of reality would destroy the very structure that defined and provided support for the least powerful. The people needed to believe in the system, needed to go along with the lies; for to criticise the system meant undermining their own security, their identity and that of the future generations.

However, it was not all one-sided. The Communist Party was in danger of hoisting its legitimacy on its own target-driven petard. While it could defer some responsibility for harvest failures and low industrial output to the climate, spies and wreckers, or, simply and most commonly, lie about figures, by raising the expectation of its citizenry to some quantifiable level and failing to deliver, it was in danger of pushing low-level discontent to more dangerous levels of collective dissent. Food shortages had worked to their revolutionary advantage in the past; there was nothing to stop the same happening again, but this time from the other side of the political fence. Hence the authorities' tolerance for pilfering at work; accessing the shadow economy, second incomes (of a limited level) thus ensured a degree of material satisfaction and helped to obviate stomach-empty protests. An observation on the irony of Soviet socialism goes: 'No unemployment but nobody works. Nobody works but productivity increases. Productivity increases but the shops are empty. The shops are empty but the fridges are full.'[70] It made collusion and delusion natural bedfellows.

The other factor enforcing denial lay in the ideological assumption that crime should decrease under the right economic conditions. While the authorities never claimed the eradication of crime, access to statistics as a means of assessing the movement of crime trends was always hard to find.[71] Despite the fact that such data come with a list of caveats, some semblance of social problems can generally be gleaned from them. Organised forms of criminality, especially economically motivated, were largely hidden, unless, as we have seen above, political advantage was to be gained by exposing such activities. Kept at arm's length, or understood as sporadic incidents rather than systemic, economic crime in it various forms was best left as a nod between officials, the furtive passing of rouble-stuffed envelopes, euphemistic conversations between workers and managers, and a whole raft of semiotic communications that saw and heard but spoke no evil of the rotting system they inhabited.

THE LEGACY

By the 1980s the Communist Party, like the Soviet economy, was stale, sterile and systemically corrupt. What successes it could lay claim to were grossly superseded by its failures, by the lies on which it fed and the hypocrisy which kept the whole system alive as if in a state of persistent vegetation. Like Lenin's preserved corpse, the Soviet people lay confined in the mausoleum of a dogma whose day was over, or perhaps had never really begun. Their most notorious (and most loved) leader had been a one-time armed robber, a Georgian bandit. The inception of the regime had been based on, *inter alia*, close collaboration with the criminal underworld of the Tsarist era, a relationship which had evolved and adapted to the new economic conditions both creating and exacerbating its failings. Throughout the history of Communist Russia criminal collaboration had been instigated and controlled by the Party, manipulated for its own ends, parts of it eradicated when expedient to do so. By the early 1980s this relationship had become so intertwined that at times it was almost impossible to distinguish the underworld from the political elite. But at all times, the balance of power lay with the latter. What came to be understood as organised crime – the merging of the entrepreneurs and the criminal groups – could only operate with the complicity, or the collusion or deliberate 'ignorance', of those who legitimately held the reins of power. They failed, or simply did not care, to understand the inimical consequences of this relationship. Most damaging to the system were the narratives of denial, the ideological rejection of organised crime, of economic criminal collaborations. But the harm went much deeper than the endemic presence of crime.

The intensification of authoritarian rule in a system driven by mechanistic concepts, in which self-identity and worth were measured, indeed *could* be measured, by economic targets, and in which the failure to meet them was obfuscated by lies and hypocrisy, plunged the Soviet people into a type of moral dyslexia. Individual creativity had no place in the system, and indeed was viciously proscribed. The 'self' could only be realised through total commitment to an economic collective, but one that was riddled with corruption. The individual as 'Soviet Man' was to be moulded according to the principles of this economic model, a product of enforced economic fraternity in which the legal and criminal were not only inextricably bound together but also given tacit approval by the 'higher authorities' (those who defined the moral conscience of the state). Clearly there was a dangerous vacuum as individual agency was compelled into subservience to a peripherally conferred 'morality', one that had been compromised by the pathological condition of the system it was supposed to qualify. Conditions were clearly ripe for further criminalisation of the economy as it moved into uncertain territory. It was not just a broken economy that Gorbachev inherited, but a broken people.

4
Shadowlands: The Gorbachev Years

Reform, said Mikhail Gorbachev in 1990, was 'not a choice. We do not have such a choice.'[1] Five years after he took on the role of General Secretary of the CPSU, and with his policy of economic restructuring in tatters, the last leader of the Soviet Union defended his decision to embark on a programme of change unseen since the inception of the world's first communist state. As much as Gorbachev might have been the man the then British Prime Minister, Margaret Thatcher, 'could do business with', he was not prepared to take on board the 'turbo-style capitalism'[2] that she and US President Ronald Reagan were keen to promote as the next stage in capitalist development. His intention was always to find a way of putting the Soviet empire on a road to genuine socialism, 'of enriching and developing our party policy and our general line towards perfecting a society of developed socialism'.[3] The reforms that followed his inauguration – *glasnost*, the relaxing of censorship; *democratizatsiya*, the establishment of meaningful franchise to the Soviet electorate; and perestroika, an overhaul, or literally 'reconstruction' of the failing economy – were specifically aimed at achieving this goal, part of the transition to return to source rather than forwards to complete change. Jonathan Steele said of his achievements, 'He opened the windows of a house whose inhabitants were slowly suffocating and let in air.'[4] However, it all came too late; the house was already in a state of dereliction, so that 'the more he tinkered with the system, the deeper the crisis became'.[5] Official figures, formerly routinely massaged, now admitted to an economic decline. A country as rich in resources as the Soviet Union, and with an agrarian capacity for self-sufficiency, had seen a steady decrease in domestic food production between 1978 and 1982. Rationing outside many of the major cities and the increase in grain imports confirmed what many Western economists had long suspected[6] – the Soviet economy was hurtling towards the cliff edge. What no one could have guessed, even then, was how close to the edge it had got by 1985.

One of the most negative effects of Gorbachev's reforms was the burgeoning of crime, especially organised forms of economic crime. By redefining the legality of private entrepreneurship as part of perestroika, he inadvertently opened the floodgates for abuses and exploitation by those sectors which previously had gained most from the shadow economy – the *nomenklatura*, or political elite, and the criminal underworld. But, as with much of all things Russian, the reforms and their consequences were riddled with ambiguities. In this environment, there arose an array of conflicting and contradictory narratives of organised crime: who it was, what it was, what it did, and who suffered most. On the one side, Communist hard-liners declared any form of private business as organised crime, or mafia; on the other, radical reformers applied the same terms to the *nomenklatura*; the public at large stuck the label on the majority of politicians whatever their ideological inclination, at young people, at the neighbours they hated and, when in international mode, at Washington and sometimes London (but never at the 'Iron Lady', Margaret Thatcher, herself: 'she could sort us out', they would say in their desire for the firm hand of authoritarianism and stability). No longer subject to censorship or ideological construction within the walls of the Kremlin, the narratives on organised crime emerged out of confusion, misunderstanding, self-preservation and fear. In their different ways, they tried to create a sense of understanding the anomic situation that the reforms had, if not instigated, then hastened into being. They drew aside the curtain of propaganda that had obscured economic reality while, in many cases, fitting new drapes to hide the painful truths they were being forced to confront. What they all shared in common, however, were the myriad ways of apportioning blame for the pathological outcomes of the modern economy, irrespective of the ideology underpinning it, and the awful reality that either model – communism or capitalism – encourages the violent and powerful to feed off the vulnerable. This chapter is about these narratives, their construction and the very real outcomes they hid, exposed or ignored, during the years of desperate reform, the last and ultimately fatal attempt to breathe life into the dying beast of Soviet communism.

TRANSITIONS

Russia's 'transition' period, as does that of other Eastern and Central European states, usually refers to the post-Soviet years of the 1990s (from 1989 in the case of the latter), described as a movement from Soviet communism to a very distinct form of capitalism (in other words, not the 'proper' version we have in the West). It is regarded as a time of draconian change and, as a consequence, one dominated by chaos, lawlessness and uncertainty, a period of intense societal change known in Durkheimian terms as a state of 'anomie', a breakdown of society's ability to contain and regulate a set of norms whose purpose is to restrain what would be otherwise rampant individual desires.[7] The breakup of the Soviet Union in 1991 was seen as the beginning of this anomic state for Russia and its former republics. For the purposes of history, the end of the Soviet Union, the 'evil empire', the twentieth-century nuclear threat to the free world, is an especially tidy affair. It was officially declared dead on 31 December 1991 as the New Year heralded in a new age for Russia as a member of the global choir and its hymn to the free market.

If transition translates as the move to another 'place' or 'space', or the conversion of one system to another, it would be more appropriate to define the Gorbachev rather than Yeltsin years as 'transitional'. Despite the failure and chaos of his reforms, Gorbachev should at least be credited with a move from the outright lie to moderate forms of transparency, from the dominance of the collective to an acknowledgement of the value of individual creativity, albeit in a restricted form. The Gorbachev years turned out to be an unintended dry run for his successor, a time for honing the skills of economic exploitation and vandalism to where they would next best fit: the free market. If any *real* transition occurred it was arguably more theoretical than tangible. The reality of the Soviet economy was that for decades it had been surviving on the back of its unofficial counterpart, the shadow or black market. It had grown up with the system, simultaneously destroying and supporting it. As one Russian academic vividly described it, 'in the West the shadow economy cohabits with the official (in various alignments). In the USSR it is intrinsic to the official economy, becoming its circulatory system, its brain, its nucleus.'[8] The transition simply legitimised parts of the black economy. Yeltsin did nothing more than bring the whole economy into the market framework. In all three models – the state-run economy, the Gorbachev hybrid and Yeltsin's *laissez-faire* – the human consequences comprised hundreds of thousands suffering the harms of not just the illegal economy but also the legitimate economy. *De facto*, there was hardly a qualitative transition, just an alteration in the scale and quality of harms perpetrated.

So why did Gorbachev's reforms end up intensifying economic criminality? How much was this simply a result of the legacy he had inherited, his attempted move away from the past, or can culpability also be attributed to a future idealised model of the free market towards which radical elements persistently tried to push change?

THE TASKS AHEAD

For decisions or reforms to be successful they have to be informed by reliable data and willing supporters. Gorbachev lacked both. The administrative-command economy[9] had been built on a mirage of inflated figures and fictitious success stories. Getting some realistic notion of the state of the economy was more or less impossible. Even when he famously broke with centuries of Russian tradition and 'went out to meet the people' as a means of discovering the conditions they lived in, Gorbachev was thwarted by centuries of that other tradition – the Potemkin effect (see Chapter 3). Nonetheless, his efforts to break down the wall of delusion continued. This was evidenced by the leadership's willingness to publicly confront social problems, including economic crime and corruption. The media were now given much freer rein to investigate and expose the consequences of decades of economic mismanagement, political decadence and public apathy as a means of garnering support for what the new regime realised would be unpopular reforms. This important gesture of openness brought home the scale of the problem, which went way beyond that imagined by the administration, as Gorbachev admitted at a press conference in 1988: 'We perhaps had not realised how widespread various negative phenomena – parasitic attitudes, levelling of pay, report padding parochialism, departmentalism, illegal actions – had become during the years of stagnation', adding, with what was at that troubled time an ever more desperate tone, 'We are waging, and shall resolutely and consistently wage, struggle for improvement, for stopping criminal activity, and ridding society of moral degenerates.'[10] However, the level of one particular negative phenomenon was well known, and this was to be Gorbachev's first major battle with social degeneracy as he saw it, one that became at best a Pyrrhic victory, at worst a fatal body-blow.

His first battle with moral degeneracy turned out to be the most unpopular. 'More people are drowned in a glass than in the ocean', runs a Russian proverb.[11] Alcoholism and its attendant problems was, and remains, a huge concern for Russian society, accounting for

.ause of unnatural deaths, either from work accidents,
rom adulterated homemade concoctions (*samogon*), or
ial violence.[12] One survey found that drunkenness in the
ion accounted for over a quarter of industrial accidents.[13]
Hence one of the most difficult tasks facing the administration was
how to deal effectively with such a sensitive and endemic issue.
Having declared its first policy initiative to raise productivity
levels by 4 per cent or higher per year[14] by increasing investment
in industrial plants and upgrading their antediluvian technology,
the administration knew that in order to achieve this overly-opti-
mistic target, investment had to be matched by an improvement
in labour performance. In 1985 the Central Committee issued the
'Resolution On Measures to Overcome Drinking and Alcoholism',
which restricted the sales of and venues for alcohol consumption.
Not only was this a hugely unpopular move, it also lost the state
revenue an estimated 37 billion roubles from the drop in sales
between 1985 and 1987, at a time when it could least afford any
dip in income.[15] A trip down America's memory lane would also
have alerted the government to the consequences of criminalising a
substance so totally embedded in the indigenous culture. During an
18-month period, more than 900,000 illegal stills were confiscated.[16]
Not only had the anti-alcohol policy angered the population, but
it had ensured that the already burgeoning shadow economy was
effectively given licence for unparalleled expansion, lining the
pockets of not only well-organised criminal groups but also a host of
individual budding entrepreneurs. As the scale of the failure became
evident, losing the administration much needed public support
and confidence as well as revenue, the anti-alcohol campaign was
quickly wound down. The next tranche of reforms brought even
greater opportunity for criminal entrepreneurship.

PRIVATE ENTERPRISE

Private enterprise had always been tolerated in a limited form.
The state sanctioned a variety of activities, particularly service
skills such as hairdressing and tutoring, where the shortages were
greatest. Some enterprising individuals even made 'a substantial
living queuing for others',[17] one service that never saw a lack of
takers. But nor had it been officially encouraged until the Law on
Individual Labour Activity, passed in 1986, intended to encourage
the untapped labour force (students, housewives, pensioners, the
disabled, and so on) into economic activity and provide incentives

for the '*democratisation* of economic life' for the populace as a whole. As with most of Gorbachev's reforms, it was ill-thought-out, failing to take into account existing problems that might impact on its successful implementation. The law was riddled with ambiguities, in particular as 'private enterprise was only supposed to act where the socialist sector had failed entirely',[18] a decision down to the local authorities. It was they, too, who were responsible for granting licences, forcing many applicants into the usual round of bribery. Those most able to 'afford' licences or to manipulate the authorities through the use of *blat* were the usual suspects, illegal entrepreneurs with black capital and strong connections with corrupt bureaucrats. Further, in an effort to stay faithful to ideological principles, hired labour was forbidden and family members only were allowed to work together in a single enterprise.

Alongside the state of the economy, it was the embedded mindset of the people that proved the most challenging. Compromises made in the above law were designed to offset opposition from those who feared the regime was selling out to the 'immoralities' of capitalism, in particular the older blue-collar workers. But this was not a homogeneous mindset. The demographic split between those wedded to the old system and those who supported economic change was, not surprisingly, largely generational.[19] A disillusioned younger generation, hungry for the lifestyles of their Western counterparts, were some of the first to take up the economic initiatives offered by Gorbachev's reforms. (Some of the most successful businessmen in Medvedev's Russia, billionaires such as Roman Abramovich, were in their late teens or early twenties during perestroika.) While this generation gap took on an increasingly political countenance, the understanding of individual economic initiative retained its Soviet ideological sense across the age ranges. Inculcating the principles of communism, and by extension, the evils of capitalism, into the younger generation remained an active aspiration of Soviet pedagogy. The 1984 Education Act declared that 'The formation of a scientific Marxist-Leninist world view in boys and girls must be paramount in all this work.'[20] This worldview regarded the workings of capitalism, of which private enterprise was a central feature, as hard-nosed exploitation, wealth acquisition with no limits. It involved charging the highest price one could possibly get away with and ruthless competition in business, the survival of the fittest. In other words, private entrepreneurship equalled business without accountability, that is, immoral economy. This mindset would remain integral to many of those who operated within the new economic reforms as well as those who criticised them.

The Law on Cooperatives adopted two years later, in May 1988, was intended as the real steer towards a functioning socialist market. Instead, it became highly divisive, provoking political scandals and grassroots protests. Most significantly in our context, it blurred even further the line between crime and economy, and in the process kickstarted the legitimisation of another form of economic vandalism.

As with individual private labour, cooperatives previously had been a small, tolerated feature of Soviet economic life. The purpose of the new law was to extend this 'to elicit the enormous potential possibilities of cooperative societies and the growth of their role in accelerating the socio-economic development of the country, intensify the process of *democratisation* of economic life, import a new impulse to collective farm development, and create conditions for involving broad strata of the population in cooperatives'.[21] Their remit included fulfilling the growing needs of the population and national economy through the production of higher-grade commodities than those produced by the state; not an especially difficult task given the latter's shoddy quality. There were three kinds of cooperative. The first operated as small-scale independent businesses, usually service shops such as hairdressers, food stalls and restaurants. Many were run as family businesses, and generally superseded the quality and service of their state counterparts. Some even provided service with a smile, a welcome change from the usual truculent manner of shopkeepers and restaurant staff. The second type of cooperative was sponsored by an official body, and would be expected to operate according to its demands. The final category was effectively the decriminalisation of the *tsekhy* (see Chapter 3), a cooperative attached to a state enterprise, run from the same premises but producing a better-quality range of goods.

Cooperatives were supposed to stimulate limited competition, but, as with the individual enterprise policy, their effectiveness was stymied by the ambiguities within the legislation, which allowed the authorities to skim off bribes in return for 'permitting' the cooperatives to function. They were further hampered by supply lines. The larger cooperatives mostly purchased their equipment and materials from the state sector, placing them in a catch-22 situation. Shortages at source had created the need for cooperatives in the first place, but also left them with exactly the same problems as the state sector and needing to seek similar solutions. They either bribed managers in the state sector to 'find' them what they required, or went directly to the black market.[22] Nor was their problem only on the supply side. For a consuming public used to artificially low state prices, the higher, market-based prices asked by the new businesses were frequently met with hostility. Their owners were classed as greedy and exploitative, particularly those operating face to face with the public, such as restaurateurs. As shortages increased and opportunity for private business grew, an emerging socio-economic division, now visible and furthermore implicitly sanctioned through the reforms, grew into violent unrest in some regions. Anti-cooperative protests broke out across the country and in May 1988 angry consumers burnt down 19 cooperatives in the Turkmenistan city of Ashkhabad.[23] However, it was not only higher prices that incensed the public.

Many rightly believed cooperatives to be legal fronts for underground business. Illegal fortunes had been made during alcohol prohibition, adding to the millions believed to be circulating in the shadow economy, capital that required investment.[24] The new economic climate provided the ideal means to do this. In 1989 it was estimated that over 500 million roubles had been paid out in bribes alone for office space, equipment, access to bank credit, the reduction of tax payments, registration documents, and so on.[25] Clearly, large amounts of capital were required before a business could even get up and running, as were the usual network alliances. To make a success of business and recoup some of this hidden 'investment' also required entrepreneurial expertise. It was clear who would gain most from the cooperative incentive.

The same alliances between corrupt politicians and entrepreneurs continued throughout the new economic climate, as had occurred previously. But now the opportunity for the politicians themselves to turn a hand to business became even more alluring and possible. The Yava cigarette factory scam was a typical example of political-business imagination. Those in charge of the Moscow-based factory got together with other state institutions in the city to create an artificial shortage of cigarettes, after which they set up their own cooperatives and sold the products at inflated prices to a tobacco-addicted population.[26] While filming for Channel 4's *Dispatches* in the capital in 1990, we were alerted to a similar scam carried out that year, but this time involving an American tobacco company in a joint venture enterprise with a local business.[27] Given the history of tobacco companies in the West, it seems not only that this was likely but, more so, that it would have been carried out with greater panache and for more profitable outcomes than the crude machinations of Soviet operations.

By 1990, cooperatives and joint ventures (legislation on the latter was also passed in 1987[28]) were said to account for approximately 4 per cent of the gross national product of the USSR.[29] A similar percentage for cooperative involvement with all theft from the domestic economy was given in official figures for recorded crime,[30] statistics which did little to move public opinion in favour of private business. Under increasing pressure from consumers and growing hard-line political opposition to the reforms, the government passed a series of resolutions in the autumn of 1989 restricting the activities of cooperatives. This included allowing local authorities to close them down if prices were fixed above those recommended by the state. Rather than improving the situation, this simply bolstered the corrupt alliance between business and politics.

COOPERATIVE CHARACTERS

So who were these new entrepreneurs? The three types of cooperative ventures mentioned above attracted people from all backgrounds, and while the intention was to promote economic egalitarianism, the flaws in the system helped to determine a clear hierarchy of winners and losers. One of the large cooperative ventures, known as the Association of the 21st Century, was rumoured to have family connections with Eduard Shevardnadze, Gorbachev's high-profile Foreign Minister (later to become a popular and controversial President of Georgia[31]), connections that would account for the scale and highly dubious nature of its early operations. Business included construction, aircraft building, the music industry and sport. The company had its office in the Intourist Hotel in Moscow, a stone's throw from the Kremlin, in what was then considered to be a prime site, sharing the top-floor rooms with a number of foreign companies keen to take advantage of the potential opened up by perestroika.[32] The Association was already estimated to have had a turnover of more than 1 billion roubles by 1989 and strong commercial links with a number of Italian firms, having been established for little more than twelve months.[33] Seven years later, a report by Guy Dunn, from the British company Control Risks, described the Association as 'one of the most powerful criminal organizations in Russia'.[34] Not all large-scale cooperatives were so easily identified as criminal, although it was assumed by many

that any successful enterprise at this level had to be as the ANT
(Automation, Science and Technology) case proved (see below).

Smaller but equally successful businesses sprung up across the
country, many of them straddling the licit and illicit. Alex and his
associates were one such company. In his mid thirties, the Lenin-
grad-born son of a high-ranking official in the local administration
sold paintings to foreign buyers through his cooperative Raduga.
Alex drove the then trademark symbol of wealth, a Mercedes,
and leased a top-storey flat in the central region, formerly three
apartments now knocked into one. Even by Western standards, the
living space was huge and lavish, including a bathroom with jacuzzi,
and a large lounge with an open fire. He entertained guests with
generous displays of food, including, in one instance, a suckling
pig.[35] His mother's contacts in the Party provided him not only
with protection from criminal investigation but also with access to
business contacts abroad. Alex's buyers, all 'respectable clients', as
he put it, from the 'capitalist abroad', would pay large sums not
only for high-quality works of art from some of the top local artists
but also for other artefacts such as icons. There was never a short
supply of interested foreign buyers, despite the fact that many of
the icons purchased for transportation were regarded as part of the
country's national heritage and hence illegal (a fact that appeared
not to concern many of the respectable and respected buyers).

Opportunities for those with some business acumen and
enthusiasm, and a small amount of seed capital, appeared to be
numerous when the cooperative initiative took off in 1987. An
enterprising and honest individual could set up a small business
as a cooperative and hope to make a modest success out of it.
Hundreds of people got involved in the early days, and not always
with powerful connections and black capital. Irina was one such.[36]
For years she had worked as a hairdresser in Leningrad but decided
to set up her own hairdressing cooperative with a shop in the
Petrograd region. She and her colleagues also made home visits to
boost their income. What savings they had were poured into the
shop. In 1989 her business came to an abrupt halt as the premises
were firebombed. Irina had refused to pay protection to another
industry growing off the back of cooperatives. She was a victim not
only of racketeering but also of the indifference and even resentment
of the local *militsiya* who refused to follow up her complaints of
harassment. The non-engaged public also resented Irina's attempt at
independence through the imposition, as they saw it, of avaricious
pricing. She had thought, naïvely, that it was possible to weather

the threats from the racketeers, trying over and over again to get the police involved. It was the principle of the thing, she explained, as well as the more pragmatic concern of being unable to meet the financial demands of the racketeers without borrowing more money. Irina, and many like her, genuinely believed in the economic reforms, but they could only work for the powerful or those willing to make moral compromises. As perestroika continued, its failure to deliver to the general public exacerbated the very situation it had tried to remedy. Initiatives such as the cooperatives, joint ventures and other forms of individual enterprise began to assume the very characteristics Soviet ideology had warned against – criminality, corruption and exploitation. The empire found itself in an ideological hiatus, attempting to extract alleged best practice from one economic model while assuming loyalty to an idealised version of another. Entrepreneurs like Irina needed the protection of the state for an activity that only a few years previously had been regarded as a heinous crime. More used to arresting *speculyanty*[37] than protecting them, the police turned their backs on the needs of the new and now legal entrepreneurs. Their unwillingness to control the spread of protection rackets was further exacerbated by poor resources, a lack of training to deal with the changing social situation and comparatively low salaries.[38] This made the police especially susceptible to bribery by those who ran the illegal protection business. In effect, a growing number of police were increasingly employed in the protection of rackets rather than their victims. There were those, like Irina, who refused to move from their principled stance. For the majority, however, illegal protection became both a necessary and useful resource as the state failed in its provision of appropriate legislation and law enforcement in the changing economic and social environment.

ILLEGAL PROTECTION

By July 1989 there were an estimated 133,000 cooperatives in the Russian Soviet Federated Socialist Republic (RSFSR),[39] of which, if the statistics are to be believed, 90 per cent were said to pay illegal protection. One client described the process as follows:

> Guys in track suits or leather jackets (the winter uniform for racketeers) go to the cooperator and say, 'You haven't forgotten that you owe us 10,000?' Interestingly enough practically

everyone remembers that they 'actually do'. Or there is another variant. Racketeers visit a cooperative and announce: We can protect you from extortionists, but you'll have to pay for this.[40]

In the contentious debates on what constitutes organised crime or mafia, Gambetta's work on illegal protection in Sicily (and Varese's adaptation of this to the Russian context) ringfences racketeering as a distinctive 'mafia' activity: 'Mafiosi are first and foremost entrepreneurs in one particular commodity – protection – and this is what distinguishes them from simple criminals, simple entrepreneurs, or criminal entrepreneurs.'[41] Their presence not as 'violent entrepreneurs' but as 'entrepreneurs of violence'[42] intensifies when the state fails or is unwilling to offer protection for private property and its owners. And yet the commodification of violence is not exclusive to mafiosi, nor is it confined to so-called 'weak' states such as Sicily and Russia. Violence, or the threat of violence, is regularly traded by powerful governments, albeit in different guises. Protection as violence, according to Charles Tilly, underlies the role of the state as simultaneously creator of danger and protector against it, epitomised most clearly in war and 'war-making' and the inevitable presence and growth of the arms industry.[43] In this respect, the designation of the term 'mafia' to non-state traders in violence serves to differentiate the legal and illegal not so much according to who is trading in what, but arguably in relation to the fragmentary nature of illegal protection, as a series of competing businesses rather than a monopolised entity. Might we then claim that the illegal protection industry, as it proliferated during the dying days of communism and early years of Russian capitalism, reflected the free market in its most pure form, allowing an egalitarian framework for the violence industry? Those who could, did enter the illegal protection market, especially those from the younger stratum of Soviet society.

As wealth acquisition replaced the building of communism as aspirations for the future the younger generation found new outlets for their energies. The Komsomol, the official youth wing of the Communist Party established by Lenin in 1918, saw its membership plummet, by 4 million in one year alone.[44] However, not all were driven to violence for financial reward only. Some, like the Lyubery group 'Rambo-style youth cult',[45] infamous for their neo-fascist behaviour, indulged in violence, as cultural criminologists would explain it, 'as a revolt against the mundane', as the need to manage a disintegrating world. They engaged in what Jock Young described as an 'intense drive for ontological certainty, for defining moments of pleasure and release ... anger fuelled by economic insecurity and deprivation'.[46] To this one could also add another reason for the willing embrace of violence. Self-identity, previously an ideological construct – the individual as Soviet citizen was also unravelling along with the system. The identity vacuum, whose impact was most marked in those living through their formative years, was being filled by these various influences; some materialistic, some nationalistic, some a combination of these and other forms of influence. From seeing Soviet youth as the hope for the future, a new generation of builders of communism, adult rhetoric became more akin to that in the West. Young people were now a 'problem', disposed towards deviancy and criminality. 'Do you know what is happening before our very eyes?', opined one crime correspondent, 'A cult of violence is becoming the norm for teenagers.'[47] And yet a cult of violence had defined and sustained the Soviet regime. Now, instead of serving the state, violence, adopted independently by some of the younger generation, was utilised in the pursuit of personal interest and, with a few exceptions, it became a profit-making exercise.

Some of the young racketeers learned their trade from family, as with Matrosynok, the son of an infamous criminal boss in the Ukrainian town of Dnepropetrovsk, who, at the age of 16, became the head of a mini-racketeering gang.[48] Others were recruited into the profession while serving time in the mixed-age cells of Soviet prisons. Afghan war veterans, *Afghantsy*, were especially open to the opportunities on offer from illegal protection. The horrors of guerrilla warfare in the unwinnable conflict with the Mujahedin provided both the psychological resilience and the physical skills required to intimidate and brutalise, attributes that readily transferred to the protection industry and served to provide some economic security in a Russia collapsing in on itself and one which had little time or resources for its returning veterans. As it required little more than muscle and bravado, the industry also recruited former sportsmen put out to graze in their twenties with no hope of stable legal employment.

Despite their disparate backgrounds, those involved in the illegal protection industry were just another example of the changing ethos within Soviet society: the emergence of an individualised consumerist society in which the commodification of skills, realised through new and diverse opportunities, was rapidly superseding the socialist principles Gorbachev was so keen to reform. A consumerist rather than communist identity appealed to Soviet youth, in part because they could see the extent to which the credo of their parents was proving to be an illusive and hypocritical reality, but also because they shared a solidarity with their capitalist counterparts who, in their own way, were also seeking identity through materialism. Western music, video and clothes were distributed by students from abroad to their Soviet peers, as gifts or currency.[49] Status, once bound up with Communist Party affiliation, was rapidly being reconstructed as access to Western brands, counterfeit or otherwise, all of which required money as well as connections (though the two were often intimately linked). In a survey carried out among senior Russian school students in 1989, one in five said they wanted to be a professional criminal[50] (in the sense of economic crime).

Some of those involved in illegal protection and other illicit trades were regarded as heroes, as much for their hedonistic lifestyles as their ability to acquire material assets. One such, Solomatin, leader of the Solntsevo group, was killed in a James Dean-style car accident during a night of joy-riding, a common pursuit amongst the suburban youth and one given an edge by switching off the car headlights. A stone was erected at the spot of the crash and became a place of pilgrimage for the young admirers of Moscow's burgeoning crime groups.[51]

Despite the rising clamour of condemnation and panic from the media and politicians over the descent into criminal chaos, many of the emerging entrepreneurial class, especially those who traded on the streets, were grateful for the services rendered by the rackets. Vulnerable to the vagaries of Soviet policing and lacking the political connections of the more sophisticated entrepreneurs, some, unlike Irina, willingly paid for illegal protection. In 1990 outside Leningrad's Peter and Paul fortress, a popular tourist attraction, traders would set up their stalls and sell an array of souvenirs to the hard-currency-laden foreign sightseers. One stallholder, a young disabled man, enthused about the level of service from the racket which ran the area. Not only did these guys keep the *militsiya* at bay, he explained, but they had offered him protection at half the going rate because of his disability.[52] Another entrepreneur who was planning a more elaborate business development, intending to open a number of restaurants in Svedlovsk, actively sought out protection:

> It was clear that the militsia would be of little use, and more than that, I knew that some of the organs of power were connected with the underworld. So we could only count on our own resources ...

So I got onto this crime boss, *avtoritet,* and even got to know a couple of *vory-v-zakone* [thieves in law]. I won't name them. We agreed that we'd admit them, and they'd not hassle us.[53]

As he explained, protection was provided in return for a part-share in the business (one of a number of distinguishing features between the Sicilian protection industry as described by Gambetta and that in the Soviet Union). It was a compromise worth having, a means of ensuring that the entrepreneurial spirit released by Gorbachev could be realised, albeit in a distorted form.

Illegal protection was thus a double-edged sword in this precarious economic environment, a facilitator on the one hand, and an obstacle on the other. As with other criminal activities that burgeoned during the breakdown of communism and emergence of capitalism, its inevitable presence testified not only to the problems of Soviet political economy but also to the pathologies of the capitalist ethos which, contrary to the intentions behind Gorbachev's reforms, was presenting itself as the only viable future. Its dual role of utility and hindrance, both before and after the collapse of communism, highlighted the ambiguities between legal and illegal economic activities in two systems that shun genuine accountability and freely chosen mutual dependency which are free from fear or violence.

Despite efforts to create a middle way, to combine socialism and the market, the overwhelming impact of binary thinking, especially as regards political economy, stymied a fusion of these ideological opposites. With hindsight, the reforms were never going to work, implemented, as they were, too late in the day and dogged by an absence of data and insight into the fundamental problems of the economy. At best they might have bought time for the Soviet leadership, and diluted the impact of what was an inevitable move towards the free market. Their failure was further exaggerated by the entrenched Cold War mindset (both within the Soviet Union itself, and in the West). Economic cooperation and individual freedom (as opposed to individualism), neither of which had manifested in a sustained positive form in either Soviet communism or Western capitalism, were hardly regarded as comfortable bedfellows. To favour one was to disapprove of the other. In this environment, the concept of the cooperative (alongside joint ventures) regarded as the most fitting form for restructuring the Soviet economy, was, in reality, bound to fail. Nowhere was this more glaringly evident than in the scandal known as ANTgate, which would put the final nail in the cooperative coffin.

DEATH OF THE COOPERATIVES

Jones and Moskoff described ANT as the 'most dramatic offender in illegal trade operations'.[54] Theirs was a view held by both the hard-line communist Ivan Polozkov[55] and the liberal Mayor of Leningrad, Anatoly Sobchak. Sobchak wrote that 'from the first pages it was clear that ANT was designed to flagrantly abuse the law'.[56] It was a measure of the complexities and confusion behind the case that two political adversaries could hold similar positions in what was a high-profile and economically crucial affair. In support of the ANT initiative stood an eclectic mix of supporters including top journalists such as Alexander Lyubimov,[57] and respected criminal investigators, including Vladimir Oleynik, from the Moscow Department to Combat Organised Crime. It even counted Oleg Kalugin, a former KGB agent who defected to the West in 1995, amongst its advocates. The significance of the ANT affair goes well beyond 1990, presaging the machinations behind Russia's privatisation programme, not least the arbitrary application of the 'organised crime' label, and their accompanying narratives.

The cooperative, or concern as it was known, ANT (Automation, Science and Technology) grew from a small venture with 60 employees in 1987 to an Industrial State-Cooperative association with a staff of approximately 5,000 by 1989. It employed top technologists and scientists working in what was referred to as the 'special regime' (the ANT State-Cooperative Industrial Corporation) aimed at improving the levels and efficiency of the USSR's dilapidated industry and technology. In May 1989 the Council of Ministers, chaired by then Prime Minister Nikolai Ryzhkov, commissioned ANT as part of the conversion programme to export decommissioned military hardware as scrap metal.[58] The hard-currency value of the scrap metal was to be used to purchase consumer goods on the foreign market, although in reality no hard currency would change hands in what was effectively a barter scheme. According to the agreement with the government, which approved the relaxation of export and licensing laws, ANT's directive was to import specified consumer and technical goods in short supply during the early months of 1990. This would have amounted to about 35 million roubles-worth of trade. The timing of this particular agreement was politically significant as republic-level elections were due that spring.

The mass import of these much-needed commodities was intended to offset the growing criticism of perestroika and show the public that cooperatives could work for the many and not just the few.

In October 1989 ANT received a request from Major-General Dovgan, Director General of Vzlot, a branch of the USSR Ministry for Radio, to purchase computers from abroad for his department. (As part of the directive and import package, ANT was to import computers which could be sold at half the usual price, thereby out-competing the mushrooming black market in information technology.) As ANT was committed to bartering rather than direct sales, it was agreed that twelve decommissioned T-72 tanks, to be converted into tractors, would be used as 'currency'. Dovgan allegedly sent the consignment from the Uralvagon plant to the port of Novorossysk where they arrived on 22 December. What rolled into Novorossysk on the train was not decommissioned hardware, nor did it have the usual accompanying documentation stating who the consignment was for. Three days later, ANT was identified as the recipient and its directors informed that the tanks had arrived as active military hardware. While ANT, suspecting foul play, tried to establish who was responsible for sending the tanks in their present state, a journalist from the communist newspaper *Sovietskaya Rossiya* visited the port after a tip-off. On 14 January 1990 the paper published a leading article accusing ANT of selling off the Soviet Union's national wealth and state secrets to foreigners. ANT had its assets frozen and all its operations abroad cancelled. *Sovietskaya Rossiya*'s 'scoop', and much of the media coverage that followed (in the days of relatively free reporting, the press was divided in its opposition to and support of ANT), used the story as a damning criticism of the cooperative initiative. As a consequence of the media frenzy, political heads rolled, most notably supporters of ANT, including the Prime Minister, Ryzhkov. ANT, now branded a 'criminal organisation', was closed down, and Ivan Polozkov, the vociferous anti-reformer, who was First Secretary of the Krasnodar region in which the non-commissioned tanks were 'discovered', was promoted to the powerful position of First Secretary of the Communist Party of the RSFSR. A few months after the scandal broke, the train guard who had accompanied the original consignment of tanks when they mysteriously disappeared was found inexplicably murdered.

It is difficult not to believe that ANT was set up given the evidence and subsequent political fallout. Oleynik described the eventual demise of ANT as the work of the 'political mafia',[59] while

Kalugin, well acquainted with the Machiavellian ways of his former employers, summed the whole affair up as:

> Either the result of a lack of coordination or rivalry between various internal sub-divisions of the KGB, which is highly improbable, or the most likely scenario here is that you have a battleground of opposing political forces ... As a result the government is kicked at and the country loses imports worth 35 million roubles. That's the price we pay for political games.[60]

The economic and political impact of the ANT scandal cannot be overestimated. The country experienced a particularly difficult winter that year and, having run out of grain to feed its livestock, was forced to import 36 million tonnes, an increase of 1 million tonnes on the previous year.[61] A year later, during an even harsher winter, the ANT affair continued to resonate in the media:

> You know that precisely in Tagil [the dispatch point for the tanks] they ration an individual to 50 grammes of bread a day. This is monstrous! The next day there is a struggle to get flour for the town. We had a chance to rectify this position that included the help of structures like ANT.[62]

There were many in the Party who had no intention of seeing perestroika work, and whose opposition to initiatives such as cooperatives was based more on the fear of losing their power base and the privileges it brought than on ideological loyalties. In February 1990, as the ANT affair was at its height, Article 6 of the constitution, guaranteeing political monopoly of the Communist Party, was abrogated. It was hardly surprising that the propaganda war between those who favoured a more rapid and market-oriented reform package and those who resisted change, was at its most acrimonious. The successful realisation of the cooperative initiative would have partly satisfied the reformist faction, some of whose members were now urging a full-scale move to the market.[63] However, it did few favours for die-hard communists, in particular those linked to the criminal economy, whose interests clearly would be threatened if such a potentially powerful concern such as ANT were to flourish. Watching their political power diminish, few of them were prepared to let go of their economic influence. As the Soviet Union prepared for its first ever genuinely democratic elections that spring, the economy continued its descent into chaos, the cooperative initiative well and truly scuppered.

Caught between two equally vociferous factions and watching his flagship policy crumbling before him, Gorbachev stepped away from the path of reform onto an authoritarian road well travelled. In doing so, he alienated himself from Soviet reformers and Western support and failed to garner support from the hard-line faction who regarded his betrayal of the Party, especially with the abrogation of Article 6, as irrevocably undermining his authority. Barely 18 months after the ANT affair, and returning to Moscow empty-handed, his request for credit from the G7 having been rejected, Gorbachev's final attempt (after much dithering) to reconstruct the Soviet economy according to more market-oriented principles, with the Shatalin-Yavlinsky Plan,[64] was running into serious problems. During his summer break in the Crimea, he was placed under house arrest, supposedly on the orders of a group of hard-line communists opposed to the Shatalin-Yavlinsky Plan and the 9+1 Union Treaty.[65] It came as no surprise that some of the leading protagonists behind the coup included those who had played a crucial role in the destruction of ANT.[66] The abortive coup, as with the demise of ANT, finally destroyed the vision Gorbachev had fought so hard to realise: the (re)construction of a genuine socialist state.

Beset by crime and corruption, and wedded, on the one hand, to a failed economic model, while, on the other, naïvely embracing the promises on offer from a model as intrinsically pathological but as yet less evident than that of communism, there was clearly no way out of the political, economic and social mess for the Soviet Union. The dichotomous framework of the modern economy – communist versus capitalist – expressed through a political discourse of hostile binaries which permits no viable middle way,[67] disqualified any form of reconciliation between the two systems, or indeed the ability to extract some vestiges of the idealism upon which each system declared its legitimacy: concern for the collective and respect for the individual. Instead, the discourse of antagonistic dichotomy prevailed, each constructing disparity 'on the basis of a parallel dehumanisation of the other'.[68] As it was clear that new forms of economic thinking were not going to emerge, it also became obvious that Russia would once again become the subject of yet another experiment of modern economy: Friedman-style capitalism, *laissez-faire*, the free market at its freest.

THE MORAL MAZE

When communism met capitalism in the dying days of the Soviet Union, years of Cold War rhetoric found a new form in the narratives of Russian organised crime (narratives that were to be metamorphosed into global concerns after the collapse of communism). It was as if each economic model, brought face to chaotic face in the Russian context, was able to pull down from the attic of propaganda the portrait of its adversary, strip bare the persona and expose the degeneracy that lay behind layers of ideological and legal discourse. Usage of the term 'organised crime', as in the West, emphasised a form of economic behaviour, or certain economic actors, which, in theory at least, represented the opposite end of the moral spectrum, the antithetical values, of the dominant model. The ideological discourse that had defined political economy in the twentieth century shaped the intensive debates and exacerbated the fragile uncertainty of policy-making now taking place in Moscow and much of the Soviet Union. In this clash of ideologies the 'organised crime/mafia' label became an important tool in the armoury of political aggression. On the one side, it represented exploitative speculation, the excesses of self-interest as realised through economic individualism; on the other, it became a symbol of the inevitable consequences of a centralised economy, the erosion of individual expression in the economic realm, the defiance of market forces which thus rendered it doomed to failure as the constant shortages in the Soviet economy proved.

Each side had sufficient evidence to argue its case. The burgeoning second economy and black market, run and/or facilitated by *speculyanty, tsekhoviki,* racketeers and corrupt officials proved the extent to which communism bred criminality. Vaksberg and Simis, harsh critics of the Soviet regime, declared that only with the dissolution of the communist state would such levels of crime, especially economic crime, dramatically decrease. In turn, perestroika, which encouraged the emergence of entrepreneurial activity, had let loose a dog-eat-dog environment. The explosion of racketeering and other examples of the growth of violence in the economy testified to the intrinsic criminogenic qualities of the market, even in the diluted form in which it was practised in the Soviet Union, seen as a vindication of the Marxist critique of capitalism.

The flexible usage of the term 'organised crime', in what was effectively an ideological stalemate, unravels many of its orthodox understandings where applied within political and legal conflicting frameworks and, in so doing, calls into question the assumptions we might hold about the different values that underpin what are ostensibly contrasting economic models (see Chapter 6). Arguably, this was one of the major problems facing Gorbachev in his attempt to reconstruct the Soviet economy. There existed neither the concepts nor the vocabulary to move the discussion beyond this binary ideological framework, itself constrained and defective and, ultimately, self-destructive. For the tools Gorbachev had at his disposal, as a legacy of Soviet communism, and the design he intended to adapt, capitalism, essentially shared the same defect, albeit manifesting in different ways. This mutual pathology, as expressed through the concept and usage of the term 'organised crime', centres on the absence of moral responsibility of economic actors, whatever their ideological persuasion, for the consequences of their actions. The conflicting narratives on organised crime describe different perceptions of similar harmful outcomes, perceptions which serve to deflect or deny the harms perpetrated by two dominant economic systems in which individual accountability for these outcomes is absent. In this *moral* context, the ideological binary discourse becomes defunct, as too does the legal/illegal dichotomy. Organised crime thus becomes the apogee of economic activity deemed antithetical to the health and values of the dominant system, the scapegoat for economic ills.

The starkness of these debates and the realities behind them reflected the complex moral world of the Soviet citizen, whose life was one long round of inconsistency and complicit duplicity. '*Homo Sovieticus*', according to Simis, inhabited 'two separate systems of morality'. In one he readily engages in the unspoken but endemic practice of bribe-giving (and bribe-taking) which is carried out 'without any burden on his conscience'. In another,

> this same citizen, in private dealings, will conduct himself in accordance with the precepts of common human morality. He will lie to a representative of the government administration, but be truthful and honest in relations with friends and neighbours; he is happy to steal twenty packets of cigarettes from a tobacco factory where he works, but will not steal a penny from another person.[69]

While a somewhat simplistic account (interpersonal property crime did occur, albeit infrequently, because there was little to steal from the average citizen), it nevertheless captures the essence of economic behaviour in Soviet life. Even those who did not blatantly engage in such behaviour nonetheless gave tacit support to those who did. A survey conducted at the Krasny Triugol'nik shoe factory in Leningrad in 1969 found the attitude to theft at work was generally one of indifference, so that if someone saw a colleague stealing, rarely would it be reported. Ten per cent believed the constant pilfering to be a direct consequence of planning deficiencies. There was, of a course, a pragmatic reason for this indifference. Somewhere along the shadow economy line, the person who witnessed the crime would inevitably benefit from the theft in the meandering network of informal exchange. And there was always the canny logic of the workers' state to alleviate any pangs of conscience. If the state owns all the property and the people are the state, so ran the argument, it is impossible to steal from oneself.

Some, however, did not successfully manage the contradictions that shaped their existence in Soviet society, and were unable to reconcile or shy away from the glaring gap between rhetoric and reality, from the slogans that declared the successful march towards utopia to the daily truth of shortages. In Ledeneva's study of informal exchange and *blat*, one of her respondents tells of the consequences of trying to avoid the unofficial manipulation of the system by acting with integrity:

> I was brought up with principles. I can't tell you how many opportunities I missed. When I was a peoples' deputy I could arrange a telephone line for myself, to solve an apartment problem I had proper connections, knew those people who were engaged in all this. And the fact that I did not use them made me even less respected. But those days I understood everything literally, believed in every slogan in the newspapers, in Komsomol and Party ideals. But the nomenclatura people I met did not pay me any respect for that. They respected those who made them feel powerful and helpful. My friends told me 'You must be abnormal. Can't you tell somebody you have a problem, they will sort it out somehow, you've been waiting long enough for a flat.' And I felt I couldn't. Not because I was honest, just silly. I simply didn't know the rules of the game.[70]

This rather disingenuous description (someone in the position of peoples' deputy would undoubtedly have had knowledge of the 'rules of the game') nonetheless illustrates the moral conflict between official and unofficial reality and the pressure placed on individuals to 'conform' to deviant behaviour. The normalisation of deviancy as a basis for the functioning of political and economic relations further nurtures 'destructive, defective and criminal relationships ... and leads to the establishment of an uncivilised order in society'.[71] Clearly, integrity and accountability have no practical presence in a society dominated by this ethos, and, as the quote illustrates, are even despised.

With this philosophy dominating the *de facto* engine of economic activity in the Soviet Union, that is, the unofficial economy, the foundations were laid for a particularly stark but *by no means erroneous* interpretation of the free market. Rather than counter the corruption and crime that had become normalised in Soviet society, the road to the market provided a framework of legality for practices hitherto proscribed, bringing with it an overt acceptance of many behaviours previously deemed intrinsically unethical. With the exception of those who were ideologically opposed to change, only a few supporters of reform, such as Moscow sociologist Simon Kordonsky, anticipated the further criminalisation of economic behaviour if market conditions were introduced in full.[72] The majority placed their faith in the alleged stability and promised prosperity that the free market would bring, swallowing Western propaganda as readily as their forebears had accepted communism. Faith was placed in the market mechanism as a force for good, rather than in the nature of those who operated within it. The impact of individuals and their moral sensibilities on the economic arena was a secondary consideration, as it had been under communism. In a society that had for years inculcated into its population the concept of free enterprise as unprincipled and exploitative, divisive and socially destructive, the transmutation of one version of economic determinism to another was bound to have adverse consequences.

Those most able to embrace the free market had acquired their entrepreneurial skills and the necessary social and monetary capital to enable their commercial success via activities in the shadow economy and its interface with the corrupt 'overworld'. This factor, in combination with the overwhelming understanding of capitalism through an ideologically hostile lens, played an important role in the emerging nature of what was to become the free market experiment in Russia. The changes in legislation, permitting various forms of private business, in most cases did not alter the mentality or interpretation of capitalism as morally redundant. For many Soviets, it was not just an economic model that was gradually being endorsed but the modes of behaviour associated with it. In other words, a green light had been given to business as exploitation, to an economic model that exhorted the pursuit of self-interest in which negative outcomes on the weaker, that is, those less capable of playing the Darwinian game of competitive business, were assumed to be a natural by-product. In the years to follow, as Russia embarked on its frenetic pace of unregulated capitalism, this attitude prevailed quite simply because *there were no real demands for a moral change in economic behaviour by the advocates of laissez-faire,* both within and beyond Russia. As with the central economy, it was not expected that individual economic actors would function as moral agents. That task would be determined by the free market which, like its ideological adversary, was regarded as a producer of moral outcomes, of democracy, justice and order, incidental rather than directed consequences. Hence when these two economic models fused during the dying days of communism, Simis's parallel systems of morality collapsed into one system of legitimised amorality. It was still acceptable to lie to and steal from the state, but in this new climate there was no obligation for principled behaviour towards one's friends and neighbours who were increasingly part of a sanctioned 'dog-eat-dog' economic landscape.

The meeting between Soviet communism and capitalism in that brief period of 'transition' under Gorbachev was experienced not as a clash of ideologies but as the melding of two streams of modern economy bound by a common pathology: the dispersion of responsibility for economic outcomes away from the individual. Neither the problem to be solved (failing Soviet communism) nor the tentative solution offered (private enterprise) demanded accountability from individual economic actors. Instead, moral agency was embedded within the economic models themselves, one which had aimed (but was clearly failing) to shape the individual as a particular type of socially responsible economic actor; the other which claimed to transform individual activity into the social good. Into this ideological vacuum of individual economic responsibility, exacerbated by the prevalent levels of legal and moral ambiguity, the conflicting narratives of organised crime vied for attention and political influence. And yet at the heart of these diverse narratives lay a common theme. Organised crime, however it was interpreted, was regarded as the embodiment of economic exploitation, of violence – physical or psychological – and ruthless self-interest. It represented the antithesis of those values underlying a basic sense of humanity, values deemed crucial to a decent and fair society. Hence its symbolic importance as the epitome of immoral economic behaviour, in which responsibility to and for the 'other' was not only absent but consciously abused in the ruthless pursuit of profit and gain.

CONCLUSION

The diverse range of activities and actors drawn into the competing discourses of organised crime in the final years of Soviet communism

– from the usual suspects of *speculyanty*, *tsekhoviki*, racketeers, and so on, to the obvious (but less visible) corrupt members of the political body, to anyone occupying the muddied spectrum of newly emerging entrepreneurs – reflected a moral uncertainty about the values of both communism and capitalism. One could argue that in such a scenario the term 'organised crime' becomes practically meaningless, too arbitrary to hold any real value in understanding different forms of collaborative economic activity and their harmful impact. But as a *representation* of the antithesis of humanity and common decency in an economic context, organised crime, in its different ideological interpretations, can still act as a mirror of the reality of society's values and the resulting harms.

The narratives of organised crime in Soviet Russia (and, as we shall see, in capitalist Russia) have been beset by what might be described as a binary dyslexia. The vocabulary available for articulating what and who comprised Soviet organised crime and its impact on reforms such as perestroika was shaped by ideological thinking and Cold War rhetoric. This allowed no real discussion about economy and crime beyond the established dichotomy of communism and capitalism, which for the most part framed debates within an 'either–or' framework. 'Get rid of the Communist Party then the "mafia" (shorthand for the collaboration between the criminal world and its political patrons) would disappear', read the popular reformist narrative; 'Reinstate the old system and the profiteering gangsters would be eradicated', was articulated as the desperate droning of a dwindling minority of conservative voices. Trapped inside this conceptual straitjacket, it was easy to ignore the meta-narrative that lay behind the conflicting narratives of organised crime: neither communism *nor* capitalism provide the most fruitful and fair economic path of the future. Remove the legal markers that imbue each system with its own moral status and they expose the pathological condition prevalent in the modern economy, in which there exists no real accountability and no sense of genuine, freely given altruistic motivation.

As the final decade of the twentieth century began, bathed in the euphoria from the tearing down of the Berlin Wall and the hubris of George Bush Senior's New World speech which presented the neo-liberal agenda as the only hope for humankind, Soviet communism, while still not yet dead, was clearly terminally ill. Barely 18 months later, one of the twentieth-century superpowers lay in the ruins of its predominantly own making. A general sense of Manichean madness pervaded the media, governments and public opinion across the developed world, including those of the collapsed communist states. Liberal democracy and the market had triumphed over the evils of authoritarianism and central economic planning.

During the autumn of 1990, I was out in Moscow working for Abraxas, an independent film company, on a documentary for Channel 4's *Dispatches* about organised crime in Moscow, alliteratively titled 'Moscow's Mafia Millions'. Despite the chaotic and criminal state of the economy there was a palpable optimism in the capital about the future of Russia, particularly amongst the younger generation. After a day of shooting general views we passed a subway entrance to the Arbat, one of the capital's most famous shopping areas. A young woman was sitting on a low wall, clearly suffering from what appeared to have been a particularly intense drinking session. We quickly filmed the unfortunate as she threw up again and again and used it in the programme as a metaphor for the state of communism, Soviet society as sick, mired in crime and corruption. Few realised the extent to which the proposed cure of *laissez-faire* would drive Russia to even greater sickness and even greater levels of corruption and crime. The vomiting Russian woman is just as appropriate as a metaphor for the toxic medicine the West delivered as an antidote to Soviet communism, poisonous not only to the Russian system, but to others too. In our arrogance we in the West also assumed that there were no lessons to be learned from this ignominious and crime-ridden end of the Soviet Union. History was to prove otherwise.

5
Comrade Capitalists: The Tale of Crime and Economy in the 'New' Russia

Shoppers of the world unite!
(Advert on the metro for a new shopping centre in Moscow, September 2003)

The Fontanka Canal in St Petersburg circles round the centre of the city they call the 'Venice of the North'. The widest and busiest of the city's waterways, it cuts across the main street, Nevsky Prospect, at the Anichkov Bridge, a strident landmark with its four equine statues known as 'horses tamed by men'. Readers of classical Russian literature know it as the place where Raskolnikov watched a drunken woman attempt to commit suicide in *Crime and Punishment,* and where the troubled Golyadkin, the main protagonist in Gogol's *The Double,* first met his terrifying doppelganger. A stone's throw from the bridge, in the Shuvalovsky Palace, one of a number that line this celebrated part of the canal, used to stand the St Petersburg House of Friendship.[1] Once the official face of Soviet culture, bringing together artists, performers, writers and such like with their foreign counterparts (under the sharp eye of a KGB-linked 'guardian') in the new Russia, it soon discovered a niche for its skills and connections in the frantic onslaught of the capitalist climate. The Party platitudes with which this group of loyal communists had greeted their overseas guests, extolling the virtues of state-directed arts, were overnight and with almost imperceptible ease transformed into commercial talk of joint-venture possibilities, the expansion of existing business contacts and cultural exchanges, but now with a distinct profitable edge. If Lenin turned, Friedrich von Hayek must have joyously jumped, in their respective resting places.

One of the House of Friendship's new business ventures – most welcome for the foreign visitor – was the café tucked away in the ostentatious surroundings which offered a variety of flavoured teas and unsweetened coffee, sheer delight after the sugared Turkish-style coffee and sickly sweet torte offered by the drab Soviet cafés. Its prices were gentle on the foreigners' purse but less so on those of the ordinary Russians. Nonetheless, some sectors of Russian society were financially able to frequent this small oasis in the early years of Russia's transformation to the free market. Amongst them were members of the Tambovsky group, leading figures in St Petersburg's burgeoning criminal world. They were quite at home drinking tea in these salubrious surroundings run by the old-cum-new *nomenklatura*; hardly surprising, perhaps, at a time when relationships between the political elite and criminal business had never been so amicable.

In these early days of the so-called 'transition' other characters went in and out of the House of Friendship, now transformed into a glorified business centre. One undistinguished British entrepreneur was a regular guest at the Shuvalovsky Palace, on the hunt for any opportunity to make a suitable killing (money, that is) in the Klondike years of Russian capitalism. He strode amongst his House of Friendship courtiers, this one-eyed king in the land of the partially blind, scattering around the names of business contacts he allegedly had in the UK and continental Europe, contacts desperately required for the much sought after foreign investment. During these visits, his interpreter informed me, he would sit in the largest room in the palace as lesser Russians, but blessed with connections to the House of Friendship, lined up to ask his advice or help with their own business or, if they were lucky, find themselves recipients of his (constrained) largesse. He was but one of thousands who bee-lined to the economically devastated states of the former Soviet Union, exploiting the wealth of cheap labour and bargain-basement deals thrown up to the foreign investor.

The House of Friendship was an interesting microcosm of Russia's economic players during these troubled years: the criminal opportunist, the state capitalist and the foreign entrepreneur. In frequent collaboration, they managed to drive the country into violent chaos, leaving ordinary Russians stripped of the little assets they owned, and even more vulnerable and weak than they had been under the failing communist system. Chrystia Freeland, a former *Financial Times* correspondent, wrote of that period: 'The biggest crimes have not been clandestine or violent or even, in the strict legal sense, crimes at all ... Russia was robbed in broad daylight by businessmen *who broke no laws*, assisted by the West's best friends in the Kremlin – the young reformers' (emphasis added).[2] This chapter is about these relationships and the accompanying messy, conflicting narratives of Russian organised crime, tales that legitimised, refuted or ignored the devastating harms visited upon an already desperate people, in the name of the free market and democracy.

TO MARKET, TO MARKET …

An enduring image of the failed August coup of 1991 was that of Boris Yeltsin standing on a tank in defiance of the die-hard communists who had tried to drag the country back to its Soviet past. As with the toppling of the statue of Saddam Hussein in Iraq twelve years later, Yeltsin's dramatic gesture became a symbol of the end of a terrible era of repression and a new dawn of freedom and hope. However, as the years rolled by, and with the benefit of hindsight, these apparently 'momentous' events have in both cases turned out to be at best a case of political myopia, at worst an arrogance-infused regard for neo-liberal hegemony. Fukuyama's book *The End of History*, like George W. Bush's famous declaration 'Mission Accomplished', assumed the historical inevitability of a New World Order dominated by Western values; ideals which would be accepted with open arms because they were inherently good, or at least, unquestionably better than whatever else was or had been on offer. 'Shock therapy' economic policies and 'shock and awe' bombing campaigns each laid the foundations for the establishment of these ideals (so declared) in erstwhile hostile societies. That they have produced such chaos in their wake cannot be attributed entirely to the toxic legacies of each society but must also point to the pathological condition of the 'cure' itself.

In 1992 *laissez-faire* was regarded as the magic bullet for the devastated economies of the former communist states in Europe and Asia. Russia's Prime Minister, Yegor Gaidar, quickly established the 'shock therapy' policies advocated by Western experts such as Jeffrey Sachs, a Harvard economist who had been instrumental in the direction of Poland's economic transition, and Anders Aslund, the director of the Stockholm Institute specialising in communist economies. The policies entailed a decisive break from the hybrid socialist market ideas of Gorbachev. This involved the liberalisation of prices, which had been held artificially low by former communist governments, to be followed by rapid privatisation of many of the state industries, with the notable exceptions of energy and minerals.[3] The aim was to stabilise Russia's economy and, after price liberalisation, achieve a budget deficit of 3 per cent or less, keeping inflation, the *bête noire* of neo-liberalism, at 3–5 per cent monthly.[4] Similar programmes had been carried out with some success in Poland and what was then Czechoslovakia. There were concerns raised, however, about the 'one size fits all' mentality that failed to take into account the diverse cultural and historical backgrounds of the different countries from the former communist bloc.[5] Nor were the anxieties of many Russian economists who, prior to the coup, had expressed misgivings about such draconian measures in a country where monopolisation was so entrenched in its economic structures and psyche, given deserved credence. To this latter objection to shock therapy, Aslund responded with 'Even reasonably knowledgeable Soviet reformers have great difficulty understanding what a market economy actually entails.'[6] So, it would turn out, did reformers out West.

The advocates of shock therapy in Russia were given formidable support from Western sources. Washington had offered unparalleled support for the market-friendly Yeltsin during the coup, anxious to ensure that its erstwhile Cold War enemy pursued the 'right' path of reform. According to the US journalist Seymour M. Hersch, such was the desire for a Russian leader dedicated to *laissez-faire* that 'President Bush ordered that essential communications intelligence be provided to Yeltsin – over the bitter protests of the National Security Agency.'[7] Barely two months previously, Gorbachev had been unceremoniously sent away from the G7 summit empty-handed, a political rebuff to his request for aid to shore up the ailing Soviet economy as it desperately sought a compromise position between socialism and capitalism.[8] His post-coup declaration 'I am convinced that socialism is correct, I'm an adherent of socialism',[9] only served to alienate him further from those who saw no alternative other than rapid track marketisation. To be 'our man', as Yeltsin clearly was for the West, brought forth the support not only of intelligence assistance, but of unquestioned billions of dollars into the biggest free market experiment in history.

Shock therapy was adopted by the 1992 April Congress after much heated debate. In the face of vociferous opposition from high-profile politicians such as Vice President Alexander Rutskoy and Ruslan Khasbulatov, Chairman of the Supreme Soviet, a compromise programme was accepted in which privatisation was given a 'socialist' bent. This involved the redistribution of the ownership of large state enterprises to managers, workers and the remaining populace through a voucher scheme. Reformers hoped that this might help ameliorate the impact of financial damage to the public, most of whom saw their savings wiped out after the liberalisation of prices. It was also an attempt to encourage investors and employees in the enterprises to raise standards and increase production, but few were keen to invest back into the ailing enterprises. Instead, machinery was left to rot and workers were laid off. With the dramatic impact of price liberalisation which saw the rouble plunge from 180 to the dollar in January 1992 to 1,200 to the dollar 18 months later,[10] those hardest hit used their vouchers as currency. Worth 10,000 roubles per shareholder in October 1992, they were sold off months later, sometimes at half their original price. The buyers were those most able to weather the storm, having stockpiled dollar currencies or with high-volume rouble liquidity cashflows. It was clear who profited most from this notional gesture of democratic privatisation. As Nelson and Kuzes discovered in their study of Russia's economic reform in the early 1990s, 'Twenty percent of the Moscow DMs [privatisation decision-makers] we interviewed told us that, although workers were ostensibly the buyers of municipal enterprises, "behind them" were "high administrators," "nomenklatura," "black marketeers," or "mafia-structures."'[11] This came as no surprise to opponents of the *laissez-faire* solution who had predicted that the more ruthless speculator would 'acquire vouchers and/or stocks from common Russian citizens, gaining controlling interests in Russia's most valuable properties, and then sell the assets of these enterprises for a quick profit without reference to the individual firm'.[12]

By 1993 a large number of Russians had been thrown into financial despair. In St Petersburg, 32–35 per cent of the population was living below minimum subsistence level.[13] Society was unravelling painfully, with no social safety net to catch the most vulnerable. People lined the streets begging or selling what they had, some the produce from their dacha garden, others what they were able to forage from the few possessions they had. Children, pensioners, the disabled – poverty was indiscriminate. Meanwhile, to the west of Russia Poland, the alleged 'success story' of shock therapy voted in a communist majority, a backlash against the social consequences of its own free market experiment.[14] The impact of the Polish election results on Russia's road to the market, rather than slowing down the frenetic pace of market reform only served to push it even faster towards further privatisation. The biggest concern was not the extent of the damage inflicted on society, but rather whether in Russia, too, the communists would gain political ground in the economic free-for-all that was effectively stealing a nation.

PROBLEM NUMBER ONE?

A number of reasons were put forward for the disastrous outcomes of shock therapy, not least the endemic presence of organised crime or the 'Russian Mafia' (sometimes spelt 'mafiya' to give it a peculiarly Slavonic touch). Racketeering, a problem during the years of perestroika, exploded alongside other predicate crimes associated with organised crime, such as drug trafficking, illegal arms-dealing, counterfeiting, money-laundering and contract killing. The first ever Kremlin Conference on Crime in 1993 was an attempt to analyse and be seen to be tackling the proliferation of crime across the country. Interestingly, it related Russia's problem of the growth of crime to that of developed democratic states, uncharacteristically stating that the growth was 'not ideological but [a result of] numerous contradictions between the individual and society'.[15] Yeltsin famously announced: 'Crime has become problem number one.' The then Vice President, Alexander Rutskoy, who headed the commission, infused his speech with hyperbolic references to an omnipresent danger in a discourse familiar to many of his Western counterparts: 'The present sweep of crime already poses a threat to the existence of the state, its institutions, and more so the people (*narod*) itself.'[16] For a country that had for decades claimed that crime was disappearing, the official declaration that it was now a priority issue appeared to confirm the gravity of the situation. The commission also included results from a sociological survey conducted in 1992 across Russia in which, to the question 'What do you consider to be the biggest problem in your town or village?', 54 per cent of respondents mentioned crime, with unemployment following closely behind at 48 per cent. No distinction was made as to what sort of crime was being referred to. To the more general question 'What in the last year has worried you most?', 67 per cent listed price rises and the fall in living standards as their number one problem.[17] In other words, for the majority of the Russian population, it was the legal economy, as understood, and the blunt violent impact of deprivation as a consequence of reform that they feared above the physical brutality of criminal groups.

For the non-entrepreneurial Russian the problem of crime consisted in 'street' or interpersonal offences such as theft and muggings, and violence in the home, especially in the bigger cities such as St Petersburg.[18] Prior to the changes of the late 1990s, most criminality was economically motivated, comprised of theft and embezzlement of state property, for obvious reasons (see Chapter 4), much of it carried out as a collaborative act between individuals – collective (socialist?) crime. The new economic climate, however, brought with it a different ethos, introducing a brutal interpersonal competitiveness based on the survival of the fittest. Olga, a female solicitor, explained how her partner in a local law consortium, a long-time friend, had been registering clients for his own consultation without telling her. 'We would always share clients,' she explained, clearly upset by this apparent betrayal, 'but now he wants them for himself.'[19] As this behaviour increasingly impacted on the changing nature of criminal behaviour in the economy, one which had hitherto steered away from crimes against the individual, it further alienated a population already reeling from the initial impact of shock therapy, from the current reforms. As in Poland and other former communist states, the maligned Communist Party saw increasing support from the disillusioned.

Problem number one as interpreted by foreign observers was clearly organised crime, not just as a domestic issue but one that took on international proportions. The Western media went into overdrive in its assessment of the threat posed to national security by this terrifying new phenomenon from the East. The murder of two Chechen brothers in London in 1993 sparked off a media frenzy. A *Daily Mail* headline read 'The Talons of the Red Mafia', while the London *Evening Standard* warned 'The Russians are Coming'.[20] Thuggish-looking, gravelled-voiced, swaggering, tattooed, gun-carrying gangsters dressed in 'Godfather'-style pinstripe suits[21] – a stark sartorial contrast to the ill-fitting drab garb of that other obstacle to economic reform, the communist remnants – were not only mean and cruel but their dangerousness was intensified by their apparent access to nuclear materials from Russia's disintegrating military-industrial complex.[22] The alleged transformation of Russia from erstwhile superpower enemy to an out-of-control mafia state was an almost overnight affair. Departments in Western intelligence agencies threatened with extinction in the friendly climate of East–West collaboration could now reinvent themselves as guardians against a new but familiar terror, while law enforcement agencies at national and international levels became the front-line offensive in what was now a global war on crime.

Of the 150 or so pages in the Kremlin Crime Commission's report, only three were dedicated specifically to the issue of 'organised crime' (of which there was no definition given). Yet this vague and small chapter, peppered with statistical data of dubious methodological origin, was uncritically accepted and constantly used by non-Russian academics and official agencies as evidence of the Russian Mafia-state.[23] One of the most quoted extracts from the report was the claim that organised crime controlled up to 40 per cent of Russia's gross domestic product.[24] Nothing was mentioned as to what exactly this entailed – which businesses, services and industries – or whether 'control' involved criminals running businesses, acting in collusion with or against the will of legitimate entrepreneurs, or, ultimately, whether or not this was necessarily a bad thing, given, as Luttwak has contentiously argued, that organised crime in Russia brought a sense of entrepreneurial spirit to an otherwise hostile and incompetent business environment.[25] Implicit in the repetitive use of statistics such as these was the idea of a collective criminal type, one that stood in opposition to the values of the 'new' Russian society, that undermined its imported neo-liberal ethos and hence stymied its healthy economic development. 'Forty per cent of business controlled by organised crime', if left unquestioned, goes a long way towards explaining the chaos and social devastation of the free market experiment as a criminal rather than a legal problem. Tapping into the stereotypes and narratives constructed around organised crime, meaningless data were reconstructed into meaningful inferences. More than 1,000 of the 4,000 organised crime groups in Russia at the time, so ran the statistics, had 'international and inter-regional connections'. Crime groups of three, four or five members? Permanently or temporarily established? Data collection based on what type of crime recording? It appeared unnecessary for Western agencies and media to interrogate these figures too closely, data that gave some of them a *raison d'être* and others a good storyline.

Problem number one was thus constructed as a concrete and familiar narrative with ambiguous references, in which it was possible to gloss over the contradictions of the free market experiment and focus, instead, on an easily identifiable scapegoat. The confusion of legal boundaries in Russia at that time exacerbated even further the propensity for clinging to these narratives, and served to imbue the economic devastation with the usual dichotomy, of good business and evil businessmen. Artificial borders were thus created in the legal vacuum, a vacuum in which the free market was clearly thriving according to its own principles. Indeed, the *real* number one problem, and one that most avoided admitting, was that Russia's 'mafia state' was actually capitalism's picture in the attic, a portrait of an economic model as ugly as its predecessor and one that also brought out the worst rather than the best in humanity.

'MERE KIDS' OF BUSINESS

We have three types of capitalists in our (city). There are entrepreneurs who have been given the chance to make real money, thanks to the changes in our system, and there are criminals who launder their dirty capital in legitimate business. But the first and second types are mere kids in comparison with our 'biznessmeni' in the official structures of power. They, in disguise, are the true masters of Moscow.

(Y. Shchekhochikin, quoted in S. Handelman, 1994)[26]

The second type of capitalist, as described by Moscow crime correspondent Yuri Shchekhochikin (above) and *part* subject of this book, attracts attention largely because of the mythical status and stereotyping that has, in itself, created a lucrative business – the 'mafia industry'. As the cover of this book demonstrates, we like our illegal entrepreneurs to be distinctive, exaggerated in their personae and business activities. However, who they are and what they do is as varied as any business circle. Nor should we always confer on them an intrinsic characteristic of willingness to employ violence, one of the distinguishing features used to differentiate legal from criminal business, unless there is a clear notion as to what is understood by violence. As the rest of the chapter shows, violence and the economy takes on different forms with myriad consequences and can lie quite comfortably on either side of the legal divide. As much of the literature on criminal business or organised crime focuses on dissimilarity, especially in the Russian context, this section of the chapter will look at shared characteristics, at the banality of criminal business amongst the 'mere kids' of Russia's early days of capitalism.

Oleg and his taciturn partner Andrey were, to extend Shchek-hochikin's analogy, the primary-school end of the criminal spectrum, relatively new to the business and among the lower echelons of the criminal hierarchy in St Petersburg.[27] Nonetheless, in their dress and manner they would have made good copy, suitably swaggering and tattooed to fulfil the image we have come to associate with 'mafia'. They ran a thriving prostitution racket in the Moskva, one of the limited number of half-decent places to stay for the foreign visitor in the days prior to the construction frenzy that gave birth to a new class of Russian billionaire and a better class of accommodation. Their business ran on the hedonistic drives of 'respectable' husbands, brothers, fathers and sons from out West, many of whom were able to claim their delights on business expenses. The Moskva is well located, standing opposite the famous Alexander Nevsky monastery and cemetery. This latter is the permanent home to some of St Petersburg's most accomplished residents, including the composers Borodin, Glinka and Tchaikovsky, and Gumilev, the husband of Anna Akhmatova, one of Russia's most loved modern poets. The beautiful grounds of the monastery, in the early years of the hoped-for economic miracle, were also the temporary home of a collection of the city's most desperate, from alcoholics with suppurating sores, to washed-out and diseased street prostitutes, the severely disabled and the grubbiest of children. It was a good spot to beg as tourist coaches pulled up frequently and rich foreigners (we were all 'rich' then) intending to taste the cultural delights of this 'Venice of the north' found themselves having to confront its underbelly, albeit for an uncomfortable but fleeting moment.

The growing supply of beautiful, young females had been nurtured by the effects of the reform, which hit, as always, women as the most economically vulnerable. Many of them could barely maintain a living at subsistence level, never mind purchase the growing stream of desirable Western imports. New dreams emerged from the rubble of communism, visions of unending wealth and foreign travel, best achieved by clinching a marriage certificate with a well-paid non-Russian. Prostitution offered a way out of the impecunious present and a possible means of future security beyond the daily travails of post-communist society. Increasing supply was also met with growing demand, as Russia's Klondike years brought a large contingent of foreign businessmen to its major cities. Oleg and Andrey's business acumen spotted a gap in the lucrative market and the profits soon followed. Occasionally they branched out into other lines of business, such as the sale of counterfeit goods, small arms, or the bigger stuff: for example, according to a probably exaggerated claim by Oleg, the odd decommissioned tank. Many of their circle were drug users (heroin was seeping into the city from the central Asian republics), but neither claimed to be involved either as consumers or as providers of narcotics, and there was no apparent evidence of drug or alcohol abuse during our meetings.

Oleg had spent three years in a prison camp in Zapoliare. He was clearly familiar with the rules of his particular game: who to pay, who not to pay, where he could work and the lines he must not cross. It was a convenient arrangement that involved the *militsiya* and more powerful criminal entrepreneurs. Once he paid a percentage of his earnings to the *militsiya* in the hotel, Oleg was left alone by the authorities to conduct his business:

They [the police] don't get mixed up in my business, unless there's been a murder. Anything else and they're not interested. If one Russian in the hotel is pissed and picks a fight with another, then they come. That's the job they're employed to do in the hotel.

His other outgoings, to those higher up the business ladder, the 'intelligent guys' as he called them, ensured that he and Andrey had monopoly control over the flesh trade in the hotel:

Here, I can take in or hurl out who I want. I can chuck out a prostitute. This is my turf, I've been here a long time. I know the scene. In the Pribaltiskaya [hotel] I can't do this. If I were to go to some of the guys there, they would chuck me out. That's how it works.[28]

It was a sensible business arrangement all round, which is why Oleg never once complained about having to pay protection to the local rackets or the *militsiya*. Oleg was less happy about his relationship with the other state structures, such as the KGB. Even at the height of *bespredel*, or lawlessness, in the new Russia, the old structures of power continued to exert control, real as well as symbolic.

It [the KGB] is the only organ of power which can contain crime. Everything comes under its heel. All the directors of the hotels are former KGB employees, the same with the managers. Everyone working in the restaurants are all with the KGB, listening and informing ... There's this guy here, he worked for the KGB, well he gets pissed. Somebody nicks his gun. So they pick up me and this girl I'm living with. They take away our passports at first, then we have to sit in the entrance hall. They say to her: 'We know you, we can fuck everything up here for you, so you're going to think about who nicked the gun.' I hadn't even been in the hotel that day. They held us for three days.

These were not the rantings of an aggrieved pimp and counterfeiter. Despite the draconian and economic changes, political transformation was more subtle. The state as such, as Vadim Volkov wrote, retained its power base despite the chaos. 'Given the size and power of the state in the Soviet Union and in previous times, stripping the state of any significance during the post-Soviet transition might seem to be a gross error ... narratives in which the state is absent and claims about self-emerging social orders should be treated with

CRIME AND ECONOMY IN THE 'NEW' RUSSIA   107

suspicion.'[29] Ironically, it was Gorbachev, rather than Yeltsin, who initiated sweeping reforms of the state's most powerful arm. Under the radical KGB head, Vadim Bakatin, initial moves were made to reduce the number of personnel and depoliticise the agency, only to be stymied by Victor Barannikov, a Yeltsin appointee, who reinstated its more traditional structures.[30] Volkov's insightful analysis of the security industry and the role played by state agencies alongside and beyond illegal business reveals the enduring power of the state and its ability to respond to the new economic climate. In commodifying state security the protection industry became legal, driving out criminal business, and assuming control of one of the most lucrative commercial ventures in post-Soviet Russia.[31]

It was the racketeering industry which, above all, defined organised crime in Russia during the 1990s. Varese, working with Gambetta's model of the Sicilian Mafia, found similar characteristics between the context and conditions of illegal protection in Italy with those in Russia, based on, *inter alia*, the absence or weakness of property rights and the endemic presence of official corruption, as conducive to the proliferation of racketeering.[32] But, as with most entrepreneurs, those that could, diversified. 'Anton', not only ran a 'firm' that managed over 60 protection operations in St Petersburg, but he expanded into prostitution rings, some international and some involving trafficking, as well as a lucrative vodka export business.

Aside from its marketability in the protection industry, violence, according to Anton, was rarely used in settling disputes amongst his competitors, running, as it often did, contrary to the sole aim of profit maximisation. 'If we are forced to use violence then we will resort to it. But this is pretty rare as it's a serious issue …Then we stop making money and everything is diverted to this conflict.'[33] If there was one part of his business empire that Anton felt least comfortable with, it was the protection industry, thriving as it did in a legally chaotic environment. His hope for Russia and the future was for greater stability, 'safety and well being. I don't want my children to live in a lawless society. It gives me no pleasure at all to live in this condition.'[34] The way out of this situation, he believed, was through capitalism itself. Anton, the racketeer, pimp, trafficker, smuggler and head of one of St Petersburg's successful crime groups, could have stepped out of the Chicago School of economics: 'Capitalism', he believed, 'is a spontaneous movement where everything is self-regulated. This is freedom, and as time passes, an equilibrium is reached.'[35] Milton Friedman would have been impressed.

As one of the more prolific sites of economic activity, the protection industry encompassed the legal, semi-legal as well as illegal spheres. Vladimir, was the head of the security company 'Okhranost', a former police officer whose contacts with the Federal Service for Counterintelligence, the Department to Combat Organised Crime and the Ministry of the Interior allowed him to operate one of the most powerful protection agencies in St Petersburg.[36] In his basement floor office, fortressed against attack by metal doors and an entourage of AK47-carrying minders, Vladimir ran his protection business that looked after foreign firms and some of the successful Russian entrepreneurs in the city. His company was legal, he claimed – 'we don't compromise ... but follow the law' – and had no business connections with organised crime. He always 'resolves problems on a correct basis', and such is his operational ethos that 'the bosses of the criminal world, in St Petersburg, in Russia, take us seriously and open conflict does not take place'. Vladimir's claim to legality and integrity was not shared by the local *militsiya*, but they were unable or unwilling to touch him. Straddling the official structures and the criminal milieu, he was sufficiently protected himself by the politically powerful in the region to enable his highly dubious activities to prosper unhindered by the criminal justice system. Vladimir and his operations summed up the state of play in capitalist 'new' Russia - business constantly moving between the legal and illegal, the *ad hoc* grasping of opportunity and the will to exploit to the full the prevailing ethos and chaos of the economic reforms.

These snapshot examples of criminal enterprise, operating at various levels of organisation, of membership numbers and influence, support the familiar descriptions of organised crime that inform the narratives of threat and violence. Celebrity characters from this world, such as Yaponchik and Mikhailov, have achieved international status in part through their ability to travel for business purposes beyond their borders, but, more significantly, because of what they represent rather than their actual activities.[37] The high levels of violence they employed, reflecting the violence woven into their indigenous society, have justifiably attracted attention and concern. However, these levels of brutality, mainly directed at those involved in illegal activities, either as competitors or partners, have often been confused with the *extent* of their influence.

Russia's criminal world cannot and could not operate successfully and over the long term without the compliance of and negotiation with the official structures. The Russian state, as Volkov notes, never collapsed in on itself. There was no revolution and no real anarchy (although some provincial regions got pretty close to it). Even at the height of its chaotic condition, the state remained powerful enough to engage in conflict with the Chechen region in 1994, and again after the rouble crash of 1998. Yeltsin retained sufficient control over the security forces to enable him to crush the 'troublesome' political elements that opposed his reforms in 1993. In other words, had the state through its security agencies genuinely wished to tackle problem number one, it could have done, as Oleg pointed out. However, official priorities lay elsewhere and, in many instances, Russia's criminal world had a part to play in the pursuit of them.

MASTERS OF MOSCOW

The most successful entrepreneurs in Russia, according to the journalist Anna Politkovskaya,[38] are

> ... those who first get a slice of the State pie – that is, a State asset as their own private property. This is why the vast majority of big businessmen in Russia are now former members of the Communist Party nomenklatura, the Young Communist League or Party workers ... the second is that once you have been successful in appropriating State assets, you stay close to the authorities – that is, you bribe, or 'feed', officials regularly. This should guarantee that your private enterprise will prosper. The third condition is to make friends with (i.e. bribe) the law enforcement agencies.[39]

The state pie was in the process of being sliced up even prior to the breakup of the Soviet Union. One of the first large-scale privatisation schemes in Moscow,[40] the year before shock therapy was officially set in motion, involved a conglomerate known as UKOSO, whose job was to transfer the whole district or *ispolkom* from the public to private sector. The conglomerate, a mix of business people and officials, planned to set up the Oktyarbrski region, the size of the London Borough of Islington, as an area of rapid investment, free from 'bureaucratic bias'. The scheme involved the sale or 'relocation' of social centres and residential accommodation, including recently constructed flats intended to rehouse large families, for the purposes of investment by interested business groups. It was a monolithic project steamrolling over residents' objections, many of whom were due to be transferred or displaced from their homes to other regions in the city.[41] Complaints to the Moscow City Council would have been futile as UKOSO had invited some of the council members into the scheme as shareholders. The scheme dragged on beyond the collapse of communism but was halted by the city mayor, Yuri Luzhkov, in late 1992 at a time when privatisation was still politically sensitive. It took only a short period of time, however, for the politically sensitive to become normal practice.

Russia's rapid privatisation programme transferred over 14,000 state enterprises to the private sector during a two-year period (1992–94), the largest transfer of property ownership in one go,[42] although the large industries, in particular energy and minerals, remained in the hands of the state. There was also a huge surge in the privatisation of residential property, especially in urban hotspots. Real estate provided not only a means of laundering criminal capital but also opportunities for criminal business to work with developers, in much the same way that the Yakuza had been instrumental in moving reluctant residents out of their prime-site accommodation in Japan.[43] The *kvartinaya* (apartment) mafia, as they were known, intimidated or even murdered those who refused to hand over their 'des res' homes to developers. Anecdotal accounts spoke of residents being hurled out of their twelfth-storey apartments by these 'clearance' groups. Yet, despite the attempt to provide a more egalitarian form of privatisation through the voucher scheme, the winners remained a small group of official-linked entrepreneurs or entrepreneurial officials. According to one public poll, nearly half of the respondents believed the privatisation programme to have benefited those in the shadow economy, and over a quarter believed it to have been in the interests of the *nomenklatura*.[44] The actual beneficiaries, however, according to another study, were more likely to be the *nomenklatura*. As the majority of privatised firms, especially the bigger state concerns were unprofitable and required substantial investment over a period of time, the report concluded that it was highly unlikely that criminal elements, driven only by profit acquisition, would be directly involved.[45] Even if they were, however, there was little that could be achieved in big business without the backing of the relevant officials. But who were these officials?

The explosion of political parties in the Russian Federation during its first year brought into the political arena diverse characters from equally diverse backgrounds. In 1992 there were 18 political parties registered, including the Democratic Party of Russia, the Peasant Party of Russia, the Russian Party of Communists and the Party of Economic Freedom.[46] The chaos of transitional politics, in contrast to the defined agenda of the Soviet Parliament, posed a challenge to onlookers. Gone were the clear lines of ideological identity and predictability of a one-party system. Outsiders, especially from the West, sought meanings that were compatible with the old system, a typical binary landscape of understanding, Cold War dichotomies playing this time as 'you're either with shock therapy or against it'. Those in opposition to the free market, either in their credo or in the underlying values that appeared to contradict those behind shock therapy, were understood as communists, or criminals or, worse still, both. As in the title of Handelman's influential text on crime and economy in 1990s Russia – alliterative, succinct and comfortably simplistic – the new enemy was a fusion of past and present: 'Comrade Criminal', synthesising the two *bêtes noires* of twentieth-century Western civilisation as defined most stridently by Washington. Communism and the mafia had now become one, an amalgamation of the major threats to the free market and, most importantly, the main reason for Russia's inability to adapt successfully to the economic programme intended to lift the country out of the ruins of an experiment gone horribly wrong. What emerged was instead a 'mafia state':

> The connection between organised-crime groups, the military industrial complex and provincial leaders recreated the criminal state inside Russia's post-communist society. Inevitably, the comrade criminals played a major role in politics. Mob money and Communist Party funds supported newspapers and certain right-wing political groups, and some provincial crime lords reputedly financed the political campaigns of anti-government candidates during the December 1993 elections.[47]

However, this was a jaundiced view, reflecting only one aspect of reality by insinuating clear boundaries between two seemingly different types of economic behaviour, when in fact none existed. Good and bad economic actors were designated according to whether their perceived roles were regarded as supportive of or obstructive to the new system. In most cases it was difficult to make any such distinctions amongst the heaving and interwoven mass of opportunists, from the lower depths of the Olegs and Andreys to the upper echelons of politics and business, The arbitrary understanding of the term 'comrade criminal' was further subjectified by its arbitrary application, formulated and employed according to the 'who' rather than the 'what'. Labelling thus had little to do with whether actors were involved in legal or illegal business, but rather with their ideological affiliations. This not only worked to create a scapegoat population such as 'criminal communists' but, on the other hand, as discussed below, enabled advocates of shock therapy to act unethically and even illegally with little or no redress because they were on the 'right' side. Nor was this confined to the jurisdiction of the Russian Federation. According to criminal intelligence in St Petersburg, the much respected Mayor of St Petersburg, Anatoly Sobchak, a vociferous supporter of Yeltsin, was detained and then released at a London airport when he was discovered to be carrying a suitcase full of undeclared paper currency during a trip to the UK to promote business between the two countries. The British authorities, it seemed, had deliberately turned a blind eye to Sobchak's attempt to smuggle hard currency in the interests of mutual economic advantage.[48]

Privatisation in Russia was largely about who could grab the most and the quickest. Human nature rather than ideological affiliation was the real issue. That the overwhelming number of those who benefited most from privatisation – the real masters of Moscow – were erstwhile Communist Party members was only relevant insofar as it provided them with opportunities to best exploit the new economic environment. By focusing on the spurious ideological identity of economic actors and their instruments (as in 'mob' money) rather than on the nature of their activities and the harms inflicted, it became easier to justify, or, more accurately, abnegate the need to justify, the problems thrown up by the free market. Ideology became little more than a means of rationalising on the one hand, and scapegoating on the other.

LAISSEZ-FAIRE DEMOCRACY

Underlying the justification for introducing the free market model to former communist states was the notion, already expressed, that it would inevitably lead to the establishment of rule of law. Olsen's argument that it is in the interests of the 'stationary bandit' to eventually create and then work within a legal business framework developed the idea as expressed by the Mont Pelerin Society that those societies opposed to free market principles and their legalising/ civilising consequences would inevitably encourage the opposite. Established by the grandees of free market philosophy, including Friedrich von Hayek and Milton Friedman, the Society had declared in its founding statement that:

Even that most precious possession of Western Man, freedom of thought and expression, is threatened by the spread of creeds, which, claiming the privilege of tolerance when in the position of a minority, seek only to establish a position of power in which they can suppress and obliterate all views but their own. The group holds that these developments have been fostered by the growth of a view of history which denies all absolute moral standards and by the growth of theories which question the desirability of the rule of law. It further holds that they have been fostered by a decline in the belief in private property and the competitive market ...[49]

The Russian experience of *laissez-faire* however, questioned many of the underlying assumptions of the Mont Pelerin Society, not least in the development of a transparent and democratic system of governance. While the legacy of communism, seeped as it was into the emerging political system, clearly stymied moves towards genuine democracy, the neo-liberal agenda actively contributed to the arbitrary implementation of the law. More worrying, it was given vociferous support by democracies in the West.

By 1993 the much vaunted shock therapy policy was facing growing opposition in the Russian government. Despite the draconian moves to pull the economy out of the communist rubble, the country found itself hit by a depression with production falling by 15 per cent over an 18-month period.[50] In April of that year a four-question referendum designed to break the impasse between the executive and the legislature on issues of economic reform and constitutional change went in favour of the pro-market President. Nonetheless, the State Duma continued to block proposed changes, a move also exacerbated by Yeltsin's demand that he should be given emergency powers. After months of publicly aired scandals and accusations flying between pro- and anti-reform factions, Yeltsin took a firm stance on the political stalemate and unconstitutionally dissolved Parliament. His action was challenged by the Zorkin, the Chairman of the Constitutional Court, which promptly led the President to order the security forces to surround the White House, the seat of the Duma. The bloody confrontation that followed between supporters of the Yeltsin camp and those behind the conservative element of the Russian Parliament, at whose head stood the Vice President, Rutskoy, broke out at the Ostankino television tower on 3 October and ended with the bombing of the White House by the security forces the following day. The death toll of those killed in the confrontation was officially put at a 176,[51] although the figures are disputed by unofficial sources, which put the figure as high as 1,500.[52]

While there were no innocent parties on either side of the conflict, two facts remained. Firstly, Yeltsin's move to dissolve Parliament was illegal, and secondly, the crushing of the anti-Yeltsin camp was disproportionately aggressive. Neither of these facts seemed to resonate with neo-liberal states out West, which gave their explicit support for Yeltsin's actions. The then British Prime Minister, John Major, assured his 'total and unequivocal support'[53] to the Russian leader, while US President Bill Clinton remarked, 'It is clear that the opposition forces started the conflict, and President Yeltsin had no other alternative but to try to restore order.' Clinton's support for Yeltsin was based on the notion that 'he is Russia's democratically-elected leader', hence 'I have no reason to doubt the personal commitment that President Yeltsin made to let the Russian people decide their own future in elections.'[54] Academics also lent their voices of support to Yeltsin, one of whom, Thomas Remington, justified the dismissal of Parliament as 'a solution to the political impasse'.[55] Given the large measure of approval of his crackdown from those who wielded considerable influence on institutions such as the International Monetary Fund (IMF) and the World Bank, both of which were enthusiastically bankrolling Russia along its free market path, Yeltsin continued one of the most vigorous strategies of power centralisation the country had witnessed by creating a new constitution which placed more power in the President's hands than *de jure* Stalin had possessed. He also outlawed a number of opposition political parties, including the Russian Communist Party, which he had unsuccessfully attempted to ban in 1991. Remington, explaining the unconstitutional sacking of Parliament as a 'solution' (above), went on to state that they improved 'the odds of democratic revolution'.[56] Yet the reality of the October crackdown and its aftermath was, as history has shown, and as Naomi Klein acerbically wrote, 'to defend Russia's capitalist economy from the grave threat of democracy'.[57]

Laissez-faire democracy in Russia was clearly shaped according to an adherence to the credo of 'private property and the competitive market'. Violence was condoned when its agents were free market supporters, even when perpetrated as a consequence of illegitimate action by the agents themselves. How different the Western response to Yeltsin's centripetal power-directing strategies to the more diluted bid for centralised power by Gorbachev, the socialist, in his creation of the Presidential Executive, where he was described as having 'rammed through measures to establish a new Soviet Presidency' which 'contains seeds for future dictatorship'.[58] Neo-liberalism in the Russian context (as in numerous others across the globe) was emerging as the very threat the founding principles of the Mont Pelerin Society declared it stood in opposition to. In other words, the ideology of neo-liberalism was creating the very conditions the Society had attributed to, *inter alia*, Soviet communism. The arbitrary exploitation of executive power and subsequent disabling of serious political opposition, both condoned in different ways by the West, revealed the extent to which the economic aspirations of a few could override the political interests of the majority. This was not simply law-making by the powerful for the powerful, but law-breaking by the powerful for the powerful, reconstituted as a political 'moral' necessity in the face of 'illegitimate' opposition. More importantly, it sent out a message that foreign governments, which vehemently criticised the practice of legal relativism in the Soviet Union, would condone the very same in the name of free market ideology.

Yeltsin quickly translated foreign support into a carte blanche for other draconian domestic policies. In the same month that he cracked down on 'former communist *apparatchiks*' (in American media parlance), an anti-crime programme in Russia's capital, ostensibly aimed at tackling organised crime, was initiated. The Mayor of Moscow, Luzhkov, declared that the intention of the programme was to

> ... clean the city with the help of enhanced police patrols, public organizations, volunteers and democratically-minded youth ... As for empty markets, we will possibly not have exotic fruit and vegetables but honest dealers will come from Lipetsk, Bryansk and other places to sell traditional Russian food. We should have open markets and not mafia controlled trading facilities.[59]

The implicit identity of these so-called criminal populations were traders from the southern republics such as Georgia, Azerbaijan and the Caucasus, main suppliers of 'exotic' foods and representative of the majority of stallholders in the capital's markets. Distinctive by their dark-skinned features, they became targets for the *militsiya*'s brutal 'problem-solving' response to the anti-crime drive. The mafia ethnic card was played to great effect in Russia, where xenophobia and racism, especially acute in times of economic crisis, lie thinly below the surface. Nikolai Modestov, author of *Moskva*

Banditskaya, summed up the general attitude when he wrote that 'the history of organised crime in Moscow, as well as Russia as a whole, was written by the representatives of the Chechen criminal communes'.[60] While there was little doubt that crime groups from the Caucasus and south were active in Russia, they were singled out as the major and most threatening population, amongst a number of even more violent and effective Russian groups.

Whipping up racism as part of a crime control strategy, particularly against Chechens, helped to prime the Russian population for the assault on Grozny, the capital of Chechnya, in late 1994. What was famously predicted as being a war of hours rather than weeks by the Defence Minister, Pavel Grachev, the first Chechen war of two years' bloody duration became a test of Yeltsin's resolve to consolidate state power within the Kremlin. Chechnya's declaration of independence three years previously threatened to set a precedent for other regions seeking secession from Moscow. Yeltsin had to be seen to be tough and decisive. There was also the issue of oil. An agreement put forward with a consortium of US and British petroleum companies in 1994, and signed the following year, promised a cash-strapped Russia millions of dollars from sales and tariffs from the Caucasian pipeline passing through Chechnya.[61] Grozny was pounded by Russian artillery, bringing the estimated death toll of civilians (both ethnic Russian and Chechen) in the city alone, according to one source, to 25,000.[62] Yeltsin's phalanx of foreign supporters raised little or no opposition. Indeed, Clinton was reminded to note that America, too, had had a civil war, and, as 'no state had a right to withdraw from our union',[63] so attempts at secession in Russia should be firmly resisted.

As the rhetoric of Islamic fundamentalist threats to democratic states (including those aspiring to democracy) became a dominant feature of international political discourse[64] towards the end of the twentieth century, the largely Muslim population of Chechnya yet again became the target of another Russian military assault. Explosions in two Moscow apartment blocks in the early autumn of 1999, killing more than 200 people, were attributed by the Russian government (with little or no evidence) to Chechen separatists.[65] Vladimir Putin, Yeltsin's anointed successor, used the Moscow attacks to justify the second invasion of Chechnya, hence consolidating his position as the new tough and decisive President. The Chechen mafia threat had metamorphosed into Chechen terrorism. This time, however, there were more Western voices in opposition to the military action and its impact on civilian life in the beleaguered region. Russia's relationship with the West had gone into decline during the last couple of years of the millennium's last decade. The free market experiment had clearly failed. Hence turning a blind eye to human rights abuses was no longer necessary as Russia appeared to be taking its own political and economic path, increasingly in opposition to that mapped out by the neo-liberal agenda favoured in Washington and London. Those once deemed friends and 'good' business partners were now the new 'mafia'.

ROBBER BARONS AND GANGSTER CAPITALISTS

The road to market upon which Russia had embarked, and which was turning out to be politically and socially as well as economically disastrous, became known by Western observers as, *inter alia*, 'wild', 'robber baron' or 'gangster' capitalism. It was as if, by inserting an adjective of a disparaging nature, moral distance could be created between capitalism in Russia and that in the so-called 'advanced' capitalist systems. The avaricious designs of Russia's entrepreneurs, the harmful outcomes of much of its business activity, needed to be understood as distinct from rather than natural to the economic model foisted upon it. In the delirium of communism's collapse, and what was subsequently understood as a resounding endorsement for capitalism, problems emanating from the shock therapy experiment needed to be explained as aberrations. The Soviet legacy bore most of the brunt of explaining the explosion of crime and corruption. The failure to develop workable models of privatisation was understood according to either the historical development of capitalism, as in the robber baron narratives, or as a combination of the enduring influence of communism and/or the peculiar nature of Russian culture. Wild or gangster capitalism played into the notion of a society at home with high levels of violence, where life was cheap, the law historically abused and exploitation and corruption a natural inclination of state institutions. While none of this was untrue, its emphatic delivery, drowning out alternative or complementary explanations, obfuscated an important additional narrative. As in any experimental situation, where the results magnify conditions or qualities of the subject being tested, the free market experiment in Russia (as in many South American states) exposed the flaws and dangers of capitalism, not least the consequences of a system that appeals to and nurtures material as opposed to ethical individualism (or individuality). Russian-style capitalism was different only insofar as it produced an exaggerated form of the economic model, but not one that differed in its qualitative attributes to those forms apparent in 'advanced' capitalist states. In other words, it exposed a myth.

'Robber baron' capitalism was used to describe the period in which a group of powerful oligarchs emerged by bankrolling the beleaguered Russian economy in an attempt to ensure the re-election of Yeltsin in 1996 and, by extension, the continuation of free market reform. It drew parallels with the so-called 'robber baron' era of American capitalism when big business and financiers steamrollered legislation they regarded as inimical to their interests, such as cutting out competition and price-fixing. It was also a period when big business often operated hand in glove with politics. The usage of this term in relation to the development of capitalism in Russia was premised on the notion that the US robber era was but a temporary phase, and that the colossi of Russian business, as with their American counterparts such as the Morgans, the Drews, the Goulds and the Vanderbilts, would be brought to heel and emerge as philanthropic and law-abiding citizens.[66] Neither the premise nor its application reflected reality.

The robber baron narrative, as with the imported mainstream narratives of organised crime, were based on a myopic vision of events within the US itself, more on myth than reality, an endorsement of the fabled landscape upon which capitalism has been perceived and understood. The taming of the American entrepreneur was little more than a mildly effective curbing of big business and its influence. The intended legal restraint came from the Sherman Antitrust Act of 1890 but, as Howard Zinn notes, the legislation not only had few teeth but ended up as a weapon against the vulnerable and for the powerful:

> The [Supreme] Court also said the Sherman Act could be used against interstate strikes (the railway strike of 1894) because they were in restraint of trade. It also declared unconstitutional a small attempt by Congress to tax high incomes at a higher rate (*Pollock* v. *Farmers' Loan & Trust Company*). In later years it would refuse to break up the Standard Oil and American Tobacco monopolies, saying the Sherman Act barred only 'unreasonable' combinations in restraint of trade.[67]

Comprised of a population sympathetic to, and often in collusion with, big business, the Supreme Court, as interpreter of US law, acted, in the words of one banker, as 'guardian of the dollar, defender of private property, enemy of spoliation, sheet anchor of the Republic'.[68] Nor did the evolution of capitalism in the twentieth century mark a significant change in attitudes and behaviour. Edwin Sutherland's definitive study *White Collar Crime*, published as a monograph in 1949, and the first of its kind to focus attention on law-breaking amongst the economic elite (followed by an initially slow but growing body of literature on the subject) exposed a level of systematic law-breaking and manipulation as a normal condition of capitalist corporate behaviour. He likened corporate business to professional criminals, in not only having a disregard for the law but in their persistent violation of it. If some form of progress from the days of 'wild' capitalism have been achieved, it is certainly not as developed as orthodox narratives describe. For Sutherland the American corporation pursued 'a truly Machiavellian ideology and policy. It has reached the conclusion that practically anything is possible if resources, ingenuity and strenuous effort are used ... [including] the objective of manipulating people'.[69] Literature on US and other advanced capitalist states' corporate activities beyond their domestic jurisdictions, especially in developing countries, provides little evidence of an evolving propensity towards the development of law-abiding behaviour, thus giving lie to the concept of a *phase* of robber baron capitalism, and Olsen's assertion that market economies *per se* encourage 'private firms and individuals [to] do much more to discourage violation of the law'.[70] Rather, the behaviour so described is simply displaced to regions where rule of law is weak, and exploitation and law-breaking can occur with impunity.

Neither is the application of the robber baron narrative to the Russian situation entirely appropriate as a historical parallel. America's nascent market, as with that in Britain, evolved within an insular and largely protectionist environment as part of the nation state,[71] unlike the global economic landscape that confronted the 'new' Russia. Nineteenth- and early twentieth-century capitalist economies were dominated by industrial production rather than finance, real or virtual, operating as the leading commodity. This latter scenario entangles different national economies in the complex web of global finance and in doing so makes it more difficult to ringfence the transgressions of dominant figures in a particular jurisdiction. In other words, the behaviour of Russian 'robber barons' cannot be isolated from those engaged in business from more advanced capitalist economies. (Perhaps advanced capitalism is best described as the point at which theft and economic abuse become more democratic?)

LOANS FOR SHARES – CRIME OF THE DECADE?

Russia's oligarchs emerged as a response and solution to the economic crisis facing the country in 1995, a year before the presidential elections. Shock therapy reform had become so unpopular that the reinstated Communist Party led by Gennady Zyuganov saw significant gains in the Duma during the 1995 parliamentary elections, raising the possibility that Zyuganov might be a serious contender for the presidency. Billions of dollars of aid from the World Bank, the IMF and USAID were being poured into Russia on the understanding that the administration would continue with its *laissez-faire* programme. A political backlash would stop or severely slow down the process. Despite the cashflow from the West, productivity levels continued to fall, and the government found itself forced to address its huge budgetary deficit through credits from the central bank, thereby causing massive inflation. There was, however, one source available from where to raise the desperately needed capital in time to stave off economic meltdown before the presidential election. Successful entrepreneurs who had made their fortunes in the cut and thrust of the early years of privatisation, including figures such as Boris Berezovsky, Vladimir Gusinsky, Mikhail Fridman, Mikhail Khordokovsky and Vladimir Potanin, agreed to lend money to the government to the tune of over £1 billion (9 trillion roubles) and became leading figures in what was known as the 'loans for shares' scheme.[72] This involved low-interest loans to the government from private banks, secured through the auction buyout to these entrepreneurs of major state-owned companies whose shares would be held as collateral by the banks until the loans were repaid. In the meantime, the enterprises would operate under the management of the shareholders. The two main goals of the scheme, from the government's perspective, were to inject cash into the much depleted reserves of the treasury and, at the same time, remove the 'red directors' in charge of the large state enterprises, including the mineral and energy industries. On the side of the entrepreneurs already having accrued vast amounts of capital, the scheme offered them a direct line to the Kremlin; as one academic put it, 'the oligarchs never needed cash, just connections'.[73] In the end they got a huge cache of the first and an even greater reserve of the second.

The scheme was initially met with suspicion by one of the leading reformers, Anatoly Chubais, the major link between the Russian government and Western donors. Faced with economic collapse at such a politically sensitive time, he eventually acquiesced while quietly acknowledging that the business elite would simply 'steal and steal',[74] which is *de facto* what more or less occurred. The plan went ahead at the end of 1995, but the auctions were clearly rigged and the industries sold well below their value, in what was effectively insider privatisation. Chubais was later to state that while the auctions were clearly fixed, the exercise was justified in the interests of preserving free market reform.[75]

The scheme was greeted with uncomfortable but tacit support from the West, despite the obvious illegality of its execution. The *Financial Times* best summed up the general attitude in its acknowledgement that, while there were 'dubious' operations behind the scheme, they had nonetheless 'injected some fresh thinking and new capital into some of the country's most managerially moribund companies'.[76] Most importantly, they achieved their political aims. Yeltsin was re-elected in what Daniel Treisman described as 'Russian Tammany Hall'[77] (a reference to the business- and criminal-linked sponsorship of the Democratic Party from Tammany Hall in New York during the late nineteenth and early twentieth centuries), and the 'red directors', as the remnants of communist influence over state assets were finally prised away from the country's industrial crown jewels.

In many ways, however, the loans for shares scheme was hardly out of the ordinary in the cut and thrust of global economics, and most evident in the light of the crisis gripping major capitalist economies in 2009. Chrystia Freeland was quick to make the connection:

> Loans-for-shares was such a naked scam, such cynical manipulation of a weakened state, that – especially now, as Russia continues to fall apart – it is tempting to dismiss the rapacious oligarchs who instigated it as just plain evil. Yet as I watched them plot and profit, I couldn't help asking myself how different the Russians really were from our own hero-entrepreneurs, the gizmo-makers and the Internet tycoons and financial wizards our society so fawningly lauds for producing an era of unprecedented prosperity.[78]

Privatisation was now steaming ahead in all sectors of the economy as the country moved even further into its 'robber baron' state. Berezovsky and Gusinsky bought up large sections of the media, Murdochising what had previously been state terrain;

Khordokovsky continued to expand his oil empire, and the remaining energy and metal industries were gradually swallowed up by the privatisation frenzy in backroom deals. In a bid to recoup some of the assets it had more or less given away, the government set business tax at nearly 40 per cent. Predictably, Russia's big businesses moved most of their capital into offshore accounts, filling the banks in Switzerland, London, New York and numerous small island tax havens. If this was Russia's robber baron 'phase', advanced non-robber baron economies were lending a proactive hand to their unscrupulous neighbours, positively encouraging the rapacity recognised by Freeland.

The growth of Russia's financial sector exploded in the 1990s, mimicking institutions in the West but with neither their economic stability (as it was then) nor reserves. Speculation on stocks and government bonds, in particular the treasury bonds known as GKOs,[79] by domestic and foreign investors was frenzied, spurred on by the ludicrously high returns. In 1997 the best-paying shares were said to be offering returns of up to 1,500 per cent, making Russia 'the world's hottest emerging market'.[80] Economists were optimistic, and publications such as *The Coming Russian Boom*[81] predicted a rosy future for Russian and Western investors alike. It was a short-term and highly illusory situation. However, in 1998, as the aftermath of the Asian economic crisis of the previous year, which had prompted a fall in oil prices and the selling of Asian-held Russian GKOs, began to take hold, Russia found itself facing an unprecedented economic crisis. Unable to meet its debts it defaulted on payments, most notably $40 billion in GKOs. With the devaluation of the rouble, the economy went into meltdown, a financial Chernobyl whose toxic clouds wafted over Russia's borders into the world's markets.

In the months following the crash, recriminations abounded and narratives changed. The oligarchs, hailed only three years previously as part of Russia's 'fresh thinking' on the economy, were now held largely responsible for the recklessness of their financial machinations. The crash had hurt world economies, investors lost billions and a number of hedge fund groups, most notably Long Term Capital Management,[82] collapsed. In contrast to the uncomfortable but nonetheless gently applauded support for the business elite's challenge to the communist directors of Russia's energy and mineral industries, the *Financial Times*, under the headline 'How Russia's Mafia Cashed In On Capitalism's Crisis', now excoriated these very same.[83] Their hitherto ability to push out the 'red directors' and instil some genuine entrepreneurial drive into Russia's economy and create the apparently frenetically lucrative financial system in the aftermath of the presidential election was now interpreted as indulging in the 'murky waters of secret deals and holding companies' – a fact that passed by many Western observers during the 'theft' of Russian assets in 1995, as they buried their heads in historical amnesia. With great irony, Boris Kagarlitsky commented how 'the Western press discovered corruption in Russia, only after the collapse of the rouble and the onset of financial crisis in 1998'.[84]

Five years after the dramatic economic meltdown, and as Russia began to establish some kind of economic stability largely through its energy resources, Vladimir Putin, the tough-talking and even tougher acting President of Russia, cracked down on the oligarch circle in a bid to assert greater state control over Russia's assets, in particular oil and gas. He ordered the arrest of Yukos CEO Mikhail Khordokovsky[85] on suspicion of fraud, tax evasion and embezzlement. The main reason given for the motivation behind his arrest (clearly selective, as the charges could have been applied to any other of the oligarchs, most of whom remained untouched by the arbitrary justice of the state) was that Khordokovsky had broken an informal deal with Putin not to use his position for political influence. It was believed he intended to fund Yabloko, one of the main opposition parties to Putin. But there is another, less trumpeted reason for his arrest. Just before Khordokovsky's detention, it was rumoured that Yukos was about to sign a deal with Exxon, a major Western oil company,[86] which would have given a foreign company major shares in one of Russia's most lucrative industries. The advantages for Western interests were clear, both politically and economically. The oligarchs, many of whom, like Khordokovsky, were looking for substantial foreign partnerships, had once again become friends of the West. Their history was rewritten, or conveniently forgotten. The oligarch 'mafia' of 1998 were now 'victims' of an emerging totalitarian state, one seemingly hostile to the interests of business out West. Khordokovsky, according to an editorial in the *Financial Times*,[87] was described as 'no saint' – the most damning statement on his biography; hardly the vitriolic tone found in the aftermath of the post-rouble crash. The new account stated that 'despite the rumours, these men did not become billionaires through violence or *mafiya* tactics. Rather, they became billionaires by playing the game more effectively and ruthlessly than anybody else during Russia's free-for-all transition to capitalism'.[88]

PICTURE IN THE ATTIC

But now that so many of us have given up on the dream of a resurrected Russia, we have been seduced by a titillating new set of images: gangsters, shootouts, drugs, prostitutes, money-laundering and kick-backs. Blaming Russia's woes on these lurid forms of crime and corruption is easy, and exciting – but it's not really true.

(C. Freeland, 2000)[89]

The devastating consequence of the loans for shares debacle went far beyond those of conventional criminality. It led Russia into even greater social and economic hardship than that experienced in the early days of shock therapy. Yet, as Freeland points out, the enduring images of Russia as a 'failed' free market economy remain dominated by tattooed, gun-toting mafiosi. It was they who were deemed largely responsible for the devastation wrought by the introduction of *laissez-faire* economics, the solution turned problem. But beyond the imagery of close-cropped male thugs, the discourse of the Russian mafia and Russian organised crime told stories of several degrees of 'otherness', of realities and values distinct from 'outside' observers and their 'inside' supporters, a discourse wrapped in ideological, political and social ambiguities and subjectivities. These extra layers of ideological and political references were especially useful when the 'insiders' betrayed, either intentionally or otherwise, the vision and idealism of the economic model sold as the panacea to communist ills by the outsiders.

Mafia narratives are based on moral distancing within a particular mode of behaviour, especially economic. While in their most simplistic form they are reiterated by a Lombrosian style focus on physical characteristics created or enhanced by certain types of images, such as the mug shot, they can be transposed onto other 'undesirables' whose physiognomy and biography might elude such facile representations. Even the oligarchs, the engine of Russia's free market, could easily be categorised, according to the moral estrangement of mafia discourses when expedient to do so, not by their physiological characteristics but by their ethnic and cultural background and heritage. That this became necessary from the Western perspective was due to the fact not that they betrayed the principles of the free market, but that they embraced them fully. Russia's aspirations of full-blooded capitalism were not a failure of the free market, but an unqualified success. For the free market experiment in Russia, like Oscar Wilde's picture of Dorian Gray (the grotesque 'true' image of the soul of the philandering and murderous

Gray hidden from the world in an attic, while the portrayed assumed a public countenance of unageing beauty and innocence), presented a true image of the inevitable harms and injustices of the free market. Thus narratives of organised crime and the arbitrary labelling of its terminologies created a veil behind which the countenance of advanced capitalism hid its true features, where socially constructed criminal acts become a distraction from, or obfuscation of, a system which amplified the human consequences of an economic model that, as Edward Skidelsky writes, 'today defines itself simply as a science of choice under conditions of scarcity [where] practitioners are debarred from talking about morality, save as an instrument of growth, as "moral capital"'.[90]

Five years before Russia plunged headlong into *laissez-faire*, Michael Douglas had brought his Oscar-winning performance as Gordon Gekko to the Hollywood screen in the film *Wall Street*. Intended as an anti-hero, the ambitious stockbroker became an inspirational figure for a new generation of entrepreneurs whose principles were based on wealth accumulation without principles. Gekko's philosophy summed up the business culture of neo-liberal America and Britain: 'Greed,' he states, 'for the lack of a better word, is good. Greed is right, greed works, greed clarifies, cuts through and captures the essence of an evolutionary spirit.'[91] It was a philosophy that resonated with a corrupt generation of the Soviet *nomenklatura* responsible for exploiting its people behind the doors of political privacy, a philosophy that endorsed a generation of underworld entrepreneurs whose callous tactics became integral to their success. The Gekko ethos marched in through the door of shock therapy and it was this that greeted Russia as it embraced the free market. In many ways, Soviet communism and Western capitalism had found their common ground.

THE RUSSIAN KLONDIKE

Larry Hagman, who played the infamous J. R. Ewing, a philandering ruthless business magnate, in the American TV series *Dallas*, a popular import to Russian TV screens, once claimed that the series was 'directly or indirectly responsible for the fall of the [Soviet] empire. They would see the wealthy Ewings and say "Hey, we don't have all this stuff." I think it was good old fashioned greed that got them to question their authority.'[92] Arrogance on the side of Hagman, perhaps, but not a million miles away from the reality.

Russia of the 1990s became a Klondike for both indigenes and foreigners. All manner of speculator was drawn to a country of massive resources and cheap and skilled labour. In 1993, Richard Poe, a self-styled, Russian-speaking business expert, published *How to Profit from the Coming Russian Boom*, a guide for those intending to do business in Russia but slightly put off by the chaotic and criminal conditions. Poe takes a sober line, exploding many of the myths attached to who constitutes the 'mafia' and how influential it is as an operation. He leads prospective gold-seekers through the maze of Russian customs, culture and mindset, providing a list of practical 'dos and donts' in a book that offers plenty of largely accurate information to do what it says in the title. Poe begins by reassuring the hesitant speculator that 'the chaotic conditions in Russia lend themselves most readily to the entrepreneur'.[93] In other words, legal ambiguity, leap-frogging on the back of economic recession, riding the frenzied rollercoaster of reform, are all conducive to the free market speculator. One of the most lucrative opportunities, he writes, is privatisation: 'Some 7000 factories ... will thus be up for grabs at bargain basement prices ... As you know, the very essence of investment is to buy cheap and sell dear.'[94] But the thrust of Poe's 'grab it while you can' philosophy, not surprisingly, was short on the human cost of these opportunities. He describes the informal sale of share vouchers by the cash-strapped poor and hungry, whose concept of value was determined according to its ability to satisfy the most basic of needs, as follows: 'Some entrepreneurs are reported to be hawking them [vouchers] in the streets and subway stations ... But such trade has its limits. When a Russian on the street sells his voucher to another Russian, the seller doesn't have enough information handy to price his voucher accurately.' Nor does he appear to note the irony of his anecdotal reference to the fact that 'Russian prostitutes – notoriously conservative in financial matters – are readily accepting vouchers in return for their favors.'[95]

Poe's world, as that of any free market entrepreneur – whether in New York or Moscow, London or St Petersburg, Tokyo or Ekaterinburg, whether an arms dealer or drugs trafficker, an importer of legal goods or person smuggler – was based on profits over people. In the Russian context, freed from the constraints of eternally resented and resisted, whenever possible, legislation curbing the 'free' in the 'market', the immoral consequences of an economic model that claimed an amoral stance, became glaringly obvious. The starkness of Russia's lawless economic and social

landscape exposed as false the concept of an embedded morality
in the socially constructed legislation that governed Western forms
of the free market, legislation designed to create a moral distance
between legitimate and illegitimate business. For in this Russian
legal wilderness, as Poe and his like discovered, the free market
could be at its most freest. It was in this chaos of transition,
the dog-eat-dog mentality that drove the economy, that the free
market realised its true potential: respectable business, able and
willing to work alongside and with its criminal and quasi-criminal
Russian counterparts. The neo-liberal picture in the Russian attic
revealed the moral ugliness of economics without responsibility,
an economics based not on human need but on human greed,
an economics that oppressed genuine freedom and democracy,
substituting these for egoism and inequality. Most importantly, it
reiterated the fact that crime, and in particular organised crime,
is a politically exploited social construction, a means not only of
creating an expedient 'threat' but of displacing accountability for
the inhuman consequences of the dominant economic model. Russia
exposed the free market not as inherently conducive to law, order
and democracy, but rather as an encouragement for law-breaking,
social disharmony and subtle forms of authoritarianism.

One of the most common forms of illegal behaviour by foreign
businesses in Russia is bribery. Despite its endemic practice, offering
and receiving a bribe is proscribed by the Russian Federation's
Criminal Code[96] (a fact that came as a surprise to a couple of members
of the foreign business community I spoke to in St Petersburg).
During the early days of shock therapy, at a British conference on
doing business in Russia, corruption was one of the topics under
discussion. The majority of the business community there were
happy to lay the blame squarely on the shoulders of the Russians:
'Their culture, not ours.' When asked what would happen if their
company refused to pay bribes, the consensus was that business
would be lost to a competitor. It was pointed out that responsibility
must then surely lie not only with Russian culture but also with the
competitive model of economics. Only one person agreed with this
assertion. The rest stated that such a claim was naïve and clearly
reflected the speaker's ignorance about business matters.[97] In another
situation a CEO defended his company's behaviour on the basis
of responsibility to shareholders. As Poe brashly acknowledges of
his own business culture, saying 'no' doesn't come easy, so other
ways are found to avoid breaking the US Foreign Corrupt Practices
Act which prohibits payments to foreign officials. Delegation of

bribe-giving to a Russian employee solves the dilemma. One of his interviewees explains: 'If part of that money goes for bribes, you tell them you don't want to know about that. That's their problem. You just pay them the fee and they get the job done.'[98]

The myopic vision of the capitalist ethos that prevailed in Russia's so-called transition manifested as denial, euphemism and calculated ignorance. The symbiotic relationship between foreign companies and Russian criminal business was refuted at every opportunity, unless the foreign company was portrayed as a victim. A risk assessment report for foreign companies in Russia highlighted the problems of racketeering, but offered a note of optimism, as in this tacit endorsement of the advantages to be gained by collaborating with illegal protection firms:

> ... the British company was eventually told that it had little choice but to accept the offer [of illegal protection] if it wanted to operate in Russia at all. Despite this inauspicious start to the partnership, the Chechen 'company' has proved able, and the British company is beginning to make a substantial profit. Apparently the British company's main competitors are also using the same distributor.[99]

The more cynical and knowledgeable observer, such as Poe, acknowledged the pragmatics of working with the 'enemy'. Journalist Tim Sebastian also delivered it straight: 'Their [Western firms] willingness to lie on their backs and be abused by Russia's organized criminal networks must rank as one of the least resisted rapes in history.'[100] Handelman was more cautious, alluding to the possibility of such collaboration but maintaining a belief in the integrity of the foreign entrepreneur: 'Without realising it – *or, at least, so one would hope* – Western businessmen flocking in to exploit the rich resources in Central Russia end up providing a cover of legitimacy to Russia's comrade criminals' (emphasis added).[101]

It was not only the foreign business community, travelling pioneers of shock therapy, that exploited this legal and moral vacuum. The shock therapy missionaries themselves, bearers of the Mont Pelerin principles, became embroiled in the very activities these principles were supposed to eradicate. Shock therapy had its origins in the Chicago School of economics, a model of *laissez-faire* that was adapted by Jeffrey Sachs, a Professor at the Harvard Business School, for countries such as Bolivia, Chile, Poland and Czechoslovakia. On the apparent (short-term) success of these experiments he turned his attention to Russia. Shock therapy, 'Iraq without the explosives',[102] as Klein cynically described it, was undertaken in Russia with the consultative and financial support of a group of experts from Harvard University's prestigious Institute of International Development (HIID). They worked alongside the Chubais clan (named after Anatoly Chubais, one of the 'golden' boys of the 'new' Russia) and his small elite of 'reformers', who had the ear of the most powerful political people in Russia, and were soon themselves to become politically powerful through the high-level links they had forged with the US.[103] A study of the *modus operandi* of Western aid to former communist states during the 1990s, focusing in part on the HIID and Chubais clan networks, was conducted by the social anthropologist Janine Wedel. Her fieldwork and findings reveal a system of corrupt clans, systemic law-breaking, nepotism, 'theft' and bribery on *both* sides in the process of establishing a free market economy in Russia. The programme of privatisation, described by one Western economist as '*de facto* fraud',[104] created highly lucrative consultancy positions for the specialist team from Harvard Business School which had direct access to the Russian President. Few of the contracts went out to tender and were largely kept within the incestuous world of the HIID-Chubais clique. Further, unpopular policies advocated by the clique, certain to incur opposition within the Duma, were often ratified by presidential decree thus bypassing the parliamentary process.

Advocating pluralism and competition in theory, the HIID and Chubais clan created the Russian Privatisation Center (RPC), 'home' of the partnership and a conduit for much of the aid and grants (according to one estimate, $4 billion was managed by the RPC). Aid was distributed in Russia according to political considerations and, as the prime player in the funding game, the RPC ensured that any policies passed by the Duma seen to conflict with their own were effectively blocked. The nature of this relationship, Wedel concludes, 'served to reinforce many communist-type practices: it strengthened the interdependence between the Russian economic and political systems, and reinforced the practice of inventing fictions to please the authorities (in this case, the donors)'. When two members of HIID were revealed to have been involved in substantial payoffs and insider dealing, it was clear that 'communist-type practices' were not confined to the Russians. The dangers of such relationships are clear, Wedel warned: 'Using "developmental assistance" political assistance to one political group or leader was a feature of the Cold War ... which continued into the post-Cold War period in the form of new elite-elite relations'; a situation, she notes with prescience, where 'the potential for political backlash is significant, serious and has potentially grave consequences ... .'[105] The backlash came remarkably quickly.

BACK TO THE FUTURE

By the end of the 1990s, with Russia reeling from the devastating impact of shock therapy and plunged into yet another financial disaster, a firm hand emerged to bring order out of chaos. Putin was no Hitler or Stalin, but he recognised the need (and opportunity) to re-instigate the centrifugal forces of power. The path back to authoritarian-style governance was welcomed by the majority of the Russian population, for whom benign dictatorship and stable prices were preferable to democracy and the vagaries of the market. Reining in those deemed responsible for the economic crisis of 1998 was one of Putin's defining acts in his early years, a Machiavellian move that would entrench the power of the state once again in the economy. For the majority of Russians who had seen their lives negatively affected by the events of the previous decade, it mattered little that the charges laid against the oligarch Khordokovsky and his company Yukos, if not entirely spurious, were certainly unfairly selective. Employing the wide-ranging presidential powers bequeathed by his predecessor, Putin was able to claw back Russia's crown jewel industries – energy and minerals – effectively under the control of the state through a series of political manoeuvres, which ensured that only those loyal to the Kremlin would sit on the boards of blue chip companies. This meant, as Lilia Shevtsova comments, that

> ... a captain of big business who is not embedded in the Kremlin's unofficial networks is a foreign body. For all his intrigues and protestations of loyalty, he is inimical to the system because he has economic clout and, not being beholden to the president for his company's wealth, may at any moment become an independent player ... He is a potential threat for the personalized regime, and given the present system, doomed. The last surviving oligarchs of the Yeltsin era have embedded themselves in the structures of bureaucratic capitalism through individual deals. One can only guess what services they now render to the authorities for the privilege of being left in peace. For all that, they can be crushed at any time and they definitely understand this.[106]

Bureaucratic capitalism operates at many levels. In Ekaterinburg, capital of the Urals region, which produces 60 per cent of the country's oil, one Russian entrepreneur, reiterating other similar anecdotal accounts, confirmed that anyone who wishes to establish a business in the city must have the approval of Lukoil, the country's largest oil producer, otherwise 'it simply won't happen'.[107] In the city of Perm, on the Western side of the Urals, a similar mantra was heard. Kremlin connections, however tenuous, are essential for ensuring security for local and regional enterprises. Money still speaks, but only though a Moscow-approved larynx.

This synergy between politics and business has also had a 'trickle down' effect on the more traditional forms of criminal business. Volkov's study points to how most protection rackets have now become private legal organisations, dominated by former state security employees with continuing links to the state.[108] Even where bandit-type rackets exist, they tend to operate at a low and local level, offering protection to new or small businesses in the locales, providing effective security against street crime and helping enforce agreements in those locales where the police and state courts are especially weak.[109] The real problem for small and medium businesses lies with the local authorities and the labyrinthine regulatory process necessary for setting up and maintaining a business. Bribes for a range of services such as the acquisition of licences or for favourable inspection reports (in some cases, as many as 22 inspections a year have been carried out on some businesses[110]) are essential for the survival of entrepreneurship. Unlike many of the protection rackets, bribe-taking can be disorganised and uncoordinated, even for foreign firms. One foreign businessman explained that he had been forced to relocate his business to China because of the *ad hoc* and arbitrary demands made by local regulators so that his premises would pass health and safety inspections.[111]

The politicisation of business has relegated most organised forms of criminal business to the status of 'underworld as servant', an employee of the business-state in much the same way as it operated under Soviet communism. Few crime groups now exist in Russia that can act autonomously, and those that do have such freedom are left alone because of their insignificance rather than their strength. Alongside the usual type of illegal business activities, they are often engaged in doing the 'dirty work' for officials and 'respectable' entrepreneurs. High-level murders, such as those of the journalist Anna Politkovskaya, a constant critic of Putin and corruption, and that of Andrey Kozlov, First Deputy Chairman of Russia's central bank, a zealous reformer who revoked the licences of a number of banks suspected of money-laundering,[112] are more likely to be from the hand of crime organisations working under the command of the bureaucratic capitalists. That no one has been prosecuted for these high-profile crimes hints strongly at powerful and untouchable 'respectable' forces behind the killings.[113] Order might have been established in Putin's (and currently Medvedev's) Russia, but this has occurred at a high cost – a *de facto* rejection of the rule of law.

SILENT FLIGHT

The hysteria surrounding an invasion of the 'Russian mafia' as a destabilising force in Western society proved to be just that – an over-reaction to a phenomenon riddled with ambiguity and misunderstandings. Crime control agencies such as the UK's National Criminal Intelligence Service admitted that the threat had been exaggerated, although not until after running a number of expensive and largely futile intelligence-gathering operations.[114] The real problem, however, was much closer to the mundane activities of the legal business world. As Shevtsova notes:

> Yet, we have to admit that a number of Western entrepreneurs, lawyers and politicians have evidently demonstrated flexibility in their partnership with the Russian state, since it is hardly likely that the Russian elite would otherwise have been able to use the West as an enormous washing machine for laundering its capital and siphoning off wealth to offshore zones. In some cases, participation of Western business in shady deals in Russia not only appears to legitimize its bureaucratic capitalism but also to spread the virus of corruption to Western economies.[115]

The 'virus of corruption' might not be as endemic in Western business as it is openly so in the Russian context. Nonetheless, it has little trouble in finding a willing non-Russian host. In an economic system where money itself is a central commodity the opportunity and encouragement for corrupting forms of behaviour are inevitable. This is evident in the selective implementation of money-laundering legislation which has largely been directed at easily identifiable, though in many cases relatively small, levels of asset cleaning, by those whose business is mainly concerned with proscribed commodities and services such as narcotics and forced prostitution. In the ever-murky world of multinational business, following paper trails through the complex virtual space of finance has led to the highly subjective and selective targeting of laundering offences. 'Who' owns the money rather than the nature of its origins has a defining impact on the execution of legislation. The science of compliance, as a banking official explained, is often based on the status of a particular client; in other words, their investment potential.[116]

The nature of the investment as well as the identity of the investor also plays a crucial role in the subjective construction of 'dirty' money. Culture, sports and other leisure activities, while increasingly run as commercial ventures, have a less hard-edged and more ethically appealing status than raw business, operating as they do, in theory, as more egalitarian ventures, involving the masses. A number of sports in Britain, including the 'beautiful game', football, have attracted generous investment from former Soviet Union sources with little regard for the colour of the money pouring into it. The lax accounting regulations in many former communist states make the already complex paper trails even more opaque, so generous investors need hardly worry themselves about investigations into the source of their profits. Few are foolish enough to attempt an exposé of these untouchable magnates. Those that do, tend to come to some sorry end, most frequently crushed by litigation.

*   *   *

At this point, a couple of case studies were going to be used as an illustration of the contentious sources and backgrounds of investors from Slavonic and Central Asian regions into the sport industry. However, the influence of money not only in the world of business and leisure but also over the civil courts in this most liberal of liberal democracies, has stayed my potentially libellous hand. Libel laws in Britain have become a most effective form of 'censorship by private interests: a sedition law for the exclusive use of millionaires'.[117] Unlike the usual practice that maintains the defendant is innocent until proven guilty, British libel law assumes the guilt of the defendant until proven otherwise. So skewed is this legislation in favour of the plaintiff, that even reference to reliable open sources, as was to be the case here, that have investigated the unsavoury backgrounds and activities of some of these investors, could be deemed libellous. Britain shares this billionaires' delight with one of the most authoritarian states in the former Soviet Union, Kazakhstan, whose libel law also places the burden of proof on the defendant. Journalists prepared to expose political corruption in their country risk driving their newspapers to bankruptcy through costly lawsuits brought by the plaintiff's bottomless pit of financial resources. The 2002 Media Sustainability Index placed Kazakhstan at the bottom of its table of 20 former communist states as the most 'unsustainable anti-free press'.[118] Such an analogous situation must be about as welcome to advocates of media freedom in the UK as Sacha Baron Cohen's parodic Kazakh film character 'Borat' is to the Kazakh tourist board.

* * *

In an adaptation of the old adage 'money has no smell', capital assumes a distinctly pleasurable aroma when offered in abundance for the interests of the powerful on the back of the exploited. What is clear, however, is that in the economic relationship between Russia and the West during these post-Soviet years, full of promise, disappointment and suspicion, the categories of 'good' guys and 'bad' guys, 'us' and 'them', have been little more than the fevered designations of minds infected by the virus of self-satisfying wealth accumulation.

CONCLUSION

In the concluding scene of George Orwell's dark 'fairy tale' (as he described it), *Animal Farm*, a group of pigs, including the leaders of the rebellion against the owner of the re-named Manor Farm, are sitting in the farmhouse with the 'enemy', landowning farmers from the region. From outside the house, gazing at the spectacle with fearful amazement, are the half-starved, overworked animals whose lives have been dedicated to following the ever-changing tenets of the rebellion. They watch as the two groups – pigs and men – drunkenly toast the achievements of the rebellion. Mr Pilkington, one of the farmers, remarks that he and his colleagues are so impressed with what he saw, 'a discipline and orderliness' and the practice whereby 'the lower animals on Animal Farm did more work and received less food than any animals in the county', that they must emulate these methods on their own farms. Orwell's novel has been largely interpreted as a sharp criticism of the hypocrisies of Soviet communism. However, it is equally applicable as a critique of capitalism, as Orwell's socialist ideals would testify. Despotic forms of governance, mass exploitation and corruption are not confined to communist regimes. An economy of greed has dominated much of the development of modern economy, an ethos which traverses spurious ideological boundaries. Orwell's fairy tale is as relevant to the demise of Soviet communism as it was to its inauguration. From this common ground of self-interest, pigs and men, communists and capitalists, criminals and the legal entrepreneurs upon which they rely flow the disastrous consequences and endemic harms of the modern economy.

As Russia creeps its way back to an increasingly authoritarian society, wounded by the failures of two economic experiments, it seems set to combine the worst aspects of each system: centralised individualism. And as the West and the rest move closer to the economic chaos Russia has experienced *in extremis*, we might ask: Could Russia's path possibly be a foreshadowing of what might happen in advanced capitalist states, and, if so, what lessons can be learned from the shared pathology that links communism to capitalism and legal business to organised crime?

6
The Sovietising of Western Society

... countries, whole continents, repeat each other's mistakes at a later date, sometimes centuries later when one would have thought that everything was so painfully obvious.

(A. Solzhenitsyn, 1972)[1]

For the idea of humanity, when purged of all sentimentality, has the very serious consequence that in one form or another men must assume responsibility for all crimes committed by men and that all nations share the onus of evil committed by others.

(H. Arendt, 2000)[2]

Russia's tragic experience of communism is not unique, nor too the destructive outcomes of its experiment with capitalism. Each economic model and examples of the suffering both have caused can be found scattered around twentieth-century history and increasingly across vast swathes of global society in the twenty-first century. Economic vandalism, the outcome of these models, is now a fact of life for millions upon millions, and the number continues to grow.[3] Its myriad manifestations, including civil conflict, war, poverty, disenfranchisement, enforced migration, unemployment, the destruction of the environment, clearly have played into the hands of those who seek to gain from the growing pile of human debris. Only when such gain is collaboratively and *illicitly* executed do we call it organised crime.

Pino Arlacchi's address at the 2000 UN Palermo Convention Against Transnational Organized Crime typically upholds such narratives:

> *Outside* threats have not only changed in nature, but have multiplied. It is such challenges as: the trafficking in illegal drugs and weapons; international terrorism; environmental degradation; the spread of diseases such as HIV and hepatitis; and transnational organised crime that are the successors to conventional war *in threatening human security from without*.[4]
> (emphasis added)

However, economy and crime, as the previous chapters have shown, are messy concepts. Consider the following, common, Saturday afternoon transaction.

A pirate DVD, according to nine-year-old Katelyn, is a film you can watch before it comes out in the cinema but is a little bit fuzzy at times. This is true because she watched *Finding Nemo* at her friend Lana's and it hadn't come out then. Lana's father got it from a 'friend' of his. ('You can still watch it at the cinema if you want to. It's probably better. Not as fuzzy.') This so-called friend, in the euphemistic way of parental discourse, was a Chinese trader selling illegal copies on one of London's East End retail estates. There was no obvious negative consequence to this transaction, other than the possibility that the goods might be of poor quality. Things turned out well, as it happened: a decent recording, good price and, anyway, the kids don't really mind the quality. They'll watch anything.

The Chinese trader was a pinched-looking individual, working alongside similar others, at the bottom end of one of the many counterfeit businesses operating around the UK. But one person's cheap buy is another's irritation. Frank from Leyton has his day disturbed by these illegal traders. 'It is getting to the stage where I have to fight my way through these people to get to ASDA's or the gym. They are not aggressive but just a pain in the arse. "DVD, DVD" is all you seem to hear when in Leyton Mills.'[5] What made a hapless Chinese trader want to leave his home and family, pay huge sums of money for illegal transport to the UK, end up locked into slave labour at his destination and threatened and intimidated if he fails to meet his daily quota of sales? The demand for cheap trainers made in a factory in Tangxia which pays below subsistence-level wages for its workers so that Frank can jog his way to the gym and have money over for an extra bottle of Bourgogne Rouge? Economic vandalism is often an invisible phenomenon. So, too, is the thread that links each of us to its perpetration. Local geography and self-interest lie at the heart of most interactions in modern economy. The bigger picture, and the responsibility it imparts to those who have knowledge of it, is hidden behind the complexities of division of labour, of distance and time, all of which remove the need for moral engagement with the economic process and its human consequences. Fed on narratives of 'outside' threats and antithetical value systems, there is no obvious connection between the purchase of an illegal DVD, stag nights in a brothel and celebrity cocaine-snorting divas, with the depraved world of forced labour, trafficked women and poverty-stricken farmers in Colombia and Peru. Such narratives aim to dissociate rather than connect, exclude rather than involve. The same is true of other serious crimes, as Dorling notes in his insightful analysis of murder in Britain:

> Murder, behind the headlines, is the story of the connected consequences to our collected actions. Murder, despite being the rarest of crimes, tells us in the round a great deal about millions of us who will never be even remotely connected to such a death directly ... behind the man with the knife is the man who sold him the knife, the man who did not give him a job, the man who decided that his school did not need funding, the man who closed down the branch factory where he could have worked, the man who decided to reduce the level of benefits so that a black economy grew ... .[6]

The 'whodunnit' pitch of his analysis brings together the most unlikely suspects, a string of actors, from top politicians to street level traders, respectable members of respectable society all of whom make up the complex web of harm causation. This is not the narrative we wish to hear, one that joins the aetiological dots that make up the social whole, revealing a picture that defies the neat socially constructed 'moral' dichotomies we hide behind. The comfort of difference, detachment and disassociation has become a defining feature of our attitudes to crime, especially in an age where, as Dorling notes, the threads of attachment are ever-present; even more so, one might argue, in our economic transactions.

So, too, in the modern economy has economic life been largely understood according to ideas rather than moral outcomes, ideas which are often detached from the tangible world they seek to explain, ideas which can conceal reality. The assumption of the ideological narrative is that ideology is a 'prime mover'. According to Foucault, however, it rather 'stands in a secondary position relative to something which functions as its infrastructure, as its material, economic determinant, etc.'[7] Ideology is little more than a tool of its narrators, one which frames perceptions, creates illusions of difference, obfuscates shared behaviours, constructs boundaries where none exist. For, ultimately, it matters not whether hundreds of thousands suffer because of the mistakes of communism rather than capitalism, or vice versa. The real issue is that they *do*. Neither communism nor capitalism has brought the desired outcomes its advocates hoped for. Gross inequalities and creeping forms of authoritarianism are more the order of the day than the realisation of inspirational goals of economic justice and social freedoms. An ineluctable propensity for harm is clearly evident in both economic systems. The outcomes of this, in its extreme form, are to be found in the many strands of illegal economy which prey on the human debris of the economic debris of its legal counterpart. The narratives of organised crime avoid this story or tone it down, failing to tell us that this is not an *outside* threat, but a symptom, a product of internal pathology.

The burgeoning of criminal entrepreneurship in the Soviet Union has been justifiably regarded as one of the dystopian consequences of the failure of economic centralisation.[8] However, the same argument has been suspiciously absent in accounts for the apparent proliferation of the illegal economy in capitalist economies, most significantly in the global context of transnational crime and the neo-liberalist agenda currently dominating world politics and economy. While there are numerous examples of hyperbole and the creation of moral panics regarding the *threat* of organised crime,[9] the evidence for a marked growth in those predicate crimes associated with criminal collaborations of this nature is less easy to dismiss. Forced migration is steadily increasing, creating larger populations of 'vagabonds' for whom choice and opportunity are denied not just at source, but in movement and at destination. Reluctant mobility has become one of the pernicious outcomes of modern economy: chasing jobs, fleeing land/resource-fuelled conflict, pursuing aspirations that cannot be fulfilled, yet must be attempted otherwise those on the move risk total exclusion even at the lowest levels of survival. Illegal entrepreneurs have cashed in on the movement industry, exploiting each step of the journey, and playing their part, too, in ensuring the journey has no end.

In the aftermath of the recent credit crunch (sounding more like a muesli bar of economic chaos than the inevitable outcome of greed, exploitation and cover-ups), the shadow economy will undoubtedly expand its activities and client base and, by definition, open up even further opportunities for brutal exploitation. And as always, the largest group of victims will come from the poorest sectors. Yet the discourse of crime as a symptom of the intrinsic pathologies of the free market remains barely audible. Despite the obvious harms inflicted by the market in its current form, many attempts to create substantive changes to the system have been opposed on ideological grounds, dragging up the old fears of creeping socialism.[10]

This obsession with ideological dichotomies obscures or detracts from pathological similarities between economic systems. Hence, the possibility of learning from Russia's experience both of capitalism *and* communism remains outside the orthodox conceptual framework. The narratives on organised crime in Russia, which have been formed out of these dichotomies, as the last chapter illustrates, have been an important tool in helping to obfuscate correspondences. Look beyond these and it becomes clear that ideology is little more than a convenient chimera. This chapter broadens the discussion of economic harm by identifying a number of social, political and ethical outcomes of the modern economy which cross the ideological divide and coagulate in a trend we might describe as the 'Sovietising of Western society'.

MODERN ECONOMY AND ACCOUNTABILITY

Economic relationships in modern society have little or no concept of the 'whole'. Division of labour, one of the defining characteristics of modernity, not only opened up the possibility of intensive and diverse production but also fragmented what had once been very personal, physically close economic ties. The pre-modern economy was confined by geography, each household and village being largely responsible for the provision of local needs. Transactions were transparent, so that each party would have an awareness of the conditions and costs involved in the goods to be exchanged, services offered, and so on.[11] In the modern economy, personal proximity between producer and consumer is rare, operating instead through a complex web of negotiations and individual histories, rendering invisible much of the economic process. While the geography of production and demand has expanded dramatically, the points of transaction have remained locally confined. Producing and purchasing still involve human interaction, but at myriad different stages of a long process and with a variety of actors disassociated from the end points of supply–demand (in the virtual age of online economy, human interaction can be eradicated altogether). In a structure defined by time and distance (where it is easier to find Nemo in the deep waters of Sydney Harbour than to trace the biographies of the products we produce and consume), the perpetration of harm through the economic process becomes a more likely possibility. Ignorance as one consumer's bliss is another's misfortune.

Division of labour as fundamental to modern economy has been understood largely through the lens of ideology. For Marx the fragmentation of work was regarded as dehumanising, one in which the labourer can no longer 'confirm himself in his work, but denies himself, feels miserable ... does not develop free mental and physical energy, but mortifies his flesh and ruins his mind'.[12] Unless there is an equitable sense of labour division within a planned economy, man becomes separated from 'his essential being', his creative self, tied instead to the demands of those who own the means of production. The negative impact of such an arrangement is not only confined to manual labour. From this perspective, white-collar workers are also subject to alienation 'where the market economy has been fully developed' because 'a man's activity becomes estranged from himself, it turns into a commodity which, subject to the non-human objectivity of the natural laws of society, must go its own way independently of man just like any consumer article'.[13] In contrast, classical economists, most notably Adam Smith, while recognising the dangers of over-fragmentation, claimed numerous benefits from division of labour. The increase in production, he argued, would provide 'that universal opulence which extends itself to the itself to the lowest ranks of the people'. Specialisation, rather than dislocating the worker from his creativity, would lead to an improvement of skills, his 'dexterity', and by implication a greater fulfilment of the 'self' through these improved capabilities.[14] Smith's positive appraisal was echoed by the sociologist Emile Durkheim who regarded such an economic arrangement as a new form of social cohesion in which mutual economic dependency supplants the old ties of kinship and hierarchy. These economic bonds are contractually determined and, in a healthy society, allow for the development of the individual through the establishment of legal rights. As societies grow larger, so too will these bonds of interdependency strengthen as the division of labour becomes more complex.[15]

In neither understanding of the division of labour is the economic actor usually regarded as an autonomous entity. The effect of his (or her) actions is determined by the nature of the economic structures in which he operates. In other words, as an individual he cannot be held accountable for the consequences of his economic activity. The ethical dimension of economic relations in modern economy as traditionally understood must always lie outside the individual. Moral agency, therefore, is sited within the social as expressed by the economic. Lenin asserted this position in response to a question about communism and morality: 'to us there is no such thing as a morality that stands outside human society; that is a fraud ...

Communist morality is based on the struggle for the consolidation and completion of communism.'[16] The same pertains for capitalism, albeit with a different entry point. It is in the capitalist division of labour that material self-interest is transformed into the common good, a redistribution of wealth through an 'invisible hand', as famously described by Adam Smith:

> It is not from the benevolence of the butcher, the brewer, or the baker, that we expect our dinner, but from their regard to their own interest. We address ourselves, not to their humanity but to their self-love, and never talk to them of our necessities but of their advantages.[17]

Morality in relation to economics is thus regarded as a product of society, the individual a passive actor and agent of unintended (or involuntary) consequences.

When, therefore, economy infiltrates other aspects of society, becoming an increasing influence on, and hence deterministic presence in, social life beyond its immediate realm, as in the hegemonic neo-liberal model, so, too, moral agency becomes further removed from the individual. The 'commodification'[18] of health, education, criminal justice, and so on, in neo-liberal societies, as in planned economies, impresses a heavily deterministic quality on those areas of social life least fitted to the economic paradigm, and in doing so increasingly erodes individual responsibility and hence the moral base upon which these sectors function. For example, to think in economic terms, in education, as in the setting of quantifiable targets for intellectual achievement, typically in schools' SATs (Standard Aptitude Tests)[19] or the research assessment exercise in higher education,[20] cost-benefit analysis, as in the economic rather than intellectual benefits of running particular courses, or contract-defined relationships where students become 'consumers', unquantifiable aspects of being human are being forced into a limited and dehumanising framework. This leads to the inevitable intensification of the Weberian snare of bureaucracy as political-managerial structures are increasingly required to ensure the 'efficient' operation of the business model structure. And as with corporate organisations, accountability becomes diffused, passed around by each link in the chain like a hot potato when things go wrong. The individual as a responsible and humanising entity in areas of soul welfare and social development becomes instead the product of dystopian reality. Criteria hostile to this type of economic paradigm of quantifiable, morally indifferent outcomes are increasingly edged out of the picture, seen as (literally) worthless. Meanwhile, those aspects of being human which support the paradigm – greed, cunning, exploitation, self-interest, and so on – are given commendable status despite their ethical deficit.

Deterministic models of economy encourage moral bankruptcy almost as a presupposed condition for membership of economic life. In the absence of accountability for the impact of our economic actions we nurture an environment conducive to harmful behaviour, both legal and illegal. It is this abnegation of accountability, *the absence of ethical individuality as integral to modern economy*, most evident in the Russian experience of communism and capitalism, that has helped create conditions conducive to organised crime, not only as an ontological reality but in the construction of narratives that condemn it as antithetical to, rather than consequent of, the normative values of modern economy.

Russia's cultural and historical propensity to subjugate the individual, his or her rights and responsibilities, has enhanced the barbaric qualities of economic models which abjure individual moral agency as a major component of their functioning. As the previous chapters have shown, these models provide ideal conditions for the maintenance of powerful elites and criminal behaviour, for arbitrary justice and legal ambiguity.

In the light of these two failed and failing economic models, in particular the neo-liberalist model, Robert Reiner calls for a different emphasis on the individual in the light of social and economic interests:

> Egoistic individualism regards individuals as responsible primarily for themselves – neighbours hold back! Reciprocal individualism sees all individuals as mutually responsible: neighbours are to be treated as oneself, requiring equal concern and respect. These two versions of the ethics of individualism suggest radically different notions of social policy, crime and criminal justice.[21]

Reiner's critique of neo-liberalism and its *de facto* rejection of the 'responsible individual' is underscored by a cautious optimism in the possible emergence of more widespread forms of social democracy, premised on the hope that centre-left institutions, albeit rapidly becoming an endangered species, will have left a sufficiently strong legacy to provide some foundation for the realisation of this alternative. My own view, while concurring with much of what

Reiner says, is less optimistic. While reciprocal individualism breaks with the traditional forms of self-serving responsibility, it does not go far enough. More radical responses are required to avert an implosion of society on the scale that occurred in the Soviet Union. For despite the unpredictable and destructive outcomes inflicted on many of its population in the pursuit of a *laissez-faire* model of economic reform, such an alternative did at least exist to stay the dissolution into bloody chaos. In the event of a global economic crash, there are not even quasi-viable alternatives strong enough to ameliorate the inevitable anarchic condition that is already bubbling under the surface in a number of struggling states.[22]

THE SOVIETISING PROCESS

The tendency points in another direction, one that could best be described as a 'Sovietising process'.[23] In other words, those negative characteristics which defined Soviet society and created conditions conducive, *inter alia*, to the proliferation of the criminal economy are present in ever-increasing frequency in the West; in particular, in those doyens of neo-liberalism, the United States and Britain. These characteristics, while manifesting in different forms, have similar inimical outcomes to those which tore apart Soviet society. While there are no doubt numerous forms of this Sovietising process, the overwhelming sense of Sovietisation as understood here comes from those factors which impose a ruthless yet stealthy erosion of genuine individual freedom, the death of *individuality* – the creative, unique and responsible self, as opposed to the notion of individualism as the promotion of self in the egoistic sense referred to by Reiner. Before discussing the Sovietising process and its relationship to criminal enterprise in more detail, we need to understand this notion of the ethical self as individuality.

Individuality and Responsibility

The individual as a moral agent is, as described here, premised on Bauman's understanding that:

> Responsibility being the existential mode of the human subject, *morality is the primary structure of intersubjective relation* in its most pristine form, unaffected by any non-moral factors (like interest, calculation of benefit, rational search for optimal solutions, or surrender to coercion). The substance of morality being a duty towards the other (as distinct from an

obligation), and a duty which precedes all interestedness – the roots of morality reach well beneath societal arrangements, like structures of domination or culture ... Morality is not a product of society. Morality is something society manipulates – exploits, re-directs, jams.[24]

The individual as an autonomous moral actor is one whose actions involve 'being for the other',[25] as Levinas describes it, an inescapable condition of freedom, which itself is born out of a commitment or responsibility to the 'other'. This is not the 'reciprocal individualism' Reiner refers to, but a step beyond. It requires a move further than the mutual to the 'other', not *as* oneself but *before* oneself. While mutual responsibility necessarily involves conditionality, a response as a contractual obligation of reciprocation, ethical individuality has no such conditions attached. Further, implicit to the concept of mutual responsibility, is a level playing field of reciprocation, one which, in reality, rarely exists. Indeed, Reiner makes this observation when describing the changeable levels of agency confronting the offender. 'Choice and responsibility – and hence the scope for condemnation and just punishment – remain. Offenders make their own histories – *but not under conditions of their own choosing*' (emphasis added).[26] In the world of the modern economy, one increasingly split by gross inequalities, individual circumstances will have an impact on the extent to which this 'being for the other' can occur, to whom and in what capacity. This translates into a duty of the powerful towards the more vulnerable; as Pemberton notes: 'if "being for the other" is unconditional, then a moral obligation is borne by the developed world, whatever ideological and historical disputes exist over the responsibility for the suffering of these people'.[27] Hierarchies of privilege thus bring a certain relativism to the active realisation of this inherent, but as yet only momentary or sporadic engagement of the responsible, ethical self with the 'other'. This in turn releases the individual from external compulsion, placing responsibility for being a responsible self in the hands of each person in their unique situation, at a specific time.

However, circumstances conducive (rather than compelling) to this active recognition can be manipulated, curtailed or threatened especially when related to economic association. Neither communism nor capitalism in its late modernity neo-liberalist development functions according to the principle of 'being for the other'. And so, consciously or otherwise, they thwart or eradicate it. One of the ways this has been achieved is by diverting attention onto a socially constructed stereotype as a representation of the very opposite of the ethical economic individual – the immoral economic individual. In Soviet Russia, it was the entrepreneur; in the West, any number of dissolute figures – the drug dealer, the thief, the pimp, the loan shark. Place these individuals into a group of similar immoral characters working together, characters who are defined according to their active commitment to being *against* the other (and whose self-interested motivations somehow strangely fail to be transformed into the common good by an 'invisible hand'), and we have 'organised crime'.

The context for Bauman and Levinas's probing of what it means to be a moral, responsible individual was the Holocaust, genocide rather than economy and its criminal consequences. Nonetheless, there are similar factors at work here, grounded in the shared space and quality of modernity. Bauman understood the Holocaust not as an aberration of modern civilisation but as 'another face of the same modern society'.[28] In other words, the Holocaust was cut from the cloth of modernity, and could only have occurred in modern society which provided the necessary instruments to carry out abuses on this scale. Rationality, bureaucracy and technology – the defining characteristics of modernity – were central to the efficient disposal of millions of victims to the death camps. This was, remarks Bauman chillingly, the civilising process in action. Closer in time, and wrapped up in the economic considerations of 'innocent' shareholders and 'non-culpable' boards of directors, atrocities akin to the suffering caused in Nazi Germany are evident around the world, not as directed forms of political and racial hatreds, but as the dull thud of indifference to suffering consequent to the pursuit of self-interested goals. The Bhopal tragedy (see Chapter 2), alongside numerous other corporate 'crimes', provides a stark and horrifying account of moral indifference encouraged by the structures and systems of modern society. This was an 'accident' waiting to happen. The indirect death toll from the toxic leak amounts to over six and a half times that of the recent terrorist attacks in New York and London. Not one person has yet been found legally accountable. As Punch states:

> The Bhopal tragedy raised issues related to industrial safety ... the transfer of technology by multinationals, the level and reliability of regulation in less developed societies, the legal muscle of western corporations and their influence via the media, and

the ethical responsibility of management for a disaster in one of their plants abroad.[29]

It was as if all the instruments of civilised society became weapons of defence for those from the offending company, Union Carbide, and the colluding Indian government, in an attempt to legitimately offset responsibility for the appalling consequences of the economic venture. 'As there was never any ownership, there is no responsibility and no liability – for the Bhopal tragedy or its aftermath', claimed a spokesman for the company that took over Union Carbide's profits in 2001 but clearly not its liabilities.[30] Technology, the rational base of law and the division of labour (blame has been located at different parts of the management/labour chain by differing parties, resulting in no genuine attempt to provide real justice for the victims and their families), facilitated the removal of direct accountability for the ongoing misery of children and their parents. This is not organised crime in the traditional sense, nor even according to legal proceedings, corporate homicide or manslaughter, because there have been no legal proceedings. No one has been found accountable, in this and hundreds of other similar atrocities worldwide. It is simply an 'unintended' outcome, alongside thousands of other unintended consequences that have caused horrendous forms of suffering, inflicted by multinational companies supported by their shareholders, by the banks which hold our accounts and the financial markets we invest in to ensure pension and other material securities. All of these provide a quality of life to us, the privileged. But at what point, we should ask, can we continue to churn out the mantra of 'unintended' consequences? How many deaths from these unintended consequences constitute 'enough', the magic number when we can no longer sustain the claims of innocence? Indeed, does there, should there, even exist an unacceptable number, and who is to decide what that number is?

In a world economy which draws together the needs and desires of millions of individuals into an inequitable whole, responsibility for the 'other' must become a tangible, constant concern. It entails understanding the human cost of human need and desire and realising the part each one of us plays in this process. This is not what those driving modern economy as it has evolved want us to do, nor is it something we individually warm to. For the majority of us in the developed world, to assume that responsibility means 'giving up something' or changing the comfortable patterns of behaviour which have been inculcated into our thinking. Accountability is clearly a burden which is inimical to the major forms of modern economy. So we buy into the narratives of organised crime, those 'immoral selves', as a form of ablution. And we buy into the compromises asked of us by those who construct the narratives and promise to protect us from them.

Responsibility for, or accountability to, someone or something requires a level of individual freedom, the ability to make choices and take on their consequences for others as well as for ourselves. As we turn to consider the Sovietising process of Western society, it should become clear that our trajectory is moving away from more freedom to less. There are many reasons for this, but some clearly have a parallel in the Soviet experiment with modernity and its attempted creation of the rational-scientific individual, free to think and free to choose, but only within the framework of those choices and thinking which adhere to the rationalist worldview. What the West most abhorred in Soviet society, the hothouse of scientific-materialism, with the brutal and systemic suppression of genuine individual freedom (a process facilitated not only by the instruments of modern society but Russia's historical legacy of authoritarian rule), is now fast becoming the West's own reality and creeping dystopia.

THE AUTHORITARIAN GAZE

In 1920, disillusioned with the direction of the Bolshevik Revolution he had previously supported, the Soviet writer Yevgeny Zamyatin published his novel, We. Its satirical content against collectivism and biting anti-utopian stance forced it into the swelling number of underground Soviet literature, until it found its way into the US and was published in 1924. Related through its main protagonist, identified as every character in the novel was only by their personal number, D-503 describes a world of cold, repressive functionality in which One State, the putative utopian world, sucks the mind and will of the people into the pursuit of its rigidly prescribed way of life. The activities carried out each hour are dictated by One State in its maintenance of harmony and stability; equality is assured through the anonymity of names as numbers; apartments and workplaces are transparent edifices where everyone remains under surveillance 24/7 except on designated Sex Days. It is a numbed totalitarian state, not so much laced with fear as passive acquiescence, an indifference to moving beyond anything other than the desires and direction of the Benefactor who 'runs' One State. This is utopia for its inhabitants, a total giving up of self, sucked into the collective of blissful ignorance where no one is responsible for anything beyond what One State requires of them. 'We comes from God, I from the Devil' is the paradisal chant of the horde of One State sleepwalkers. Fear comes only from the unpredictable, that which One State does not control. Constant surveillance holds no disquiet for a public where 'We have nothing to hide from one another.'[31] Heard that one before?

The outer accoutrements of the dangerous move towards authoritarian governance in the West, with special reference to Britain and the US, are well documented. A growing body of literature on surveillance society and the threat it poses to civil liberties has occupied columns of newspapers and an abundance of articles for academic journals and books (and with room for even more radical analyses).[32] Debates on the threat to human rights with the introduction of draconian-style legislation related to terrorism, as in the Patriot Act in the US or a series of anti-terrorism and organised crime-linked legislation in the UK introduced since 2000, go a long way to vindicating Nils Christie's Cassandra-like tone of over a decade ago that 'the major dangers of crime in modern societies are not the crimes, but that the fight against them may lead societies towards totalitarian developments'.[33] Infused with an irrationality that defies the reasoning stance upon which civilised society claims its strength and virtue, as official statistics in the US and UK show a steady decrease in crime,[34] crime control measures follow the opposite trajectory. Prison numbers are up in both countries,[35] by popular demand it seems. And while more of us are affected by 'ordinary crime' than that linked to terrorism or organised crime, we swallow the narrative of a pan-threat and clamour for policies that could make any one of us an easy victim of the never-ending potential for miscarriages of justice.

There is at work here a strange kind of do-it-yourself totalitarianism. We ask of those who assure of their capability to protect us that they take more freedoms away from us, never quite trusting their declared competence as being sufficient but nonetheless finding reassurance in their presence, always wanting to further empower the state and its armoury of crime- and war-fighting mechanisms. We are becoming more and more like children, needing patriarchs and tsars (which we now have many of – a drugs tsar and ironically one each for civil liberties and privacy) to lay our trust in and throw responsibility at. One State utopias, abhorrent in the crude, brutal mode of Soviet communism, are temptingly attractive when they manifest as gentle, almost unobtrusive forms of coercion that guide us to a place not of our choosing but chosen for us. In conscience-stirring times of global warming, food shortages, glaringly obscene economic inequalities, and daily acts of violence which are often reported as having no logical motive, in these uncertain times that question the democratic and economic paradigm we cling to and try to foist on the 'undeveloped' world, relinquishing freedom and the responsibility that goes with it by slipping into an anaesthetised state of soul and moral indifference, appears to be a small price to pay for 'peace' of mind.

Peace, not just of mind, but of a social kind, is in short supply, so we are told, in the midst of all the wars currently being fought. The 'war' on organised crime, as on terrorism, drugs, and so on (with the exception of poverty – a noticeable retreat is evident on that front), has provided a semantically induced sense of patriotism and with it an acceptance of the use of so-called 'emergency powers' by the state. The former British Prime Minister, Tony Blair, during one of his final assaults in the 'war' on organised crime, implicitly invoked such powers, claiming that

> these big organised crime trees can't be dealt with in the same way as volume crime like burglary or anti-social behaviour ... We've got to be hard, efficient and, if necessary, ruthless as they are trying to do to us ... My impression sometimes is that the system is struggling against a presumption that you treat these crimes like every other type of crime and that you build up cases beyond reasonable doubt ... To require everything beyond reasonable doubt in these cases is very difficult ... I think people would accept that within certain categories of case, provided it's big enough.[36]

And they do. Alongside the proposal to undermine habeas corpus, another cornerstone of rule of law, by extending detention without charge to 42 days (in a recent poll supported by 65 per cent of the public[37]), the British government, like their US counterparts, are pushing us ever deeper into a totalitarian state not just of being but of thinking.

The official narratives that construct the threats from organised crime and terrorism and the compromises we are asked to make for the protection of our freedoms against such adversaries are in fact the *real* danger to those very freedoms. The Racketeer Influenced Corrupt Organizations Act of 1970 (RICO), designed ostensibly to counter the alleged high-security risk from illegal business in America, set the ball rolling for the unravelling of established legal safeguards:

It muddied the traditional separation of civil and criminal procedures by allowing civil suits, brought by the government or by private parties, to strip mobsters of the businesses they controlled and to impose on them treble damages. Not least, whereas with most criminal law the presumption is for strict interpretation, the RICO statute was designed to apply widely and be interpreted liberally.[38]

RICO was, according to Naylor, 'strong stuff'. Its liberal application extended to phone-tapping and harassing an array of people, including those suspected of political activism, such as human rights organisations and charities.[39] Since RICO, other legislation specifically targeting the proceeds of crime have been passed, and passed on, as examples of best practice (with little evidence that this approach is effective) as Britain and other countries have followed America's lead. 'Dirty money' is riddled with definitional ambiguities and can include tax evasion from legal business, as Mitsilegas points out. Inextricably tied into the global discourse on threat and security, money-laundering measures, which give financial and security agencies a broad remit of intrusion in privacy 'makes derogation from established legal principles seem acceptable'.[40] This steady infiltration of state control over the affairs of the individual gathered pace after September 11th. The Patriotic Act and subsequent legislation on security has left democracy and freedom in America in a parlous state as Michel Chossudovsky's analysis shows:

If emergency measures are maintained, the militarization of civilian institutions, as distinct from an outright Military Coup d'Etat, would essentially lead America in the same direction, while maintaining all the appearances of a 'functioning democracy'. In this regard, the contours of a functioning Police State under the façade of Constitutional government have already been defined:

- the Big Brother surveillance apparatus, through the establishment of consolidated data banks on citizens;
- the militarization of justice and law enforcement;
- the disinformation and propaganda network;
- the covert support to terrorist organizations;
- political assassinations, torture manuals and concentration camps;
- extensive war crimes and blatant violation of international law.[41]

This emerging dystopia is not just driven by social and political responses to an apparent threat from criminal elements and the 'wrong' kind of fundamentalists. It is also about ensuring the economic status quo; in other words, maintaining the dominance of and subservience to a malfunctioning economic model. The real threat, as viewed from the Olympian heights of free trade elites, is not organised crime, although they are usually vociferous in their open condemnation of its negative influence on the world economy. Illegal entrepreneurs, as in the Soviet Union, play an important role in the maintenance of the status quo. As in Soviet Russia, they provide proscribed goods and services upon which areas of the dominant economic system are dependent. For example, illegal migration for forced labour, an increasingly profitable business for criminal groups, has been estimated to be worth up to $3.8 billion worldwide, much of which is based in developed countries, holding up parts of numerous industries including construction, agriculture, clothing, food packaging and the service sector.[42] So too is the arms industry in not infrequent collusion with criminal entrepreneurs as a means of bypassing embargoes or shoring up regimes publicly deemed 'enemy'.[43] As long as crime groups are able to facilitate the agendas of the powerful when called upon, they will be tolerated or, perhaps, in some cases, only selectively targeted for the sake of expediency.

The real problem for many of the economic and political elites (increasingly indistinguishable as separate categories) is the ordinary consumer or producer, those who might not want to play ball according to the rules created by the elites. The Bolsheviks resolved their problems of reluctant players in the newly introduced state-ownership game through swift and brutal repression. Once large-scale opposition had been crushed, the next step was to maintain the support of the repressed. What worked best was fear and propaganda. The same goes for those living under the shadow of neo-liberalism, albeit in ways more subtle, but no less brutal in their consequences. The following section looks at how the 'free' and 'democratic' West applies similar techniques to its own and other economic citizens, methods of repression which in turn create conditions conducive to the proliferation of the criminal economy.

ECONOMICS AND COERCION

The above form of creeping authoritarianism is what Thomas Mathiesen describes as 'noisy'. It is blatant and tangible, crude almost, in its open propensity for the curtailing of rights and liberties. However, there are other forms of repression or coercion, those that involve a 'silent silencing' of opponents of the dominant ideology. This creation of acquiescence, as Mathiesen writes, is 'structural; it is a part of our everyday life; it is unbounded and therefore engraved upon us; it is noiseless and therefore passes by unnoticed; and it is dynamic in the sense that in our society it spreads and becomes continually more encompassing'.[44] Its subtlety makes it more conducive to democracies, where open displays of coercion, especially of a physical nature, are more liable to provoke organised forms of resistance (the treatment of detainees at Guantanamo Bay and Belmarsh Prison rightly provoked a clamour of criticism and pressure on the relevant governments to at least be seen to be doing something about the situation). More insidious, however, are the mechanisms that eradicate resistance to authoritarian governance by encouraging forms of self-censorship, through a banal but pervasive paralysing of criticism and struggle against the status quo. Self-censorship is undoubtedly the most effective means of 'resistance to resistance', especially when it occurs 'through the forms of perception and expression that he [the censor] has internalized and which impose their form on all his expressions'.[45] This internalising, as with most forms of control, is most effective during the formative years of childhood.

Control through early socialisation, especially as a means of offsetting deviance and crime[46] (as socially constructed phenomena, they also translate as 'resistance'), was one of Lenin's most pressing concerns during the nascent period of Bolshevism; 'a tool for the transformation of contemporary society', as Nadezhda Krupskaya, Lenin's wife, wrote in *Public Education and Democracy*.[47] The same need to educate out of ideology has taken hold in US education, famously set out in the letter from Marc Tucker, then president of the National Center on Education and the Economy, to Hillary Clinton in 1992, urging that educational reform should 'remold the entire American system for human resources development', one that will 'develop one's skills that literally extends from cradle to grave and is the same system for everyone'.[48] Those skills for the development of human resources, that is, fodder for the economy, are to be developed in compliance with the needs of the corporate elite. Resistance is not an option, freedom of expression outside the service of the status quo is taken seriously and punitively:

Students who lack the proper corporate school spirit do so at considerable risk. When Mike Cameron wore a Pepsi shirt on 'Coke Day' at Greenbrier High School in Evans, Georgia, he was suspended for a day. 'Coke Day' was part of the school's entry in a national 'Team Up with Coca-Cola' contest, which awards $10,000 to the high school that comes up with the best plan for distributing Coke discount cards.[49]

The school curriculum in the US, Moore continues, is increasingly devised according to the content designated by innocuous-sounding 'sponsors': 'Teachers have shown a Shell Oil video that teaches students that the way to experience nature is by driving there – after filling your Jeep's gas tank at a Shell station', is just one example of indoctrination, this one parading as a lesson on ecology. Instead of plastering posters of well built Stakhanovite workers reaching up with their hammers and sickles to the heavens of a future communist paradise, every available space in these schools is transformed into some sort of advertising hoarding. Nor does propagandising stop at school. Television advertising for children, embraced by Britain with less fervour than in the US, but still enjoying the most relaxed advertising laws in Europe, ensures that neither age nor location can shield society's most impressionable from the onslaught of capitalist dogma. As one expert on the psychology of advertising notes:

> By seeding their products and images early, the marketers can do more than just develop brand recognition; they can literally cultivate a demographic's sensibilities as they are formed. A nine-year-old child who can recognize the Budweiser frogs and recite their slogan (Bud-weiser) is more likely to start drinking beer than one who can only remember Tony the Tiger [a cartoon character advertising breakfast cereal] yelling, 'They're great!' … This indicates a long-term coercive strategy.[50]

The pursuit of happiness as wealth acquisition, an established cultural norm throughout most of the developed world and a value ruthlessly exported to developing countries, lies at the heart of this dogma. In the global economy failure to subscribe to this tenet, on the terms set by the wealthy nations, can result in myriad forms of punishment. For the reality is that the developing world is little more than a number of satellite states whose purpose is to serve the interests of the *nomenklatura* of the global economic party: the World Trade Organization, the International Monetary Fund and the World Bank (see below). Pressure to adopt the free market doctrine is applied not as military crackdowns but rather as a series of often damaging formulations of economic policies between the rich and developing nations where 'Investment capital ... is the equivalent of firepower ... R&D [research and development] ... of weapons innovation ... market penetration ... has replaced military bases and foreign garrisons on foreign soil; and trade barriers are now the most formidable of all artillery'.[51] Even when developing countries are aware of the inappropriateness of the programmes 'offered' to them by the economic giants, they dare not refuse for fear of reprisals such as the suspension of loans, the establishment of trade embargoes or the raising of tariffs by the rich nations on goods from developing countries. In other words, they are intimidated and threatened by a well organised group whose sole aim is to spread its octopus tentacles across the globe in the interests of money and power while forcing its ideology on the reluctant and the resistant.

Those joining the free trade bonanza late on in its history – either voluntarily, such as China and some of the former communist states of the Eastern bloc, or under more external pressure as in the countries of South America such as Chile, Brazil and Argentina – have either experienced rising rates of economically linked crime or the poverty/income inequality-induced movement of people abroad.[52] In either case, criminal groups in slum areas such as the Brazilian *favelas* or the so-called 'snakehead' networks of Chinese human traffickers have clearly profited from the vast opportunities made available as a consequence of free market economics.[53] But it is not just with the newcomers that coercion and illegal entrepreneurship are on the increase. Established market economies intimidate their own and punish dissidents in subtle but equally ruthless ways to those meted out by the Soviet regime against internal political opposition.

Exclusion is one of the more common forms, not just as removal, but as an internalised sense of unworthiness, where the individual is castigated as a failed consumer and/or producer, and hence a failed human being. This is acutely realised in our ability to exist as 'consumer-beings' in an economic age dominated by debt. Without a certain level of credit *worthiness*, access to the realisation of the consumer-being is blocked or constrained, and with it, happiness. Belonging, being and getting on amount to operating according to the system that requires us to be (credit) card-carrying members of the consumer party. In the Soviet Union, failure or deviation from communist norms was understood according to individual pathology, one which could be rectified once a programme of rehabilitation was completed and the offender was forcibly integrated into the system (with the exception of sanctioned deviation). Compulsion to integrate in capitalist systems is an equal necessity, but the pressure comes from within, from what Paul Willis describes as 'individualizing and internalizing a structural problem'.[54] In other words, punishment for failure is applied by those least able to enter the marketplace of employment to themselves, driven home by a sense of inadequacy. Like Boxer, the faithful workhorse dedicated to the revolution in George Orwell's *Animal Farm*, they are led into destructive self-recrimination: 'It must be due to some fault in ourselves.' Nor is this confined to the unemployed. As Richard Sennett points out, the 'specter of uselessness' has been absorbed by a work culture created by neo-liberalism, in which experience and talent in professions have been replaced by the 'production of results'.[55] In this way, the demeaning of self by the self in collusion with policy-makers and employers inculcates a sense of frustration and hopelessness and, with it, an inability to look at the bigger structural pathology. Happiness as wealth acquisition thus becomes both an economic and emotional goal; its failure, a tie that binds.

Silencing through failure and hopelessness is as effective as the more brutal methods of fear used in authoritarian regimes such as the Soviet Union. But the silencing of protest does not stop there. In the very remedy offered to a way out of exclusion, silence is (literally) bought by providing resources for temporal inclusion into the system, one which boosts the potential for a plethora of illegal business.

'Gulags of Debt'

In July 2005, Mark Johnson, a loan shark or illegal money-lender, who had charged his victims 8,000 per cent interest on loans, threatening those who could not pay, was sentenced to nearly four years in prison. The Recorder who sentenced Johnson told him, '(Your) business inevitably preyed on the weakest members of the community, *these were people who had no one else who would lend them money*' (emphasis added).[56] He was one of a growing number of successful prosecutions brought against loan sharks by Birmingham City Council's Loan Shark Unit, set up in 2004 to combat the spiralling business of unauthorised money-lending in the UK. This was before the 'credit crunch' of summer 2007.

The comments of the Recorder are interesting not for the opprobrium they lay on the offender but for the nature of the reference to the victims. The marginalised status of the victims, refused money by legitimate lenders, receives no qualitative attention. Perhaps the court was not the place to do so. But on a more general scale the reporting of loan sharking follows the traditional media pattern of focusing on the crime and victim rather than causalities. Illegal money-lending, however, like most economic crimes, has a direct relationship to the official economy. The culture of debt, which feeds local and global economics in the age of neo-liberalism, has created a new class/social structure: debt for need and credit for greed. The former is sub-divided into those tied into debt bondage with legal lenders, from high street banks to quasi-legitimate private lenders to those like Johnson (who killed himself in his prison cell five months later), whose interest rates and willingness to employ brutal methods of retrieval classify him as 'criminal'. The brutality described, however, is the stentorian narrative that booms over the crucial issue of marginalisation. Being inculcated into the culture of debt, of worthiness as understood through credit ratings, those who fail to acquire this worthiness according to impossible criteria set (for them), are often *pushed*, with as much brutality as they receive at the hands of the loan shark, into the shadow economy. Those who drive them to desperate measures – the banks who refuse credit, the advertisers who pummel their children's minds with an insatiable appetite for material goods (Christmas is one of the most lucrative periods for loan sharks, the time when parents, especially single mothers, try to make up for the hardships visited on their offspring because, as they are told, their children are 'disadvantaged' by their family status, evident in their inability to provide the financial symbols of love and care), utility companies which threaten to turn off basic amenities if increasingly high bills are not met, and the governments which make debt a respectable condition while penalising those unable to deal with it, parade as the respectable protagonists of the legal economy. Many receive bonuses for their profit-making skills, some receive rewards for their money-losing skills. Adam Applegarth, the former boss of Northern Rock, which recklessly lost £167.6 million of its investors' money, accepted a £750,000 'payoff' for financial incompetence. Clearly, there is no fear that someone of this stature will commit suicide, in a prison cell he will never be required to occupy, for ruining the lives of thousands.[57]

The potential for the proliferation of loan sharking in the current economic climate, long considered one of the lucrative activities of illegal business in the US,[58] hardly needs elaboration. Further exacerbated by the increase in the movement of people at the more vulnerable end of the global 'family', Bauman's 'vagabonds',[59] whose status automatically excludes them from authorised loans, illegal money-lending and its conditions of brutal bondage, will benefit not only loan sharks but those others whose illegal industries depend on clients having access to capital.[60] Nor should this latest crisis come as a surprise. Peter Warburton warned of the folly of creating an economic system based on credit with an alarming prescience seven years before the US subprime mortgage disaster. In his doomsayer book *Debt and Delusion*, he wrote:

> A deterioration in any aspect of the credit system ... poses a threat to the whole system ... With a complacency found only in those who inhabit a dream-world of analytical purity, central bank officials have applauded financial innovation as the harbinger of greater economic efficiency. They seem not to have considered the possibility that the unfettered credit and capital markets might have damaging side-effects.[61]

Now they have, and there is widespread damage, but few are recommending a radical restructuring of the economic model that encourages such destructive outcomes. When a debt crisis is termed as a 'credit crunch' this testifies to the head-in-the-sand mentality of a scale that eventually brought the Soviet Union to its knees.

The tinkering of the neo-liberal economic model, as with Gorbachev's attempt at re-establishing the ideal socialist model, can at best buy time, but, as a small yet growing number of academics and practitioners are realising, it cannot be sustained.[62] A decade ago, the radical critic John McMurtry examined the state of capitalism in the immediate aftermath of the Asian economic crisis. *The Cancer Stage of Capitalism*, as the title of his book suggests, provides an illuminating and accurate analogy with the processes of cancer within the physical body:

> A world *coup d'état*, one might say, has occurred, and still unfolds without social populations yet awakened to it ... Its full implications are still not recognized even by those who see its political nature. The new system can be defined simply in the first instance. International money capital seeking to become maximally more has been accorded well-defined and overriding transnational rights to rule the world's production and distribution, uncontrolled by any limit of social, individual

or environmental life-host. Tens of thousands of pages of secretly negotiated regulations bind societies and legislatures to a transnational order making illegal whatever life claim 'does not honour trade obligations'. Few people have any idea of what has been signed. Fewer still have read a page of them.[63]

McMurtry's analysis is as relevant now as it was then; more so as the pathogenic agent of debt has infiltrated even deeper into the global economic body. The symptoms he identifies are known to the majority of us in privileged positions of choice-making, but active protest against the system and demands for the necessary draconian changes are strangely muted. One explanation for this is the silent silencing by debt itself, that is, debt as a form of social control. The ability of pathological indicators, such as debt, to exercise a dual function of exposing pathology and arresting effective responses to it was also apparent in the Soviet Union. Queues in the Soviet Union, the irrefutable symbol of a failing command economy, helped maintain public order and acquiescence. According to a report in *Pravda*, 37 billion hours a year were spent queueing. As Lance Morrow noted in reference to the figures given by the Soviet newspaper, 'To enforce a wait, of course, is to exert power. To wait is to be powerless. The Soviets have turned waiting into a way of life ... To bind an entire people to that kind of life is to do a little of the work of the Gulag in a different style.'[64] While also ensuring that a good number of the Soviet population would be occupied and publicly visible in an ordered fashion, queues focused attention on the micro-problem, the immediate issue of procuring food and other basics. (There was always sufficient (just) to stave off the angry protests that had precipitated the bread riots of 1917 which in turn led to the revolution.)

Debt in the West acts in a similar way. It concentrates the mind and energy on the immediate, imprisoning not literally through time but through uncertainty and fear of default. Combined with the new work culture of temporary contracts (according to Sennett, in real terms, about one fifth of the American labour market[65]), debt ensures that people literally cannot afford to protest too strongly. In all walks of life, subservience to structures and behaviours many of us feel uncomfortable with, and morally sell out to, is achieved through the vice-like grip of debt that impacts on every aspect of our lives. The plaintive excuse 'I would object to this or that injustice but I have a mortgage to pay' locks so many of us inside a prison the marginalised are desperate to enter. Even the privileged choice-makers must live with this uncertainty, and in doing so sacrifice real choice for freedom for its chimera, born out of subtle coercion. Totalitarianism is as easily inflicted by the self as by power structures, making us simultaneously both inmates and guards.

Targets and Deviance

In an indirect way, the coercive impact of debt has helped encourage further aspects of the Sovietising process: the subsuming of all aspects of life to the positivistic gaze. In other words, we in the West (and Britain stands as an especially strong example) are increasingly prepared to lie back and be counted – One State citizenry – in a world identified and defined by numbers, through the pervasive culture of target-setting, auditing, performance indicators and other equally inappropriate means of measuring the human condition in its myriad aspects. Vocal dissent exists, but effective resistance remains weak. In the economic realm alone, the Soviet experience has shown the problems incurred by rigid target-setting and the subcultural behaviours that emerged as a consequence. Targets, while having validity as motivators and measurements of economic development, lose their efficacy when they become an end in themselves. In services such as health, education and criminal justice, when valued input is increasingly determined by measurable output, target-setting can easily become a force for repression. The *raison d'être* for professionals is increasingly to reach the prescribed targets in areas which, by their very nature, defy mathematical precision. To fail to do so risks a series of subtly punitive responses, such as being overlooked for promotion or endangering the possible renewal of contract work. A debt-run economy ensures that risk aversion is even more crucial and compliance more entrenched. In an increasingly competitive environment where institution is set up against institution and individual against individual, in the punitive employment of target-produced tables of 'excellence', energies are therefore directed towards goal achievement rather than opposing its divisive and destructive consequences. Production to target rather than quality of work becomes the overall motivation. In the loss of self as agent of creativity through work, so, too, is responsibility, to anyone or thing other than the mathematical formula of output as a form of self survival, gradually eradicated.

In a critical attack on the impact of the British government's obsession with targets, Hillyard et al. analyse its effect on criminological research and, by implication, teaching:

Academics are now less free to investigate a range of pressing social problems. In criminology, perhaps more than most disciplines, this means benign commentary and empirical research that lacks any sociological imagination. It means an endless conveyor belt of predictable and auto-suggestive findings, often generated by large scale, publicly funded, state-sanctioned, evaluation-oriented research projects that are ultimately self-serving and self-legitimizing.[66]

This creeping utilitarianism not only affects the content of much criminological research, but has an equally inimical effect on academics themselves, on their individual integrity, and on the quality of their relationships with one another, their students and the institutions in which they work. This reflects a pattern across other disciplines and professions, where state and increasingly corporate interference[67] determines the nature of what and how we teach, investigate, heal, police and discipline. As with the Soviet regime, the burden of compliance towards often unrealistic targets brings with it a predilection for deviance – the falsification of figures, the cutting of corners (especially dangerous in the health profession), background wheeling and dealing to achieve, or at least look as if one is achieving, the prescribed quotas. Creative accounting and other imaginative devices, worthy of the most deviant Soviet practices, are now becoming part of British culture. As one report observed, 'targets for A&E minimum waiting times were being circumvented by imaginative fixes where trolleys either had their wheels removed or were re-designed as "beds on wheels" and corridors and treatment rooms are re-designed as "pre-admission units"'.[68] In an environment where deviance increasingly becomes common practice, the gradual erosion of ethical behaviour facilitates the extension of the deviant into the criminal, not just in the workplace but, as Weber's 'spirit of capitalism' argues, into the very heart of the individual. As Zinoviev observed about his own people, Soviet Man (*Homo Sovieticus*), 'It is easy to be moral if you live in conditions which do not force you into morally reprehensible actions.'[69]

As yet, the privileged of neo-liberal states cannot claim to be 'forced' into the 'morally reprehensible'. Our unwillingness to take up responsibility for our role in the economy, to pursue the short-term easy solution, is, however, leading us ever more into a position where force takes a more direct and brutal form. Then choices will be limited not between profit and loss, but between survival and collapse. Holding on to the human, at work and in other areas of the economy, is a crucial issue for each of us. The disinclination to do so is further encouraged by those who lead the neo-liberal agenda, and for whom moral indifference becomes the fertile ground for it.

'VULGARIAN SELF-SEEKERS': THE CAPITALIST *NOMENKLATURA*

The proliferation of crime groups in Soviet and post-Soviet Russia has, in large part, been accounted for by the endemic corruption of the elites.[70] It was these 'vulgarian self-seekers' and their expedient alliance with the criminal sector that nurtured the criminogenic environment which eventually helped destroy the Soviet economy and lead Russia into gangster or 'wild' capitalism. This elite class or *nomenklatura*, created at the behest of Stalin, was granted a number of privileges including access to better-quality and larger quantities of goods and services than the rest of the population, as a means of securing loyalty to the paranoid leader. But as a system it continued long after the demise of its innovator. Its entrenchment as part of the system created a two-tier society in which 'the gap in living standards (housing, food, and possessions) between the nomenklatura and "simple Soviet people" reached the magnitude of the gap between dignitaries of similar rank and the ordinary people before the Revolution'.[71] The *nomenklatura* as a concept and more so as reality was a serious deviation from the ideological roots of Marxism and its Leninist adaptation, and consequently attracted those prepared to collude with what eventually became a black market in the 'buying' and 'selling' of political status and employment.[72] So brazen was the behaviour of the *nomenklatura* in their rapacious pursuit of (hidden) wealth and power, and so disregarding of the law, that it became difficult to distinguish them from the criminal world that provided the goods and services essential to this hedonistic lifestyle. In reality, the only distinction lay in the balance of power between the *nomenklatura* and the underworld, quite categorically in favour of the former. In the 'new' Russia, as Ledeneva notes, the old *nomenklatura* show themselves to be 'objectively more capable of handling management problems' and, further, 'their experience and their connections are needed in post-Soviet conditions',[73] the very conditions, that is, that nurture our own *nomenklatura*.

Political and corporate elites are no strangers to capitalist societies, nor too are the abuses and criminal activities in which these elites engage. What is new, perhaps, is the intensification of this fusion between politics and the corporate world, to the extent that political and economic interests are increasingly difficult to separate to the point that global capitalism is unashamedly reducing politics, and hence democracy, to a secondary, or even superfluous, status.[74] One of the most blatant examples of the symbiosis between politics and economics was the 'remarkably close relationship' between the Bush administration in the US and the multinational company Halliburton. Up until 2000, when he was appointed US Vice President, Dick Cheney had held the position of Chief Executive Officer at Halliburton. As Vice President he became one of the major architects of the Iraq War. Halliburton found itself in a position of favoured status in the Iraq oil carve-up, secured in the no-bid game, which netted the company profits of over $150 million. Hardly serendipitous.[75] The US cannot claim the only title to this mother of all mergers. George Monbiot's disturbing appraisal of corporate Britain lists no less than 44 business-related government appointees to positions of political influence in what he calls his 'fat-cat directory'.[76] Most disturbing of all is the fact that the appointments listed were granted after the election of the Labour government in 1997 rather than by the business-friendly Conservative Party. 'New' Labour's willingness to embrace the neoliberal agenda as a means of returning to government (after a 19-year absence) is just one example of the creeping deference to economic elites across the West, one which is leading the developed world towards yet another Soviet phenomenon: one-party system politics.

So too is bribery, endemic throughout Soviet and post-Soviet Russia politics, insinuating itself ever more deeply into the political arena in Western democracies, except we call it something else: party donations. Lamely following the sole superpower example, other democracies have bought into the circus of political spin, producing media-groomed, sound-biting candidates whose electoral success is based more on image than policies (which have all melded into one anyway). As costs for these political 'productions' spiral (the 2000 Bush campaign cost over $191 million[77]), it behoves would-be leaders to court media and other business moguls with silent promises of post-election gifts, such as the delay or abolition of unfavourable tax legislation or the tweaking of international relations to accommodate sponsor interests. In this way economic censorship squeezes out other parties as democracy goes to the highest (and numerically decreasing) bidder. C. Wright Mills wrote in 1956, 'A society that narrows the meaning of "success" to the big money and in its terms condemns failure as a chief vice, raising money to the plane of absolute value, will produce the sharp operator and the shady deal.'[78] The current scenario *demands* a sharp operator and shady deals, which probably accounts for why Donald Rumsfeld, former US Defense Secretary, quoted directly from the Chicago gangster Al Capone when offering advice on international diplomacy: 'You get a lot more with a kind word and a gun than you do with a kind word alone.'[79]

Bribery in politics also enables the circumvention of law and a symbiosis of the *nomenklatura* with the underworld. Unlike the Soviet Union, however, constraints in domestic law and other mechanisms of control limit the extent of these collaborations within indigenous jurisdictions, for now. Nonetheless, examples of collaboration are in no shortage, as with Alan Block's investigation into the dangerous liaisons between Attwoods, the British waste disposal company, whose Board members included the late Denis Thatcher (husband of the more famous Margaret) and an Illinois-based waste company known to be involved in racketeering.[80] However, the egotistical drives of neo-liberalism threaten to chip away the increasingly fragile legal constraints on the powerful elites in their own backyard. But beyond the civilised world of rule of law, in the developing countries or industrialised states where legislation is weak, the Western *nomenklatura* find ample opportunities to pursue their self-interest with the help of the criminal underworld. Case studies are plentiful, but here are just a few. British American Tobacco has been linked to crime groups smuggling cigarettes in Asia,[81] the US government and military had strong affiliations with drug cartels in South America[82] (now relocated to Afghanistan[83]), and the arms industry is notoriously linked with the criminal underworld which can act as 'broker' in politically sensitive trading.[84] As Chossudovsky notes of the age of the global economy:

> Under the New World Order, the demarcation between 'organized capital' and 'organized crime' is blurred. In other words, the restructuring of global trade and finance tends to favour the concurrent 'globalization' of the criminal economy, which is intricately tied into the corporate establishment. In turn, the state apparatus is criminalized.[85]

This is not the narrative that makes headline news, as it rarely did in the Soviet media – unless, of course, it was politically expedient to do so. The paradox of a Soviet elite thriving in a two-tier system betrayed the very core of the regime's ideological foundations. So too has the ideological premise of wealth distribution upon which capitalism and its neo-liberal evolution are based, as in the 'invisible hand' or the so-called 'trickle-down effect',[86] failed to materialise in an acute betrayal of the system's underlying principles. In fact, the opposite has occurred – a seeping upwards of capital. On American society, John Gray commented that it 'is no longer a bourgeois society. It has become a divided society in which an anxious majority is wedged between an underclass that has no hope and an overclass that denies any civic obligations'.[87] As the world's richest country, it also has one of the fastest levels of wealth inequality, which, according to the Economic Institute, has grown from the richest 1 per cent owning 125 times more wealth than the average household in 1962, to 190 times more by 2004.[88] Its Atlantic neighbour has also seen a continuing increase in income inequality.[89] As with the string of communist-state failures across the globe, so too has the free market left a trail of economic injustice through the ever-widening poverty gap in whichever country it has been adopted.[90] It is this environment, more than any other, which has provided the gamut of opportunities for organised crime as understood through the orthodox narratives.

THE DISAPPEARING SELF

The final aspect of the Sovietising process and its implications for modern economy and organised crime is found in the dystopian nightmare articulated by Trotsky as a utopian aspiration:

> What is man? He is by no means a finished or harmonious being … surely we cannot improve on man? Yes, we can! To produce a new, 'improved version' of man – that is the future task of communism. And for that we first have to find out everything about man, his anatomy, his physiology and that part of his physiology which is called his psychology. Man must look at himself and see himself as raw material, or at best as a semi-manufactured product and say: 'At last my dear *homo sapiens*, I will work on you.'[91]

For liberal democracies this was the ultimate horror of Soviet communism, the annihilation of self in the service of the state, the Frankenstein construction of a 'utility being'. Man as a 'semi-manufactured product' is anathema to liberal society, in whose institutions, political, economic and legal, the individual stands as a free agent capable of autonomous choice-making and account-ability to the self and state. Even with the impact of positivism as a redress to liberalist absolutism, individual agency remains at the hub, in theory at least. In practice, however, the individual as an *ethical* and genuinely accountable figure is being pounded into dust by the course of capitalist economy and its development as neo-liberalism. The gradual disappearing of self and hence the capability of ethical autonomy has become a pervasive feature of the modern liberal economy. The comparative study across various market economies by Karstedt and Farrell on what they term crimes of 'everyday life' found clear evidence of the erosion of individual morality as integral to the marketplace, an erosion which was pervasive as an individual and structural phenomenon operating within the economy as a tense interplay between the two.[92] What is clear from this and other studies is that the self as *individuality*, rather than individualism, as that which can in any situation choose moral responsibility to an 'other', both seen and unseen, over the interests of self, finds its existence increasingly difficult in current economic conditions. In contrast to the Soviet perception of the individual as 'unfinished', to be processed and completed according to the dictates of communist political economy, capitalism seeks to create the individual as 'unfinishable', as a product always seeking to construct itself through the never-ending process of consuming. The consumerist message, as Baudrillard puts it,

> is precisely that *there is no one there – no person* ... The 'person' as an absolute value, with its indestructible features and specific force, forged by the whole of Western tradition as the organizing myth of the Subject – the person with its passions, its will, its character (or banality) – is absent, dead, swept out of our functional universe. And it is this absent person, this lost instance, which is going to 'personalize' itself. It is this lost being which is going to reconstitute itself *in abstracto*, by force of signs in the expanded range of differences, in the Mercedes, in the little light tint, in a thousand other signs, incorporated and arrayed to re-create a *synthetic individuality* ... .[93]

The paradox here is that at least Soviet communism saw the creation of the individual in its political economic likeness as a feasible end product. The individual, albeit manufactured by state ideology, would eventually emerge as a completed project. Not so in consumer society, where the realisation of a genuine self must be eradicated to be replaced by the synthetic, product-defined individuality who can only hope to realise this 'self' through the eternal act of consuming. 'I shop, therefore I am' can promise but never fulfil the sought-after long-term gratification, offering only a transitory sense of self, quickly dissolved as the next, even more efficient and better product comes along, promising (but never granting) greater fulfilment of being. Further, the irony of the consumer self, notes Baudrillard, is that by identifying each as unique and special, 'discover yourself through ...', 'because you're worth it', there is imposed a conformity, or what he calls *'monopoly concentration of the production of differences'*, in which the pursuit of self through branded goods and labels produces an homogenisation. We become a collective, one might say, of artificial individuals.

Consequently, to be unable to consume at the ever-increasing levels required, punitively excludes the self-in-search-of-self not only from the collective, from the chimera of a society of free individuals, but from one's own putative 'being'. The pursuit of the material hence becomes an issue of life and death (of the synthetic self). If, therefore, consuming becomes our *raison d'être*, or, indeed, us as selves, then the legal/illegal divide of the act of consuming is superfluous. It matters only to be able to consume, to sell, to produce. And everything of worth must then be measured and defined according to this criterion, everything we consider as human, including morality. As Karstedt and Farrell conclude from their findings:

> commodification is a distinct characteristic of institutional anomie: the economic model tends to dominate all other relationships in society. The extent to which individuals transfer the 'economic metaphor' into all their social relations and outside the realm of markets, and allow 'economic values' to govern their daily lives is a strong predictor of anomic tendencies and subsequent intentions to offend ... .[94]

Nor, as their study crucially points out, does offending take place by a marginal few, but rather by the so-called 'law-abiding majority'. The same pertains also to central economies as illustrated in the

Soviet context. In both, values are constructed and negotiated around the economic and material, driven either by the self-interest of the incomplete self or the survival of self as state-determined self. In neither case is ethical individuality, the positioning of the economic 'other' over and above the self (of which we are consistently denied real knowledge of), considered an important constituent of the economy.

CONCLUSION

When the human condition becomes a victim of materialist reductionism, as it clearly did under Soviet communism, more so arguably in the new Russia, and increasingly in Western neo-liberal societies, the ethical self has little chance to develop, or is gradually pummelled into oblivion. This ethical self, which manifests as will expressed through free choice and individual accountability for the consequences of that choice, not just on the self but on the 'other', provides the basis for economic fairness and by extension social justice. To will for the individual 'other' as an economic gesture is the antithesis of what we read into the term 'organised crime' and its effect on civilised society. Human, drug and arms trafficking, racketeering, loan sharking; indeed, the whole gamut of illegal enterprise linked to the illegal economy, all obliterate the sense of an 'other' as an object of entitlement and rights. Such activities not only exploit the other but, in their most brutal forms, set out to obliterate it too. The representations contained in the orthodox narrative of organised crime, however, do not tell of the reality behind the 'coal face' of harm inflicted through criminal business and the role of the dominant economies behind it. In the narrowing continuum between the ever-more 'non'-human aspect of modern economy and the 'inhuman' activities of those we label 'organised crime', activities which are direct products of both communism and capitalism, lies a meta-narrative of the pathological state of modern economy. For the West to avoid a collapse of its entire economic system, as occurred in the Soviet Union, but with even more dire consequences, it needs to pump up the volume of the meta-narrative and turn down the stentorian narratives of binary difference, whether criminological or ideological, otherwise we risk an increasingly probable situation in which 'a deepening international anarchy is the human prospect'.[95]

7
From Fear to Fraternity

It would be interesting to know what it is men are most afraid of. Taking a new step, uttering a new word is what they fear most...

(F. Dostoevsky, 1991)[1]

Brotherhood is not so wild a dream as those, who profit by postponing it, pretend.

(E. Sevareid, American journalist, 1946)[2]

The narratives on organised crime, like any narratives of a 'malicious other' serve a number of useful functions. They reinforce the legitimacy of the state and its institutions as a purveyor of violence in the defence of its citizens' interests, justifying the expansion and occasional contraction of security and crime control mechanisms. They help create cohesion between disparate and sometimes conflicting groups in the face of a common adversary. They can also distract attention away from awkward or painful realities that the powerful, as narrators, would rather the rest not know about; in particular, realities which expose the weakness of the dominant system, achieved by reinforcing what is good about society through the threatening presence of its moral antithesis. All these facilitate the transference of mass culpability to the 'malicious other' as a scapegoat for the abnegation of responsibility.

Similar narratives have been used to explain the Holocaust. Told at local, national or international levels, each narrative carries the same purpose: to create moral distance between the crime and the narrator, as well as those for whom the narratives are intended. They function as roadblocks on the path to individual conscience, helping retain the status quo by relocating culpability either to a small group of 'monsters' or to a national psyche. In reply to these narratives, critical analyses of the Holocaust, such as those referred to in Chapter 6, claim that it is impossible to isolate blame. Crimes of this scale by their very nature enfold each and every one of us to greater and lesser degrees. Modernity and its structures no longer permit such isolation of responsibility, but bind individuals together through division of labour, technologies and intricate bureaucracy. To reiterate the words of Hannah Arendt, 'in one form or another men must assume responsibility for all crimes committed by men and that all nations share the onus of evil committed by others'. Nowhere is this more apposite than in the modern economy.

NARRATIVES OF DISTANCE AND PROXIMITY

Geider writes of modern capitalism: 'irresponsibility is generalized now, thanks to the mechanisms and relationships institutionalized by modern business and banking and often codified in law. Irresponsibility is passed around to all.'[3] To be irresponsible is to be negligent, not to intend harm, but nonetheless to create, albeit passively, a situation in which harm is perpetrated. The difference between criminally induced economic harms and those brought about by all 'our' irresponsibilities, from a legalistic point of view, is one of conscious knowledge and hence intention. *Mens rea* is the cornerstone of criminally defined acts across the majority of criminal justice systems. This is most easily identifiable with one-on-one harmful acts, where the perpetrator can see or hear the pain and suffering he or she inflicts on the victim, that is, acts committed within a limited distance between individuals. While technology has facilitated the perpetration of more spatially expansive harms, such as detonating bombs at a distance, there remains an innate moral indignation, reflected in the response to certain types of offences and offenders by the majority of criminal justice systems, at the infliction of harm at close quarters. The 'monster' is the person who carries out one-on-one harmful acts, whose conscience remains unmoved by his or her act(s) of causing pain to another at close quarters.

One of the results of Stanley Milgram's (in)famous experiments on obedience showed that the further away the participants were from sensory perceptions of the 'pain' inflicted on their alleged victims, the greater the likelihood that they would continue to inflict pain when commanded to do so.[4] In other words, conscience is mitigated by distance. The further one is from the impact of one's actions, the less responsibility one is expected to take. Reiman, however, counters this orthodoxy by viewing harm not from the perspective of the perpetrator, but rather from those upon whom certain harmful acts impact. 'There is no moral basis for treating *one-on-one* harm as criminal and *indirect* harm as merely regulatory.'[5] His argument, put forward in the context of white collar and corporate crime, appeals for a reconsideration of indirect harm (by definition, infused with mitigating factors) as that based on the unmoved conscience, but one in which distance can no longer act as a tool of amelioration.

Not to care is as devastating as to deliberately injure, especially if an act not intended to cause harm does so nonetheless. Not to intend harm does not lessen its impact. Indeed, it allows for further harms to be perpetrated in the absence of conscience and responsibility.

According to a 2008 report on world hunger, 5 million children are dying every year from poor nutrition (1 million below the number of Jews killed in the Holocaust over a three-to-four-year period), despite the fact that food (grain) production is currently at a record high.[6] Civil war and corrupt third world politicians are some of the more visible factors that carry blame for these deaths in places such as the African continent. But as the report states, other, what we would describe as indirect, perpetrators have a hand in this huge death toll. Populations in rich countries 'consume more volume' than those in developing regions, and changing consumer behaviour such as the demand for all-year-round produce or the growing level of food wastage in restaurants as high-income groups eat out more, put undue pressure on food supply. So too has the free market and its inconsistencies, such as speculation in food and related industries in the face of falling real estate values or the emergence of international food cartels, further contributed to the growing inequality of food availability and distribution.[7] Structural factors presuppose individual agency. Violence is most effective and widespread not through guns, threats or direct physical abuse, but through lifestyles, which lack *imaginative* conscience and respon-sibility extending beyond the proximity between perpetrator and victim to imagined consequences of our individual behaviours.

This propensity for indirect violence is reinforced by the ethos that detaches responsibility from the individual, turning it inwards to the self rather than outwards, to the 'other'. As Bauman notes:

> The concepts of responsibility and responsible choice, which used to reside in the semantic field of ethical duty and moral concern for the Other, have moved or have been shifted to the realm of self-fulfilment and calculation of risks. In the process, the Other as the trigger, the target, and the yardstick for a responsibility accepted, assumed, and fulfilled has all but disappeared from view, having been elbowed out or overshadowed by the actor's own self … The possibility of populating the world with more caring people and inducing people to care more does not figure in the consumerist utopia.[8]

Hence morality in a complex global economy is dangerously archaic, defined according to spatial relations that no longer exist as economic reality.[9] The configurations of the modern economy facilitate this, providing a series of 'escape routes' along which responsibility can be diffused. Division of labour in a global economy is one such route. In the lengthy chain of supply and demand, often spanning thousands of miles, incorporating numerous and diverse cultures and serving equally disparate local and national interests, violence and exploitation can remain hidden to all but the few. They can occur at various points of the complex chain without going beyond the space of sensory perception, invisible to the majority of economic links. Violent outcomes, thus concealed, allow a detachment and hence abnegation of responsibility according to traditional understandings of conscience and morality, understandings based on proximity between the harming body and the body harmed.

As Bauman states, aspirations towards a consumerist utopia cannot entertain responsibility for the 'other' if consumer society is to sustain itself. The 'actor's own self' must now become the primary driver underlying economic agency. The self as a consuming, materialist subject, that which, as Baudrillard claims, can never be fully realised but only promised, is the illusory self which has taken centre stage in economic relationships. The resulting carnage of these insatiable materialist desires therefore requires other explanations that distract attention away from the anarchy that assuming individual responsibility through conscience might bring. Organised crime as a repository of economic immorality is one such distraction, understood through these narratives, which engage with the familiar, traditional concepts of crime, violence, accountability and values, constructs which are no longer relevant even if they were, at one time, appropriate.

FEAR AND FICTION

The diverse narratives on organised crime, deepened and challenged in the context of Russia, are united by the fear factor. Illegal enterprise, we are told, threatens social stability, preying on the weak, touting its destructive wares to the innocent, undermining the integrity of respectable public bodies by corrupting its members, and constantly seeking opportunities to penetrate and infect the legal business sector. It is a proactive force against which increasing protection by the state is required. More legislation, more crime-fighting agencies with greater powers and more sophisticated technology are all essential. These narratives stoke up the industry of fear. Yet they do not tell outright lies but rather present a highly disproportionate version of a distorted truth. This distortion is as much about legitimate business as it is about the illegal. It is based on connections that have been made for us via the media, legislation, crime control policies, and so on, concerning certain behaviour and activities with associated agents, with who does what, and who, by implication, does not. Take, for example, money-laundering.

Since the 1990s one of the prime ways of tackling illegal business organisations has been to chase and confiscate criminal assets, to 'hit them where it hurts'. This was instigated as a specific policy in the 'war on drugs' and became inextricably linked with organised crime. But as Mitsilegas comments, 'dirty' money is not only criminal money: it may be legitimate money rendered illegal through tax evasion, or even legitimate proceeds which are tainted by their use to support terrorist organisations.[10] The disproportionate focus on money-laundering as a 'mafia' activity not only reinforces the notion of danger from without, but obfuscates the dangerousness from within and, as with many instances of the organised crime narrative, in doing so inserts fictional principles into the identical activities of *sanctioned* agents. Levi's succinct example sums up this process: 'When the CIA move money via BCCI, the Americans call it facilitating the national interest; when the Mafia do the same thing, we call it money laundering.'[11]

From this understanding of money-laundering the concept of 'clean' and 'dirty' money translates respectively into 'security' and 'threat'. 'Clean' money makes the economy go round, offers investment opportunities, sustains consumer spending and thus the status quo; 'dirty' money is bad for domestic and international trade, bad for the reputation of the international banking industry and bad for effective government and the rule of law.[12] In reality, however, money has no normative qualities. Those lie with the user, how they source their income or the nature of their expenditure. In the narratives of organised crime, however, as Levi points out, the identity of the user becomes essential to this normative process. 'Clean' and 'dirty' are references to users rather than the *de facto* outcomes of how money is sourced and used. From this perspective it is possible to question the assumptions that money-laundering is indeed a dangerous activity given the fact that, once in the system, capital provides financial institutions with the commodity they require. Or from a different angle, we could ask why is tax avoidance not regarded in the same light as tax evasion, a frequently used legal device for prosecuting criminal entrepreneurs (most famously Al Capone), given that both activities divert much-needed public revenue away from national treasuries and back into the hands of the user?[13]

If the current global financial crisis teaches us anything, it is that we should fear the familiar, the 'us' and the very institutions to which we look for social protection and economic security. But we are frozen by the fear of 'taking a new step, uttering a new word', of pulling the thread of these narratives and unravelling their content. We find ourselves trapped within these narratives, as Soviet Russians were with theirs, increasingly dependent on external authorities, the powerful, as narrators of our 'reality'. In colluding with them in the fictionalising of economic reality, we fear not so much the growing presence of authority, but rather its absence. Loss of the narrator and of the narratives that we have allowed to define economic reality risks an identity lacuna and the possibility of annihilation of self.

While the fiction of the free market as a promoter of democracy, freedom and wealth has been severely challenged over the past year, the fundamental discourse remains the same. The immoral 'other' continues to feature in these narratives, not only as organised criminals or Mafiosi, but now extended to include bankers, hedge fund managers, corporate executives, 'city boys and girls' of all descriptions. Blame has simply been scattered across a broader field. Responsibility, as always, lies outside and beyond the remit of the individual; it remains as always incumbent on the 'other' to be responsible for 'me', and never 'me' for the 'other'. The modern economy, so far, has allowed no space for individual moral autonomy. Morality has been conspicuously absent in debates on the economy unless relating to its criminal counterpart. Yet, as Adam Smith wrote, 'How selfish soever man may be supposed, there are evidently some principles in his nature, which interest him in the fortune of others, and render their happiness necessary to him ... .'[14] If the 'invisible hand' rendered these principles defunct in capitalism, which was clearly not what Smith envisaged, they need to be reappraised as a means of emerging out of the economic devastation that appears to be capitalism's inevitable legacy.

FRATERNITY

There is only one way to include the distant stranger: to define the threshold of the intolerable as *exactly the same for everybody*. The starting point is not pseudo-universalism or touchy-feely empathy, but a recognition of the radical and irreducible differences that do matter. These differences derive not from my ethnicity, culture, income, world-view, age, sexuality or gender, but from the primeval facts that *my children have not and will not die from hunger* and that *I have not or will not be forced from my home after watching my wife hacked to death with a machete.* It is precisely because these differences are so profound that the most ignored of revolutionary principles has to be invoked: not liberty, not equality, but *fraternity.*[15]

In his concluding chapter of *States of Denial*, Stan Cohen addresses the thorny question of the suffering 'distant stranger'. How do we bridge the gap between knowledge of the suffering of others beyond our circle of familiar proximity and actively respond to that suffering? In other words, how do we deal with the endemic culture of denial, our diverse attempts to detach ourselves from responsibility towards the suffering of those we do not know but know about? Such a response requires a time and spatial expansion of moral responsibility from a place of common familiarity to that which remains unseen yet recognised. This involves the fundamental acknowledgment that suffering cannot be differentiated or graded according to different contexts of identity. The single viable context is that of the human, a universal starting point for each and every one of us. Only then can we imagine as real the suffering of the others and, in turn, respond appropriately. Fraternity is thus conceived as a moral issue; more importantly, an individually motivated issue, a Ptolemaic universe of principles in which 'I' becomes the reference point for comprehending and responding to the suffering of the 'distant stranger', where the suffering of the hidden, distant other is understood through its absence in my own personal universe, the one I know and feel.

The same principle of fraternity pertains to the distant stranger in the economy. Fraternity has an even greater relevance in the global economy than in other social relations because each individual is to the distant other through a complex chain of material needs and desires and the tangible means of their fulfilment. Division of labour, like the myriad devices of denial (and, indeed, as one of them), in the two major models of modern economy experienced in Russia, has divided society into its separate economic components. In so doing it has diffused responsibility either outwards into a meaningless collective of dispersed accountability in which no one person can be held answerable, or inwards as a form of enclosed responsibility to self for self and no other, in a false conception of consumer autonomy. In neither case is the individual actor the prime source of moral accountability for the whole.

To this structural facet of modern economy we need to bring a morality based on imagination, not as a device of the fictitious, but one in which we can imagine in, through and beyond the differing and dividing layers of economic activity. This imaginative activity allows us to place ourselves as an economic actor at every point of interaction in the chain of production and consumption. It involves recognising that the physical and material distress of others, either through hunger, poverty, or economically induced crime, will at some point and in varying degrees have a connection back to our own individual actions. There can be no tolerance of the fact that my material well-being and that of those close to me can be enhanced at the cost of the other who I do not see or consciously know of, but who must have an existence as part of the satisfaction of my material needs and desires. The Fairtrade movement is an attempt to draw attention to the play of each link in the economic chain, raising the consciousness of consumers whose spending power allows them to make choices based on the global impact of their needs or desires. Yet, as crucial as such an initiative is, addressing many of the immediate needs of hitherto highly exploited, abused workers, it is still confined to operating within the same economic model that pits individual against individual, within a structure which paradoxically defines itself according to the interdependency of its component parts.[16]

But it is not just in the growing acceptance of product accountability that fraternity must occur. In the virtual world of finance, the most powerful commodity in global economics, division of labour has been deliberately exploited as a means of concealing 'irresponsible' high-risk investment. This has operated in an esoteric world of hedge funds, derivatives, ninja loans, private equity mega buyouts, and so on, whose *modus operandi* even the experts themselves cannot explain. Called to account for their role in the collapsing state of the global economy, bankers, hedge fund managers, corporate executives and any number of the powerful deemed in control of this arcane world have now become objects of public opprobrium.[17] They are the ones we hold responsible. And clearly, they must carry their share of accountability. Ringfencing blame, however, will not solve the problems we face in the global economy today. It puts us in danger of reproducing the same narratives of economic harm that have come to frame our perceptions of organised crime, Russian or otherwise, and 'bad' capitalists in the post-Soviet chaos of the 1990s. The problem simply becomes displaced. By refusing to challenge the economic status quo, or doing so in a limited manner, we increase the speed of the ineluctable deterioration of capitalism, playing the same game of denial in much the same way as occurred in the Soviet Union.

More importantly, and dangerously, however, displacement undermines the possibility of radically reconfiguring the economy and instead provides continued support for the 'mafia-style' dominance of the economic convention that denies pluralism and heterodoxy in economic thinking. As one economist put it, 'the pre- and post-war repression of heterodox economics and economists' resulted in the dominance of a worldview of economics in which

> the [neoclassical] community accepted a single, relatively homogenous body of ideas or theories, shared the same set of standards – theoretical, technical, and empirical – for evaluating research and publications, engaged in a network of inter-institutional and interpersonal ties that promoted communication, reciprocated employment and conference participation opportunities, and rejected or suppressed all else.[18]

This paradigm has not only dominated economic thought, but in the process rendered what should be a practical discipline arcane and disturbingly opaque. As with the old religions, which governed every aspect of the daily lives of the people in unquestioning obedience to the leadership of the high priests, so too have the workings of modern economy, both as Soviet communism and Western capitalism, become impermeable to all but a select few. The dangerous reality, however, that faces us today, is that these so-called high priests who demanded that we trust in their knowledge of matters unintelligible to the common economic actor have themselves turned out to be little more than sorcerers' apprentices. Holding them entirely to account simply endorses the spurious narratives that got us into this mess in the first place.

Once the global economy eventually rediscovers a level of composure, but on an even more fragile foundation than with previous crises, amnesia will set in, and the city elite, now seen to be working again in the interests of the populations of advanced capitalist states, will no longer be objects of blame. The old narratives of organised crime will undoubtedly resume their dominant place whenever we need to ameliorate the discomfort of moral dissonance brought on by an economic system riddled with ethical inconsistencies. Unless, that is, genuine accountability becomes inculcated into the perception of self as an economic actor.

BALANCING ACCOUNTS

Accountability in both human and economic terms involves creating equilibrium between two sides. Expenditure needs to be balanced by income and vice versa, otherwise there arises a disparity which renders both sides dysfunctional: expenditure becomes irredeemable debt, and income, unless recycled, loses its value. A graphic image of the human consequences of this imbalance is easily imagined: the bony child in developing countries, about to become another statistic in the 5 million annual deaths of the undernourished, and the obese Western child, threatened with early diabetes and a premature heart condition. What seemed to be an illogical demonstration of this account sheet was uttered during my childhood on Monday evenings as a means of exhorting my brother and I to eat potted meat sandwiches: 'There are children starving in Africa, you know.' And, as did millions of youngsters facing the same emotional blackmail, we retorted 'Well give it to them then', though I remember feeling that this almost amounted to cruelty with our particular fare. As the first post-war adult generation to experience consumerist growth, my parents were more concerned about wastage than economic injustice. They also believed that the plight of the starving in Africa would be solved by the economic system that was starting to distribute its largesse amongst the lower classes in Britain and the rest of the West. We resorted to similar tactics with our own children (brown rice and vegetables – one child is a voracious meat-eater now) at a time when Live Aid fed the world images of starving African children and unkempt rock stars bellowing that we must all put our hands in our pockets 'and fucking *give*'. Nothing had changed. Indeed, things had become worse.

The imagined transportation of plates of stale uneaten food and actual donations of millions of currency, however effective one might regard the latter, are nonetheless symbolic of a conscience that can be stirred when the global human accounting system is exposed in all its horrific inequity. But beyond the symbolic and the momentary pang of conscience, nothing has really altered on our side. We either did not notice or did not care enough to realise that the economic crisis that now calls for heads to roll in advanced capitalist countries has been around for an awfully long time, picking away at the vulnerable in countries far and near. *Their* voices of outrage and despair have been silenced under the loud clamour of Western consumerism. Only when economic harm has come home to roost, albeit temporarily, have the high-risk antics of the financial world and the political will that tacitly encouraged them engendered mass moral disapproval. Responsibility to the self still remains the central ethos.

Debates about the future of the global economy – whether to regulate more or adapt the present system to these difficult times – has as yet not moved beyond the old dichotomies of socialism versus the free market, or with merely a nod to social democratic forms of compromise. We still think in terms of deterministic economic models rather than allowing free human agency and individual moral responsibility the input that is required to make genuine change.

In addition, too much focus has gone onto the tools behind economics, such as mathematical formulae rather than the reality created by the users. Perhaps we are asking all the wrong questions, or failing to understand what economics really means. Are we prepared to make room for heterodox approaches that critique the use of these rarefied, abstract formulae in economics,[19] or require a rethink of familiar concepts such as surplus value and profit and the impact on society?: 'The real question is whether the profit is calculated before or after the true costs of an activity have been met, including in particular any costs it avoids by passing them onto society's balance sheet, underpaying people, cheating customers or destroying nature.'[20] Within these heterodoxies comes the possibility and encouragement of individual awareness as to the nature of economics, and with it choices as to individual needs, as opposed to those dictated from without, that satisfy the self but work for the economic whole.

In comparison with debates on other forms of mass injustice and human rights violations, which the global economy is constantly generating, the discourse on economic accountability and agency is years behind that of genocide. And yet similar patterns in human behaviour, harm and suffering are applicable to both. In her report on the trial of Adolf Eichmann in 1961, Arendt noted that in the narratives on the Holocaust there is 'the reluctance evident everywhere to make judgements in terms of individual moral responsibility'.[21] Much has been done since then to understand the relationship between the social conditions, personal circumstances and moral choices in situations as extreme as those in Nazi Germany, Stalin's Russia or Pol Pot's Cambodia. One common aspect that has come out of these studies is not only the propensity to abnegate individual accountability, but also the ability to accept it and act out of it. Just that knowledge alone is a step towards unravelling the narratives of disengagement and disempowerment. It could also have a place in unravelling the narratives of organised crime and economy.

CONCLUSION

Judge Giovanni Falcone, murdered by members of the Sicilian Mafia, wrote of his nemesis: 'if we want to fight the Mafia organisation efficiently, we must not transform it into a monster or think of it as an octopus or cancer. We must recognise that it resembles us.'[22] The Russian tale of crime and economy has taken Falcone's observation a step further. The resemblance, it tells us, is actually part of the identity of the modern economy, inextricably bound up with it. In the tale told, we are confronted with a question which brings its own answer: What should we, faced with economic chaos perhaps not yet as drastic as that endured in Russia but with the potential for even greater turmoil, fear most – the very real threat of an increased criminal economy or the conditions in its dominant counterpart that create it?

The road to the free market out of the rubble of communism has led Russia along the path towards a new form of authoritarianism. It neither inspired the democratic structures it claimed it would, nor provided greater wealth for the majority. Its experience of the modern economy has exposed the pathology of two models, the ideals of which are admirable and necessary. However, in isolation from individual responsibility to the other as an essential component of economic agency both have resulted in endemic criminality and systemic immorality. Yet with this human quality as a central feature in economic life, then perhaps economic brotherhood as a freely chosen condition, rather than one imposed from without, has a chance of diverting the global economy from its lemming-style rush towards the cliff's edge. If the fate of the Russian people, as the adage heading Chapter 1 states, is to show the rest of the world how *not* to live, perhaps the Russian tale of crime, economy and modernity provides a vital signpost away from the cliff's edge.

Notes

INTRODUCTION

1. 2nd Annual European Serious and Organized Crime Conference, BT Convention Centre, Liverpool, UK, 9–10 March 2009.
2. D. Hobbs (1994) 'Professional and Organised Crime in Britain', in M. Maguire, R. Morgan and R. Reiner (eds), *Oxford Handbook of Criminology*. Oxford, Oxford University Press, p. 459.
3. According to national statistics published by the UK's NHS Information Centre for health and social care in 2008, deaths from illicit drug misuse numbered 1,573 in 2006, http://www.ic.nhs.uk/webfiles/publications/Drugmisuse08/Statistics%20on%20Drug%20Misuse%202008%20final%20format%20v12.pdf. Cancer Research UK estimated that in 2005, cancer-related deaths alone from tobacco smoking were as high as 46,000, http://info.cancerresearchuk.org/cancerstats/types/lung/smoking.
4. P. Hillyard, C. Pantazis, S. Tombs and D. Gordon (2004) *Beyond Criminology: Taking Harm Seriously*. London, Pluto Press, p. 11.

CHAPTER 1

1. This was John Kerry's reference to the perceived threat of organised crime as a global phenomenon, but with particular reference to the emergence of criminal groups from Russia and their 'invasion' of established democracies. It transferred the concept of 'monolithic threat' from the Cold War to the war on crime, and in doing so provided legitimacy to the reorganisation rather than dismantling of Western intelligence agencies in the post-communist era (*Newsweek*, 'Global Mafia', 13 December 1993).
2. Living space was severely limited in the Soviet Union, the official standard being 9 square metres per person, although in reality it fluctuated over time, from 4 to 8.1 metres (J. R. Short (1984) *An Introduction to Urban Geography*. London, Routledge, p. 124), leaving little room for impoverished and potentially homeless relatives. Even when children did move with their parents, cramped conditions and the inevitable conflicts could push them into early 'independence'. See also *Petersburg in the Early 90's: Cold, Cruel and Crazy* (1994). Charitable Fund 'Nochlezhka', St Petersburg.
3. The polyclinic (introduced in the Soviet Union and also used across other countries such as France and Germany) offers a range of outpatient services, such as X-rays and general practitioner support. Polyclinics would often be attached to factories to serve the local workforce.
4. N. Christie (2000) *Crime Control as Industry: Towards Gulags, Western Style*. London, Routledge (3rd edn), p. 22.
5. R. Skidelsky, 'The Moral Vulnerability of Markets', http://www.project-syndicate.org/commentary/skidelsky3.
6. W. D. Casebeer (2008) 'The Stories Markets Tell', in P. J. Zak (ed.), *Moral Markets*. Princeton, Princeton University Press, p. 6.

7. The same year that serfdom was abolished in Russia, the American Civil War broke out over the question of slavery.

8. O. Figes (1996) *A People's Tragedy: The Russian Revolution 1891–1924*. London, Pimlico, p. 217.

9. Marquis de Custine (1990) *Empire of the Czar: A Journey through Eternal Russia*. New York, Anchor Books, p. 50.

10. UN Convention Against Transnational Organized Crime, http://www.unodc. org/unodc/speech_2000-12-12.

11. C. Sterling (1994) *Crime Without Frontiers: The Worldwide Expansion of Organised Crime and the Pax Mafiosa*. London, Little, Brown and Company, p. 1.

12. S. Handelman (1994) *Comrade Criminal: The Theft of the Second Russian Revolution*. London, Michael Joseph.

13. 'Toward a New World Order', Address before a joint session of Congress, Washington, DC, 11 September 1990, US Department *Dispatch*, 17 September 1990.

14. J. Gray (1998) *False Dawn: The Delusions of Global Capitalism*. London, Granta, p. 152.

15. M. Olsen (1995) 'The Devolution of Power in Post-Communist Societies', in R. Skidelsky (ed.), *Russia's Stormy Path to Reform*. London, The Social Market Foundation.

16. R. Williams (2008) 'Face it: Marx was Partly Right about Capitalism', *Spectator*, 24 September 2008.

17. D. Downes and P. Rock (2007) *Understanding Deviance*. Oxford, Oxford University Press (5th edn), p. 323.

18. E. Hobsbawm (1994) *Age of Extremes: The Short Twentieth Century 1914–1991*. London, Michael Joseph, p. 496.

19. http://www.marxists.org/archive/shachtma/1950/03/russia.htm#ms1.

20. S. Cohen (2001) *States of Denial: Knowing about Atrocities and Suffering*. Cambridge, Polity, p. 39.

21. Other aspects of the research process for parts of the book have been discussed elsewhere: see P. Rawlinson (2007) 'Mission Impossible? Researching Organized Crime', in R. King and E. Wincup (eds), *Doing Research on Crime and Justice*. Oxford, Oxford University Press; P. Rawlinson (2008) 'Look Who's Talking: Interviewing Russian Criminals', *Trends in Organized Crime*, 11(1): 12–20.

22. Some of the most interesting ethnographic work has been done on underworld business and its links with the legitimate world, such as Chambliss's study of corruption and crime in Seattle (W. Chambliss (1988) *On the Take: From Petty Crooks to Presidents*. Bloomington, Indiana University Press) and Hobbs's work on illegal business in the East End (D. Hobbs (1988) *Doing the Business*. Oxford, Clarendon Press).

23. L. Piacentini (2004) *Surviving Russian Prisons: Punishment, Economy and Politics in Transition*. Cullompton, Willan Publishing.

24. A. Zinoviev (1986) *Homo Sovieticus*. London, Paladin, p. 128.

CHAPTER 2

1. V. Vitaliev (1990) *Special Correspondent: Investigating in the Soviet Union*. London, Century Hutchinson, p. 101.

2. F. Engels (1950) *The Condition of the Working Class in England*. London, Allen & Unwin, p. 130.

3. J. Albini (1997) 'The Mafia and the Devil: What They Have in Common', in P. J. Ryan and G. E. Rush (eds), *Understanding Organized Crime in Global Perspective: A Reader*. Thousand Oaks, Sage Publications, p. 65.

4. A. Dolgova and S. Dyakov (eds), *Organizovannaya Prestupnost'*. Moscow, Yuridicheskaya Literatura, p. 9.

5. Emile Durkheim, regarded as the father of sociology, took a rather unusual view of crime and one that conflicted directly with the Marxist concept that believed given the proper economic conditions crime, like the state and law, would 'wither away'. For Durkheim, not even the most 'perfect' society (as in his cloister of saints) would be free of crime as there will always be some level of behaviour regarded as unacceptable and hence proscribed. What was important for Durkheim were the *levels* of crime which served as an indicator of the health of a particular society. Too little crime, as in his example of the cloister of saints, reflects a severity of social control, in which the norms applied are too restrictive on the individual; too much crime is an indictor of the loosening of normative values to the extent that the collective morals of society; its glue, so to speak, no longer have any impact on restraining deviant behaviour. 'Normal' society will have levels of crime appropriate to its collective conscience, which operates according to a consensus of acceptable behaviour. See E. Durkheim (1964) *The Rules of Sociological Method*. New York, Free Press.

6. A. Vaksberg (1991) *The Soviet Mafia*. London, Weidenfeld & Nicolson, p. 19.

7. President's Commission on Law Enforcement and Administration of Justice (1967) *Task Force Report: Organized Crime*. Washington, DC, Government Printing Office.

8. M. Woodiwiss (1990) 'Organized Crime USA: Changing Perceptions from Prohibition to the Present', *BAAS Pamphlet*, 19.

9. D. C. Smith (1991) 'Wickersham to Sutherland to Katzenbach: Evolving an "Official" Definition for Organized Crime', *Crime, Law and Social Change*, 16: 135–54.

10. Ibid.: 139.

11. The spread of communism after the Second World War into Eastern and Central Europe and China, alongside a small number of high-profile 'spy' cases in the US, sparked a number of investigations into possible affiliations between US citizens and communist organisations. These culminated in the infamous witch hunt for communist sympathisers led by Senator Joe McCarthy.

12. E. Kefauver (1968) *Crime in America*. New York, Greenwood Press, p. 14.

13. Ibid., p. 326. Three of the recommendations in the report related to immigration. As well as urging the faster processing of deportees, the committee asked for more severe punishments for those aiding illegal immigration.

14. D. Bell (1962) *The End of Ideology*. New York, Free Press.

15. F. Bovenkerk, D. Siegel and D. Zaitch (2003) 'Organized Crime and Ethnic Reputation Manipulation', *Crime, Law and Social Change*, 39: 23–38.

16. C. Sterling (1994) *Crime Without Frontiers: The Worldwide Expansion of Organised Crime and the Pax Mafiosa*. London, Little, Brown and Company.

17. A. Wright (2005) *Organised Crime*. Cullompton, Willan Publishing, p. 160.

18. Louise Shelley, http://www.wilsoncenter.org/index.cfm?fuseaction=events. event_summary&event.

19. R. Hofstadter (1966) *The Paranoid Style in American Politics, and Other Essays*. London, Cape.

20. http://www.whitehouse.gov/news/releases/2001/09/20010911-16.html. This was the statement by the President after the attacks on 9/11. George W. Bush went on to pitch the 'evil' and 'worst of human nature' against 'the best of America', in a rhetorical style that defined subsequent announcements of America's reaction and response to terrorism.

21. Z. Sardar and M. W. Davies (2003) *Why Do People Hate America?* Cambridge, Icon Books Ltd, p. 141.

22. http://usinfo.org/wf-archive/2001/010124/epf305.htm.

23. P. Rawlinson (2001) *Russian Crime and Baltic Borders: Assessing the Real Threat*. Final Report/Translation. ESRC L213252013.

24. J. O. Finckenauer and E. J. Waring (1998) *Russian Mafia in America: Immigration, Culture and Crime*. Boston: Northeastern University Press, p. 254.

25. M. Levi (1998) 'Perspectives on "Organised Crime": An Overview', *Howard Journal of Criminal Justice*, 37(4): 335–45.

26. Quoted in CARPO Regional Project (2007) *Update of the 2006 Situation Report of Organised and Economic Crime in South-eastern Europe*, Annex 'The Concept of Organised Crime'. Strasbourg, European Commission Recommendation PC-TS(2007)6.

27. The readiness to use violence varies from culture to culture and also depends on the type of crimes being committed (leaving aside the different interpretations of what constitutes 'violence'). Racketeering is clearly the commodification of violence or the threat of its use (see D. Gambetta (1993) *The Sicilian Mafia: The Business of Private Protection*. Cambridge, MA, Harvard University Press; F. Varese (2001) *The Russian Mafia: Private Protection in a New Market Economy*. Oxford, Oxford University Press), but for those involved in other forms of criminal business it can often be costly in terms of the resources required (see Chapter 5) .

28. A body of literature exists on the use in legal business of intimidation, violence and other activities designated intrinsic to organised crime, even as routine behaviour. See especially S. Hills (1987) *Corporate Violence: Injury and Death for Profit*. Maryland, Rowman & Littlefield; and R. T. Naylor (2002) *Wages of Crime: Black Markets, Illegal Finance and the Underworld Economy*. Ithaca, Cornell University Press; G. Slapper and S. Tombs (1999) *Corporate Crime*. London, Longman; V. Ruggiero (2000) *Crime and Markets: Essays in Anti-Criminology*. Oxford, Oxford University Press.

29. L. Shelley (2007) 'Human Trafficking as a Form of Transnational Crime', in M. Lee (ed.), *Human Trafficking*. Cullompton, Willan Publishing.

30. Quoted in Wright, *Organised Crime*, p. 55.

31. V. Ruggiero (1996) *Organized and Corporate Crime in Europe: Offers that Can't be Refused*. Aldershot, Dartmouth.

32. United Nations Convention Against Transnational Organized Crime (A/55/383), http://www.odccp.org/palermo/theconvention.html.

33. Gambetta, *The Sicilian Mafia*.

34. A weak or 'failed' state describes those sovereign states which fail to meet a series of criteria defined according to the US think tank The Fund for Peace.

The concept has been contested by radical academics such as Noam Chomsky who regard it as a heavily politicised label which serves to legitimise aspects of US foreign policy. See N. Chomsky (2006) *Failed States: The Abuse of Power and the Assault on Democracy*. New York, Metropolitan Books.

35. http://www.fundforpeace.org/.

36. W. Chambliss (1978) *On the Take: From Petty Crooks to Presidents*. Bloomington, Indiana University Press; M. Punch (1996) *Dirty Business: Exploring Business Misconduct*. London, Sage; B. Bullington (1993) 'All About Eve: The Many Faces of US Drug Policy', in F. Pearce and M. Woodiwiss (eds), *Global Crime Connections: Dynamics and Control*. Basingstoke, Macmillan.

37. Naylor, *Wages of Crime*, p. 105.

38. Ibid., p. 91.

39. Interview with Tony Quigley, Birmingham Loan Shark Unit, March 2005.

40. P. Hillyard and S. Tombs (2004) 'Beyond Criminology', in P. Hillyard, C. Pantazis, S. Tombs and D. Gordon (eds), *Beyond Criminology: Taking Harm Seriously*. London, Pluto Press, p. 13.

41. A. Grayling (2008), *Prospect*, June.

42. Hillyard and Tombs, 'Beyond Criminology', p. 15.

43. In their report on work-related deaths Tombs and Whyte include road traffic deaths from 'at work' vehicles and a number of occupational deaths from diseases which are not reported by the Heath and Safety Executive under the criteria set out by the Reporting of Injuries, Diseases and Dangerous Occurrences Regulations. According to their data this inclusion brings the total for work-related deaths in 2006–07 up to 1,400 compared to 755 recorded homicides – S. Tombs and D. Whyte (June 2008) *A Crisis of Enforcement: The decriminalisation of death and injury at work*, Centre for Crime and Justice Studies, King's College London, Briefing 6.

44. B. Proia (2007), PhD research, London School of Economics.

45. D. Lapierre and J. Moro (2003) *Five Past Midnight in Bhopal*. London, Scribner.

46. Pablo Escobar, former head of the Medellin Cartel in Colombia, was widely known as a ruthless druglord, to whom more than 4,000 murders have been attributed. However, according to some sources, most notably the poorer sections of Colombia, Escobar, a hugely negative force in Colombia, was also responsible for building houses and providing jobs for the disenfranchised. See M. Ceasar (2008) 'At Home on Pablo Escobar's Ranch', BBC News, 2 June, http://news.bbc.co.uk/1/hi/world/americas/7390584.stm. Clearly this offers no excuse for the murderous and destructive business he ran but does raise the question as to how money is judged to be 'dirty' or 'clean'. Do we assess its impact according to how it is earned or how it is spent, or are the two inextricably linked?

47. http://www.lawcom.gov.uk/conspiracy.htm.

48. Punch, *Dirty Business*, p. 64.

49. See Centre for Corporate Accountability, http://www.corporateaccountability.org/press_releases/2007/nov21sentproposal.htm.

50. Paul Lashmar (2007) 'Law Lords Slam Crime Agency for Freezing UMBS Payments', *Independent on Sunday*, 27 May.

51. Smith, 'Wickersham to Sutherland to Katzenbach'.

52. Z. Bauman (1989) *Modernity and the Holocaust*. Cambridge, Polity, p. 214.

53. Ibid., p. 207.

54. As Punch (*Dirty Business*) and others have shown, successful prosecutions for corporate-related deaths and injuries are difficult to achieve because the law is largely designed (in liberal democracies) for offences by the individual. For a comprehensive and thought-provoking discussion of the issues on criminal responsibility and corporations, see C. Harding (2007) *Criminal Enterprise: Individuals, Organisations and Criminal Responsibility*. Cullompton, Willan Publishing.

55. Poverty-induced participation in criminal business, whether as sellers or consumers of the products and services, is not always due to exclusion from the labour market, but in what Jock Young refers to as 'a recasting of the lines of social exclusion within the market economy' (see J. Young (2007) *The Vertigo of Late Modernity*. London, Sage, p. 121) – low-paid menial work which usually falls to the most socially vulnerable, such as immigrants, can push people into the rational motivation of choosing to work in the illegal economy because it pays an affordable wage. As an illegal migrant reasoned, why work twelve hours a day for a wage that barely pays the rent, never mind food, when you can work in a brothel? (Interview with the author, October 2008.)

56. V. I. Lenin, 'The Tasks of the Youth Leagues', *Collected Works*, Vol. 31, http://www.marx.org/archive/lenin/works/1920/oct/02.

57. Ironically, we often acknowledge the individual 'other' when a scapegoat is needed for these negative outcomes: Stalin's pursuit of those responsible for the failure to meet impossible targets, 'wreckers' and 'enemies of the people', so-called rogue traders such as Nick Leeson blamed for the collapse of Barings Bank, and Adam Applegarth, former chief executive of Northern Rock, the first British bank to be nationalised after collapsing in the aftermath of the US subprime mortgage disaster..

58. A. Block (1997) 'On the Origins of Fuel Racketeering: The Americans and the Russians in New York', in P. Williams (ed.), *Russian Organised Crime: The New Threat*. London, Frank Cass.

CHAPTER 3

1. A previous, shorter version of this chapter appeared as 'A Brief History of Crime', in P. Williams (ed.) (1997), *Russian Organised Crime: The New Threat*. London, Frank Cass.

2. G. Orwell (1989) *Animal Farm*. London, Penguin Books, p. 102.

3. D. Hobbs (1997) 'Criminal Collaboration: Youth Gangs, Subcultures, Professional Criminals, and Organized Crime', in M. Maguire, R. Morgan and R. Reiner (eds), *The Oxford Handbook of Criminology*. Oxford, Clarendon Press.

4. S. Kucherov (1953) *Courts, Lawyers and Trials under the Last Three Tsars*. New York, Frederick Praeger.

5. 'The Great Patriotic War' is the term used by Russians to describe their involvement in the Second World War. It covers 1941–45, when Stalin's Soviet Union, a hitherto ally of the Third Reich as agreed under the terms of the Ribbentrop-Molotov Pact, came under attack from Germany in the ruthless attempt to overrun and crush the communist East as part of the policy of *Lebensraum* and Hitler's contempt for yet another race he considered inferior.

6. As Figes writes, it was not the intention of Eisenstein to praise the tyrant but rather emphasise the contrite side that emerged towards the end of his bloody reign as a means of influencing the ever ruthless leadership of Stalin. O. Figes (2002) *Natasha's Dance: A Cultural History of Russia*. London, Allen Lane, p. 497.
7. Ibid., p. 496.
8. M. Shcherbatov (1969) *On the Corruption of Morals in Russia*. Cambridge, Cambridge University Press, p. 69.
9. M. Walker (1987) *The Waking Giant*. London, Abacus/Sphere Books, p. 69.
10. Marquis de Custine (1990) *Empire of the Czar: A Journey Through Eternal Russia*. New York, Anchor Books, p. 125.
11. In 1864 the liberal-minded Alexander II introduced trial by jury alongside the establishment of the Public Prosecutor's Office and Justices of the Peace. It was an attempt, amongst other things, to provide the disenfranchised with a fair system of criminal justice as well as attempting to curb rampant bribery within the criminal justice system.
12. Kucherov, *Courts, Lawyers and Trials under the Last Three Tsars*, p. 238.
13. M. Dixelius and A. Konstantinov (1995) *Prestunpny Mir v Rossii*. St Petersburg, Bibliopolis, p. 44.
14. V. Chalidze (1977) *Criminal Russia: Crime in the Soviet Union*. London, Random House.
15. E. Hobsbawm (1972) *Bandits*. London, Penguin, p. 26.
16. R. Pipes (1977) *Russia Under the Old Regime*. Middlesex, Peregrine, pp. 298–9.
17. L. Trotsky (1911) *Why Marxists Oppose Individual Terrorism*, Marxist archive, http://www.marxists.org/archive/trotsky/1911/11/tia09.htm.
18. Pipes, *Russia Under the Old Regime*, p. 161.
19. Ibid., p. 161. See also O. Figes (1997) *A People's Tragedy: The Russian Revolution 1891–1924*. London, Pimlico; in particular, ch. 3, 'Icons and Cockroaches'.
20. In his famous political pamphlet, *What is to be Done*, Lenin justified the vanguard movement of Russian socialism, leading from above rather than below, on the grounds that the consciousness of the workers' movement amongst the Russian people amounted only to the trade union struggle against economic conditions within the existing system rather than a revolutionary movement. To bring the working class to full revolutionary consciousness rather than subjugation to a bourgeois ideology of a 'spontaneous' agitation required education from 'without' by those already working to develop the socialist path, that is, 'the revolutionary socialist *intelligentsia*'. See 'The Spontaneity of the Masses and the Consciousness of the Social Democrat', ch. 2 in *What is to be Done*, Marxist archive, http://www.marxists.org/archive/lenin/works/1901/witbd/ii.htm.
21. Russian language usage tends towards objectification of the subject (though not always), where in other languages s/he would be the undisputed subject, especially in relation to personal conditions and characteristics. So, for example, to be hot, to be cold or to need something is expressed through the dative case – 'to me it is hot/cold'; 'to me is needed/required something', and so on. The idea that the structure of language and how the world is perceived are related phenomena is known as the linguistic relativity principle, a thesis put forward by Edmund Sapir and Benjamin Lee Whorf. Clearly this is a

contentious issue, but the lack of an entrenched consciousness of the individual as secondary to the collective, and the impact of this in modern Russian history as entrenched in grammar and syntax, deserves some consideration.

22. The commune remained a fixed feature of rural life after the abolition of serfdom. More substantial changes occurred at higher levels of governance, with the creation of the *zemstva* in 1864, structures of local government whose tasks partly replaced that of erstwhile serf owners. Closed to peasant representation, they attracted liberals from the intelligentsia and conservative landowners.

23. Esther Kingston-Mann (1991) 'Peasant Communes and Economic Innovation: A Preliminary Inquiry', in Esther Kingston-Mann and Timothy Mixter (eds), *Peasant Economy, Culture, and Politics of European Russia 1800–1921*. Princeton, Princeton University Press, p. 34.

24. Lenin, *What is to be Done*.

25. The abolition of the commune by those opposed to radical land reform (which demanded the expropriation of surplus land from the nobility by the peasants) was intended to dismantle what the nobility regarded as a potential structure for organising peasant resistance to the increasingly brutalised conditions they and urban workers were suffering. The First Duma had been established after the countrywide mass unrest provoked by the killing of protesters, including women and children, by Tsarist troops, as they marched in peaceful demonstrations to the Winter Palace to ask for Nicholas II's support in alleviating their distress. Fear of further unrest was not unreasonable, particularly as the reluctance of the state to cede real power to an elected representative body saw the dismissal of the first Duma only weeks after its inauguration, a clear volte-face of promises made. As it turned out, however, there was little political resistance from below. That would come a decade later.

26. Figes, *Natasha's Dance*, p. 437.

27. See also T. Shanin (1971) 'A Peasant Household: Russia at the Turn of the Century', in T. Shanin (ed.), *Peasants and Peasant Societies: Selected Readings*. Harmondsworth, Penguin.

28. P. Lyashchenko (1949) *History of the National Economy of Russia to 1917*. New York, Macmillan; A. Nove (1980) *An Economic History of the USSR*. Harmondsworth, Penguin.

29. *Artels* were cooperatives or economic associations, a Russian term used at the end of the nineteenth century.

30. D. Golinkov (1971) *Krakh vrazheskovo podpol'ya*. Moscow, Izdatel'stvo Politicheskoy Literatury, p. 76.

31. R. Tucker (1973) *Stalin as Revolutionary 1879–1929: A Study in History and Personality*. New York, Norton and Company.

32. V. S. Ovchinsky, interview with the author, December 1994.

33. The Cheka was the predecessor to a line of brutal state machinery (from the dreaded NKVD, or People's Commissariat of Internal Affairs, to the Committee for State Security – the KGB) tasked with bringing order to anarchic Russia, using terror as its main instrument of control.

34. V. Orlov (1932) *The Secret Dossier: My Memoirs of Russia's Political Underworld*. London, G. G. Harrap & Co.

35. The White Army was comprised of counterrevolutionaries who fought against Bolshevism in the Civil War (1918–21).

36. Golnikov, *Krakh vrazheskovo podpol'ya*.

37. V. I. Lenin (1917) 'Speech Delivered at a Meeting of Soldiers of the Izmailovsky Regiment, April 10 (23), 1917', http://marxists.anu.edu.au/archive/lenin/works//1917/apr/10.htm.

38. R. Pipes (1994) *Russia Under the Bolshevik Regime 1919–1924*. London, Harvill, p. 387.

39. Commission of the CC of the CPSU (ed.) (1939) *History of the Communist Party of the Soviet Union*. Moscow, Foreign Languages Publishing House, p. 256.

40. Pipes, *Russia Under the Old Regime*, p. 370.

41. L. Sheinin (c. 1956) *Diary of a Criminologist*. Moscow, Foreign Languages Publishing House, p. 87.

42. 'Collectivisation' was the name given to the process of creating collective farms or *kolkhozi*, most notoriously implemented as the forced migration to the farms of those who resisted, and the annihilation of the rich peasants, or *kulaks*, upon whose land these huge collectives were established. The most aggressive surge occurred between 1929 and 1933. Estimates of the death toll of Stalin's modernising of agriculture through collectivisation show an average of 5 million. See S. Rosefielde (1984) 'Excess Collectivization Deaths 1929–1933: New Demographic Evidence', *Slavic Review*, 43(1) (Spring): 83–8.

43. *Ugolovny Kodeks RSFSR* (1987). Moscow, Yuridicheskaya Literatura.

44. A. Dolgova and S. Dyakov (eds) (1989) *Organizovannaya prestupnost'*. Moscow, Yuridicheskaya Literatura.

45. P. Juviler (1976) *Revolutionary Law and Order: Politics and Social Change in the USSR*. New York, The Free Press, p. 47.

46. N. Murray (1950) *I Spied for Stalin*. London, Odhams, p. 185.

47. L. Piacentini (2004) *Surviving Russian Prisons: Punishment, Economy and Politics in Transition*. Cullompton, Willan Publishing.

48. A. Gurov (1995) *Krasnaya Mafia*. Moscow, Samotsvet' MIKO 'Kommerchesky Vestnik.

49. C. Sterling (1994) *Crime Without Frontiers: The Worldwide Expansion of Organized Crime and the Pax Mafiosa*. London, Little, Brown.

50. A. Solzhenitsyn (1975) *Gulag Archipelago 1918–1956: An Experiment in Literary Investigation*, Vol. 2. London, Collins, p. 238.

51. Numbers of inmates in Stalin's gulags have been subject to much analysis. Nils Christie speaks of 'some 2.5 million prisoners' in the 1950s. As his work shows, however, it is what one does with the numbers, how they were 'read', that is important. See N. Christie (2000) *Crime Control as Industry*. London, Routledge, p. 79.

52. Dixelius and Konstantinov, *Prestunpny Mir v Rossii*, pp. 75–81.

53. E. Maksimovsky (1992) *Imperiya Strakha*. Moscow, Zeleny Parus; A. Gurov and V. Ryabin (1991) *Ispoved' vora v zakone*. Moscow, Rosagropromizdat.

54. Commission of the CC of the CPSU, *History of the Communist Party*, p. 341.

55. J. Berliner (1952) 'The Informal Organization of the Small Firm', *Quarterly Journal of Economics*, LXVI(3).

56. There are special verbs in Russian to denote the origin of goods. *Dostat'* means 'obtained', as opposed to *kupeet*, 'bought in the official way from a shop'.

57. A. Ledeneva (1998) *Russia's Economy of Favours: Blat, Networking and Informal Exchange*. Cambridge, Cambridge University Press, p. 71.

58. K. Simis (1982) *USSR: Secrets of a Corrupt Society*. London, J. M. Dent, pp. 104–5.
59. V. Vitaliev (1990) *Special Correspondent: Investigating in the Soviet Union*. London, Century Hutchinson.
60. S. Laudan (1989) *Galina Brezhnev and Her Gypsy Lover*. London, Quartet Books.
61. Chalidze, *Criminal Russia*.
62. A. Vaksberg (1991) *The Soviet Mafia*. London, Weidenfeld & Nicolson, pp. 5–6.
63. M. McCauley (1991) *Nikita Khrushchev*. London, Cardinal, p. 39.
64. M. Voslensky (1984) *Nomenklatura: Anatomy of the Soviet Ruling Class*. London, Bodley Head.
65. Konstantin Simis I believe provides one of the most insightful and illustrative accounts of corruption in Soviet Russia. In *USSR: Secrets of a Corrupt Society*, based on his experience as a Soviet lawyer who was forced daily to negotiate the labyrinthine networks of corrupt relationships and practices, he brings a human approach to the oppressive (and sometimes positive) outcomes of living in a world of double standards, political intrigue and economic uncertainty. As with Ledeneva's work (cited above) the Russian perspective on corruption provides many challenges to what those of us in rule-of-law states understand as 'good' and 'bad' behaviour in office, its impact on the public and the processes of rationalising certain types of behaviour designated 'corrupt' in different contexts. See also Ledeneva, *Russia's Economy of Favours*.
66. 'Corruption of Soviet Officials', *Struggling Russia*, 29 November 1919.
67. A. Zinoviev (1986) *Homo Sovieticus*. London, Paladin, p. 68.
68. S. Cohen (2001) *States of Denial: Knowing about Atrocities and Suffering*. Oxford, Polity Press, p. 64.
69. J. Millar (1990) *The Soviet Economic Experiment*. Chicago, University of Illinois Press, p. 185.
70. Ledeneva, *Russia's Economy of Favours*, p. 72.
71. Juviler, *Revolutionary Law and Order*.

CHAPTER 4

1. D. Doder and L. Branson (1990) *Gorbachev: Heretic in the Kremlin*. London, Futura, p. 90.
2. 'Turbo-capitalism' is the term used by Edward Luttwak to describe the evolution of accelerated capitalism which has stormed across numerous aspects of society, driven by, amongst other conditions, increasing deregulation and technology, an oftentimes destructive force (E. Luttwak (1999) *Turbo Capitalism: Winners and Losers in the Global Economy*. London, Orion Business Books).
3. M. Gorbachev (1996) *Memoirs*. London, Transworld Publishers, p. 173.
4. J. Steele (1994) *Eternal Russia*. London, Faber & Faber, p. 19.
5. R. Sakwa (1993) *Russian Politics and Society*. London, Routledge, p. 2.
6. A. Aslund (1991) *Gorbachev's Struggle for Economic Reform*. London, Pinter Publishers.
7. E. Durkheim (1960) *The Division of Labour in Society*. New York, The Free Press.

8. K. Ulibyn (1991) 'Znakomaya neznakomaya', *Tenevaya Ekonomika*. Moscow, Ekonomika, p. 7.

9. 'Administrative-command economy' was the term used by Gorbachev as a criticism of the system that had developed from the central planning of Stalin to the clumsy administrative hierarchy that marked the Brezhnev era of stagnation.

10. U. Feofanov (1988) 'It Couldn't Be, But It Was', *Moscow News*, 11.

11. S. White (1996) *Russia Goes Dry: Alcohol, State and Society*. Cambridge, Cambridge University Press.

12. Most research indicates a drop in alcohol-related deaths and illness during the period 1985–87 coinciding with the alcohol ban and its short-term impact on the country's drinking habits. During the early years of the economic reforms post-1991, alcohol-related harm, including death, increased dramatically, albeit with notable regional variations (A. Nemtsov (2000) 'Estimates of Total Alcohol Consumption in Russia 1980–1994', *Drug and Alcohol Dependence*, 58: 1133–42).

13. R. Boyes (1990) *The Hard Road to Market: Gorbachev, the Underworld and the Rebirth of Capitalism*. London, Secker & Warburg; P. Gregory (1987) 'Productivity, Slack and Theft Time in the Soviet Economy', in J. Millar (ed.), *Politics, Work and Daily Life in the USSR. A Survey of Soviet Citizens*. Cambridge, Cambridge University Press.

14. Aslund, *Gorbachev's Struggle for Economic Reform*.

15. P. Hanson (1992) *From Stagnation to Catastroika: Commentaries on the Soviet Economy 1983–1991*. New York, Praeger, p. 178.

16. 'Ostanovit' samogonshchika', *Izvestia*, 11 March 1987.

17. Gregory, 'Productivity, Slack and Theft Time', p. 259.

18. Aslund, *Gorbachev's Struggle for Economic Reform*, p. 164.

19. D. Bahry (1987) 'Politics, Generations and Change in the USSR', in J. Millar (ed.), *Politics, Work and Daily Life in the USSR. A Survey of Soviet Citizens*. Cambridge, Cambridge University Press.

20. J. Morrison (1987) 'Recent Developments in Political Education in the Soviet Union', in G. Avis (ed.), *The Making of the Soviet Citizen*. London, Routledge, p. 24.

21. W. Butler (1991) *Basic Documents on the Soviet Legal System*. New York, Oceana Publications, p. 355.

22. T. Koryagina (1991) 'Yest' li v SSSR "tret'ya sila"?' *Argumenty I Facty*, 26 (July).

23. Soviet Labour Review, June 1989: 3.

24. RFE/RL, 'The "Black" Millions', 17 July 1997.

25. A. Jones and W. Moskoff (1991) *Koops: The Rebirth of Entrepreneurship in the Soviet Union*. Bloomington, Indiana University Press, p. 83.

26. Ibid., p. 80.

27. In 1990 I worked as a TV researcher for the independent film company Abraxas on a Channel 4 *Dispatches* commissioned documentary on organised crime in Moscow. During the initial stages of research we were informed by a number of people that the cigarette shortage, a dire situation in a country so heavily addicted to tobacco, was largely strategic. While we were in Moscow a flood of imported cigarettes came onto the market, thereby partially scuppering one of our major forms of currency!

28. In January 1987 a decree was passed on 'The establishment and operation of joint ventures on the territory of the USSR with participation of Soviet organizations and firms from capitalist and developing countries' and was gradually adapted to allow an increasingly higher percentage of shares for foreign investors. The unintended consequences of this piece of legislation, were to create conditions conducive to money-laundering and capital flight from the Russian side. (For further information on joint ventures see C. Fey (1995) 'Important Design Characteristics for Russian-Foreign Joint Ventures', *European Management Journal*, 13(4): 405–15.)

29. 'Ne navredy! Razmishleniye o privatizatsii', *Ekonomika i Zhizn'*, 12 (March), 1991.

30. J. Serio (1992) *USSR Crime Statistics and Summaries: 1989 and 1990*. Chicago, Office of International Criminal Justice, p. 15.

31. Eduard Shevardnadze served as Minister of Foreign Affairs from 1985 to 1990, acting as a crucial influence on the attitudes taken by the Kremlin towards satellite communist states in their bid for independence by encouraging a more tolerant stance. His drive against corruption within Georgia, his native republic, also increased his popularity. However, there were rumoured links between members of his family and criminal business, especially through the Association of the 21st Century.

32. See P. Rawlinson (2009) 'Look Who's Talking: Interviewing Russian Criminals', *Trends in Organized Crime*, 11: 12–20. This article gives a brief description of a largely abortive interview with the Association of the 21st Century.

33. A. Gracheva (1989) '21st Century', *Moscow News*, 48.

34. Guy Dunn (1997) 'Major Mafia Gangs in Moscow', in P. Willimas (ed.), *Russian Organized Crime: The New Threat*. London, Frank Cass.

35. Invitation to Alex's by a friend.

36. Irina took a colleague and I to her burnt-out premises near Gorkovskaya metro. Understandably bitter about the whole experience, she was even more angry with the lack of support from the *militsiya*.

37. *Speculyanty* were those who sold goods at a personal profit, illegal at the time in the Soviet Union (what we call entrepreneurs or businessmen).

38. According to Louise Shelley, low-ranking *militsiya*, those more likely to be called upon to deal with racketeers, earned half of the 600 roubles a month paid to private guards (S. Shelley (1996) *Policing Soviet Society: The Evolution of State Control*. London, Routledge, p. 90).

39. 'Ready to Fly: The Search for Decentralised Socialism', *The Economist*, 28 April 1990.

40. V. Vitaliev (1989) 'Skval', *Krokodil*, 28 (October).

41. D. Gambetta (1993) *The Sicilian Mafia: The Business of Private Protection*. Cambridge, MA, Harvard University Press, p. 19.

42. Ibid., p. 77.

43. C. Tilly (1985) 'War Making as State Making as Organized Crime', in P. Evans, D. Ruesschemeger and T. Skocpol (eds), *Bringing the State Back In*. Cambridge, Cambridge University Press.

44. S. Solnick (1990) 'Does the Komsomol Have a Future?', *Report on the USSR* (21 September): 9–13.

45. J. Riordan (1989) 'Teenage Gangs, "Afghantsy" and "Neofascists"', in J. Riordan (ed.), *Soviet Youth Culture*. Indiana, Indiana University Press, p. 124.
46. J. Young (2007) *The Vertigo of Late Modernity*. London, Sage, p. 20.
47. Y. Schekhochikin (1988) 'Before the Mirror', *Soviet Sociology*, 28: 6–17.
48. V. Vitaliev (1989) *Special Correspondent: Investigating in the Soviet Union*. London, Century Hutchinson.
49. As with the famous Marlboro cigarettes, they became a form of currency in the culture-starved USSR.
50. S. Khokiyakov (1989) 'Mafia Leaves Us Lost for Words', *Soviet Weekly*, 22 July.
51. The *Dispatches* TV crew visited the site in the summer of 1990.
52. Interview with the author, August 1990.
53. 'Krutiye parny:ispoved' kooperatora ubivshevo ugolovnovo avtoriteta', *Ekonomika I Zhizn'*, 1, January 1991.
54. Jones and Moskoff, *Koops*, p. 87.
55. 'Man on the Right', *Moscow News*, 26, 1990.
56. A. Sobchak (1991) *Khozhdenie Vo Vlast*. Moscow, Novosti, p. 56. It was also stated in the *Financial Times* (15 March 1990) that Sobchak was reported to have taken payments from cooperatives and used ANT as a political opportunity to implicitly rebuff some of the accusations.
57. Lyubimov, presenter of one of the most popular and liberal topical issues shows, *Vzglyad*, in 1990, was an influential voice in the ANT debate. During an interview with myself and Nick Anning in September 1990 he warned of the influence of high-level government figures in an orchestrated scandal designed to destroy ANT.
58. Gorbachev's conversion programme was an attempt, where appropriate, to direct resources away from the production of military hardware into the much needed sphere of consumer goods. It was a policy he was able to promote as the Cold War began to subside. However, it never reached anywhere near the expected level of success.
59. This and other interviews, including off-the-record discussions with Pyotr Shpyakin, one of ANT's directors and those journalists who reported on the scandal, as well as documents and reports, were given to the Abraxas film crew with whom I worked in the summer and autumn of 1990.
60. 'KGB poka ne meniayet printsipov", *Komsomolskaya Pravda*, 20 June 1990.
61. 'Kremlin Battle Over Reforms', *Guardian*, 14 May 1990.
62. 'Delo ANTa', *Izvestia*, 5 November 1991.
63. L. Abalkin (1989) *Current Digest of the Soviet Press*, XLI(46).
64. The Shatalin-Yavlinsky Plan or '500 Day' plan presented a programme of transition to the market, including many aspects of privatisation, banking reform and market pricing according to a designated timescale. According to Nelson and Kuzes, it also factored in the problem of the criminal economy and corruption, something that Gaidar's privatisation and price liberalisation programme clearly failed to do (L. Nelson and Y. Kuzes (1995) *Radical Reform in Yeltsin's Russia: Political, Economic and Social Dimensions*. Armonk, NY, M. E. Sharpe, p. 76).
65. The 9+1 Treaty was intended to devolve power to the leaders of nine of the Soviet republics, a move initially opposed by Gorbachev who had increasingly

centralised power, but one he was too politically weak to challenge. The agreement also contained plans for greater market reform in the Union.

66. Filip Bobkov was one such. A former director of one of the KGB's most hated departments, the Fifth Directorate in charge of the suppression of dissent, he had actively worked against ANT in 1989 and 1990 and was a prime mover behind the August coup.

67. Despite the socialist democratic alternatives in a number of countries such as those in Scandinavia, many of them have been gradually subsumed by neo-liberalism, or heavily impacted by it, over the past two decades.

68. Young, *The Vertigo of Late Modernity*, p. 156.

69. L. Simis (1982) *USSR: Secrets of a Corrupt Society*. London, J. M. Dent, p. 210.

70. A. Ledeneva (1998) *Russia's Economy of Favours: Blat, Networking and Informal Exchange*. Cambridge, Cambridge University Press, p. 82.

71. I. Bunich (1992) *Zoloto Partii*. St Petersburg, Istoricheskaya Khronika, p. 22.

72. S. Kordonsky (1990) 'The Party and Soviets: Possible Option of Acting at Local Markets', *Postfactum*, 4–10 August.

CHAPTER 5

1. All capital cities in the Soviet Union had a *Dom Druzhby* to promote cultural exchange with non-Soviet countries, especially capitalist states. Their cultural mission had an ideological drive, to propagate the ideas of Soviet communism through the arts. Consequently, many of their employees were KGB-linked.

2. C. Freeland (2000) *Sale of the Century: The Inside Story of the Second Russian Revolution*. London, Little, Brown, pp. 163–4.

3. V. Mau (1996) *The Political History of Economic Reform in Russia 1985–1994*. London, Centre for Research into Communist Economies.

4. SWB report, SU/1418, June 1992.

5. G. Eyal, I. Szleny and E. Townsley (1998) *Making Capitalism Without Capitalists: The New Ruling Elites in Eastern Europe*. London, Verso.

6. L. Nelson and Y. Kuzes (1994) *Property to the People: The Struggle for Radical Economic Reform in Russia*. Armonk, NY, M. E. Sharpe, p. 36.

7. Seymour M. Hersch, quoted in J. Dunlop (2003) 'The August 1991 Coup and its Impact on Soviet Politics', *Journal of Cold War Studies*, 5(1): 94–127.

8. C. Wallender (2003) 'Western Policy and the Demise of the Soviet Union', *Journal of Cold War Studies*, 5(4): 137–77.

9. 'After the Coup: The Gorbachev Account: A Coup "Against the People, Against Democracy"', *New York Times*, 23 August 1991.

10. P. Rutland (1994) 'The Economy: The Rocky Road from Plan to Market', in S. White, S. A. Pravda and Z. Gitelman (eds), *Developments in Russian & Post-Soviet Politics* (3rd edn). Basingstoke and London, Macmillan, p. 152.

11. Nelson and Kuzes, *Property to the People*, p. 50.

12. M. McFaul (1995) 'State Power, Institutional Change and the Politics of Privatization in Russia', *World Politics*, 47(2) (January): 210–43.

13. L. Panova (1994) 'The Standard of Living in Petersburg', in *The Early 90s: Crazy, Cold, Cruel, St Petersburg*, Charitable Foundation 'Nochlezka', p. 158.

14. K. K. Chan (1995) 'Poland at the Crossroads', *Europe-Asia Studies*, 47(1): 123–45.

15. E. Andrushenko et al. (1993) *Prestupnost' – Ugroza Rossii*. Moscow, RAU Corporation, p. 16.

16. Ibid., p. 13.

17. Ibid., pp. 18–19.

18. Y. Gilinsky (1994) 'Crime in St Petersburg', *The Early 90s: Crazy, Cold, Cruel, St Petersburg*, Charitable Foundation 'Nochlezka'.

19. One of the numerous informal conversations with friends and associates during the summer of 1992 and autumn of 1994.

20. *Daily Mail*, 3 March 1993; *Evening Standard*, 15 April 1994.

21. P. Rawlinson (1998) 'Mafia, Media and Myth – Representations of Russian Organized Crime', *Howard Journal of Criminal Justice*, 37(4): 346–58.

22. One of the biggest fears with the breakup of the Soviet Union was the potential for the illegal sales of nuclear materials by 'mafia' groups. Much of this was based on speculation and prevailing Cold War attitudes. An especially potent rumour circulated about a mysterious substance known as 'red mercury', which was said to be a potential component for creating nuclear bombs, and to which various illegal groups claimed to have access. It disappeared from the radar of concern as quickly as it appeared.

23. One of the most quoted parts of the report relates to the estimated 40 per cent of businesses in Russia said to be 'involved' with organised crime. This figure, based on a vague notion of 'involvement', was batted around various Russian and Western reports on organised crime as if it were hard data, for at least eight years with little or no critical analysis.

24. Andrushenko, *Prestupnost' – Ugroza Rossii*, p. 54.

25. E. Luttwak (1995) 'Does the Russian Mafia Deserve a Nobel Prize for Economics?', *London Review of Books*, 3 August.

26. S. Handelman (1994) *Comrade Criminal: The Theft of the Second Russian Revolution*. London, Michael Joseph, p. 134.

27. Regular meetings in and outside the Moskva hotel were conducted with Oleg and Andrey over a three-week period in 1992.

28. See P. Rawlinson (2007) 'Mission Impossible: Researching Organized Crime', in R. D. King and E. Wincup (eds), *Doing Research on Crime and Justice* (2nd edn). Oxford, Oxford University Press, for an account of some of the methodological issues on conducting fieldwork in Russia. See also P. Rawlinson (2008) 'Look Who's Talking: Interviewing Russian Criminals', *Trends in Organized Crime*, 11(1) (March): 12–20.

29. V. Volkov (2002) *Violent Entrepreneurs: The Use of Force in the Making of Russian Capitalism*. Ithaca and London, Cornell University Press, p. 127.

30. Dunlop, 'The August 1991 Coup'.

31. Volkov, *Violent Entrepreneurs*.

32. F. Varese (2001) *The Russian Mafia: Private Protection in a New Market Economy*. Oxford, Oxford University Press.

33. M. Dixelius and A. Konstantinov (1995) *Prestupny Mir Rossii*. St Petersburg, Bibliopolis.

34. A. Konstantinov and M. Dixelius (1997) *Banditskaya Rossiya*. St Petersburg, Bibliopolis.

35. Ibid., p. 259.

36. Interview, December 1994.

37. Yaponchik's claim to fame (real name Vyacheslav Ivankov) came about through his migration to the US in 1992. Arrested three years later by the

FBI for extortion activities and sent to prison for over nine years, Yaponchik was turned into a 'Russian mafia' stereotype, seen as tough, ruthless and powerful. However, the reality of Ivankov's association with crime is best explained by Finckenauer's sober account that although 'He is probably the toughest Russian criminal in the United States ... it is doubtful that he is or was the head of a major criminal organization or mafia boss. There is no evidence that he systematically used violence or corruption' (J. Finckenauer and E. Waring (1998) *Russian Mafia in America: Immigration, Culture and Crime.* Boston, Northeastern University Press, p. 114). A similar myth grew up around Sergei Mikhailov, known as 'Mikas', the leader of the Solntsevskaya gang in Moscow. The attempt by a Swiss court to prosecute him for, *inter alia*, money-laundering in 1998 was unsuccessful. His name appears to have been more ubiquitous and flourishing than his criminal business activities.

38.   A fierce critic of the Putin regime, murdered in 2006.
39.   A. Politkovskaya (2004) *Putin's Russia.* London, Harvill Press, pp. 151–2.
40.   Prior to the August coup, the RSFSR had adopted the Law on the Privatisation of State and Municipal Enterprises in the RSFSR.
41.   T. Djokaev (1992) 'Politikonomiya ot Il'l ili fenomen UKOSO', *Rossisskaya Gazeta,* 26 September.
42.   A. Shleifer and D. Treisman (2000) *Without a Map: Political Tactics and Economic Reform in Russia.* Cambridge, MA, MIT Press, p. 21.
43.   Luttwak, 'Does the Russian Mafia Deserve a Nobel Prize'.
44.   T. Gustafson (1999) *Capitalism Russian-Style.* Cambridge, Cambridge University Press, p. 43.
45.   J. R. Blasi, M. Kroumova and D. Kruse (1997) *Kremlin Capitalism: Privatisation of the Russian Economy.* Ithaca, NY, ILR Press, p. 119.
46.   S. White, G. Gill and D. Slider (1993) *The Politics of Transition: Shaping a Post-Soviet Future.* Cambridge, Cambridge University Press, p. 156.
47.   Handelman, *Comrade Criminal,* p. 284.
48.   As one of the leading voices of democratic reform in the late 1980s, and a popular Mayor of Leningrad and St Petersburg, Anatoly Sobchak became the subject of an investigation by the St Petersburg police into a number of alleged incidents of corrupt practices including this incident of unauthorised capital flight. As with many police investigations in Russia of high-profile figures, there is often a political agenda driving them. In this particular instance, however, the investigation appeared to be motivated by the genuine pursuit of justice. The St Petersburg police had been alerted to the incident by a member of the Metropolitan Police who mentioned it in passing and not as part of a formal investigation. Further attempts to elicit information and support from London, and which at one point I was involved in as an informal 'go-between', were constantly stymied. During a closed conference I mentioned this situation to a number of criminal intelligence officers from Europe and the UK. Some of those present declared that their police work was often stonewalled by the government and security services if the outcome of an investigation had the potential to threaten national 'interests'.
49.   Founding statement of the neo-liberal Mont Pelerin Society, in D. Harvey (2007) *A Brief History of Neoliberalism.* Oxford, Oxford University Press, p. 20.
50.   J. Hough (2001) *The Logic of Economic Reform in Russia.* Washington, DC, Brookings Institution.

51. According to the Committee for Democracy and Civil Liberties in Russia, one newspaper, *Nezavisimaya gazeta*, estimated that between 800 and 1,000 people, including children, were killed. Censorship around the death toll both in Russia and the West and the support given to Yeltsin's actions in the name of democracy was, according to John Pilger (quoted in the report), a travesty of democracy itself which, up until the bombing of Parliament, was working through the very objections of the legislature to the hugely unpopular reform programme, as well as seeking to curb the powers of the President (Democracy and Human Rights in Russia, *The Attack on Parliament*, from the Committee for Democracy and Civil Liberties in Russia).

52. Former freelance journalist Ingela Bylund, at that time a resident of Moscow, described the almost indiscriminate use of firepower by Yeltsin's troops as she and others hurried away from the Ostankino television centre (personal communication).

53. 'World Leaders Rally to Back President's Tactics', *The Times*, 5 October 1993.

54. 'Yeltsin Crushes Revolt', *Guardian*, 5 October 1993.

55. T. Remington (1993) 'Representative Power and the Russian State', in S. White, G. Gill and D. Slider (eds), *The Politics of Transition: Shaping a Post-Soviet Future*. Cambridge, Cambridge University Press, p. 79.

56. Ibid.

57. N. Klein (2007) *The Shock Doctrine: The Rise of Disaster Capitalism*. London, Penguin, p. 228.

58. B. Ruble (1991) 'Stepping Off the Treadmill of Failed Reforms?', in H. Balzar (ed.), *Five Years That Shook the World: Gorbachev's Unfinished Revolution*. Boulder, CO, Westview Press, p. 190.

59. ITAR-TASS, 15 October 1993.

60. 'Russia: Book on Chechen Criminal Network in Moscow', FBIS-SOV–96 *Daily Report*, 3 April 1996.

61. 'Britain is Set to Cash In On the Oil Rush in Azerbaijan', *Independent*, 27 September 1994; 'Oil and Blood in the Caucasus', *Washington Post*, 1 October 1995.

62. R. Johnson (2005) 'Quagmire of Convenience: The Chechen War and Putin's Presidency', Canadian Institute of International Affairs, *Behind the Headlines*, 62(4): 1–18.

63. Quoted in Michael McFaul (2003), 'US Foreign Policy and Chechnya', http://www.stanleyfoundation.org/publications/archive/EAIrussiaB03p.pdf.

64. Most famously, Samuel Huntington's 'Clash of Civilizations?' highlighted the possibility of the 'centuries-old military interaction between the West and Islam' as not only 'unlikely to decline' but as threatening to 'become more virulent', thereby almost setting out the US foreign policy agenda in the post-Cold War era (S. Huntington (1993) 'The Clash of Civilizations?', *Foreign Affairs*, 72(3) (summer): 22–49).

65. In September 1999 two bombs went off in Moscow apartments killing more than 200 people. With little or no evidence, the Russian government blamed Chechen rebels for the carnage. In the proliferation of anti-Chechen sentiment that followed, the government more or less had the blessing of the Russian public to resume hostilities against Chechnya, which it did within weeks, culminating in the second Chechen war. Not long after the second bomb went off, on September 13 another explosive device was found in the city of Ryazan, east of Moscow, again in an apartment block. A clash of statements

between the *militsiya* and the FSB (*Federal'naya Sluzhba Bezopasnosti*) roused the suspicions of some that the security services had planted the device, leading to speculation that they were also behind the other two explosions. Alexander Litvinenko, the former KGB agent who was poisoned with Polonium 210 in London in 2006, was about to publish a book about the incident set to expose Russian government collaboration in the explosions.

66. The US Sherman Act, passed in 1890, was an attempt to curtail the powers of big business in America. Its main objective was to break monopolies, conspiracies, price-fixing and other practices that might restrain free trade.

67. H. Zinn (1980) *A People's History of the United States*. London, Longman, p. 252.

68. Ibid., p. 254.

69. E. Sutherland (1983) *White Collar Crime: The Unexpurgated Version*. New Haven, CT, Yale University Press, p. 236.

70. According to Mancur Olsen, once sound property laws are established, democracy and rule of law will follow. It behoves these 'rational stationary bandits', as Olsen termed the criminal entrepreneurs, to eventually opt for stable governance as a means of ensuring greater economic productivity. Taxation rather than arbitrary theft is clearly conducive to the creation of greater wealth, therefore self-interested (criminal) owners of private property will wish to reduce theft (of their own property) and hence support government legislation that protects everyone's property (see M. Olsen (1995) 'The Devolution of Power in Post-Communist Societies', in R. Skidelsky (ed.), *Russia's Stormy Path to Reform*. London, Social Market Foundation).

71. H.-J.Chang (2008) *Bad Samaritans: The Guilty Secrets of Rich Nations and the Threat to Global Prosperity*. London, Random House Business Books.

72. For an interesting biographical account of some of the major players in the Russian oligarchy, see D. Hoffman (2002) *The Oligarchs: Wealth and Power in the New Russia*. New York, PublicAffairs, Perseus Books.

73. P. Halloran (2001) 'Russian Capital Markets 1994–2001: A Ground Level Account', in P. Westin (ed.), *The Wild East*. London, Reuters, Pearson Education.

74. C. Granville (2001) 'The Political and Societal Environment of Economic Policy', in B. Granville and P. Oppenheimer (eds), *Russia's Post-Communist Economy*. Oxford, Oxford University Press, p. 32.

75. Ibid., p. 43.

76. 'International Equities. Russia Resumes Privatisations', *Financial Times*, 10 February 1997.

77. D. Treisman (1996) 'Why Yeltsin Won: A Russian Tammany Hall', *Foreign Affairs*, 75(5) (September/October): 64–77.

78. Freeland, *Sale of the Century*, p. 180.

79. GKOs (Gosudarstvennye kratkosrochnye obligatsii) were first issued in 1994 to the banks as a means of stabilising the financial system.

80. For a potted history of the complex workings within the Russian market by an experienced journalist in and outside Russia, see A. Meier (1999) 'The Crash: The Russian Market from Start to Crash', http://www.pbs.org/wgbh/pages/frontline/shows/crash/etc/russia.html.

81. R. Layard and J. Parker (1996) *The Coming Russian Boom: A Guide to New Markets and Politics*. New York, The Free Press.

82. For a detailed and readable account see R. Lowenstein (2000) *When Genius Failed: The Rise and Fall of Long-term Capital Management*. London: Fourth Estate.
83. *Financial Times*, 10 November 2003.
84. B. Kagarlitsky (n.d.) '"Political capitalism" and Corruption in Russia', *Links: International Journal of Socialist Renewal*, http://links.org.au/node/86.
85. Khordokovsky was suspected of plotting to bankroll opposition political parties in defiance of a deal supposedly made between Putin and the oligarchs as part of a compromise between the two sides. More significantly, Khordokovsky's arrest occurred prior to a deal between Yukos and Texaco Chevron, hardly a coincidence given that the deal would have enabled a much greater influence by Western multinationals on the Russian economy and by definition would make Khordokovsky 'so powerful as to be untouchable' ('Kremlin Threat to US-Yukos Deal', *Guardian*, 4 August 2003).
86. B. Bean (2004) 'Yukos and Mikhail Khordokovsky: An Unfolding Drama', in D. McCarthy, S. Puffer and S. Shekshina (eds), *Corporate Governance in Russia*. Cheltenham, Edward Elgar, p. 349.
87. http://www.ft.com/cms/s/0/34a9bed6-d4e8-11dc-9af1-0000779fd2ac.html.
88. 'Russia: Hapless Victim in Heist of the Century', *Times Online*, 5 November 2003.
89. Freeland, *Sale of the Century*, p. 163.
90. E. Skidelsky (2008) 'The Return of Goodness', *Prospect*, 150 (September).
91. *Wall Street* (1988) Amercent Films.
92. 'How Dallas Won the Cold War', *Washington Post*, 27 April 2008.
93. R. Poe (1993) *How to Profit from the Coming Russian Boom: The Insider's Guide to Business Opportunities and Survival on the Frontiers of Capitalism*. New York, McGraw-Hill Inc., p. 10.
94. Ibid., p. 72.
95. Ibid., p. 76.
96. Articles 290 and 291 of the Russian Federation Criminal Code relate directly to bribery, with punishments of up to twelve years' imprisonment and a fine of 1 million roubles for accepting a bribe. The courts are conspicuously quiet on what is a national pastime.
97. The discussion was prompted by a paper I delivered in March 1993 at the London/Norwegian Club for a conference entitled 'Recognising Organized Crime in the CIS'.
98. Poe, *How to Profit from the Coming Russian Boom*, p. 237.
99. G. Dunn (1997) 'Major Mafia Gangs in Russia', in P. Williams (ed.), *Russian Organized Crime: The New Threat?* London, Frank Cass.
100. T. Sebastian (1995) *Sunday Express, Night and Day*, 5 March.
101. Handelman, *Comrade Criminal*, p. 80.
102. Klein, *The Shock Doctrine*, p. 239.
103. J. Wedel (1998) *Collision and Collusion: The Strange Case of Western Aid to Eastern Europe 1989–1998*. New York, St Martin's Press, p. 142.
104. Ibid. This was the reference to the fact that shares given to the public did not in reality allow them any control over the enterprises they allegedly 'owned', as this remained in the hands of the managers (p. 132).
105. Ibid., pp. 188–9.
106. L. Shevtsova (2007) *Russia Lost in Transition: The Yeltsin and Putin Legacies*. Washington, DC, Carnegie Endowment for International Peace, p. 110.

107. A number of people, including a successful local businessman, confirmed the extent of Lukoil's political and economic influence over the affairs of Ekaterinburg (August 2008).

108. Volkov, *Violent Entrepreneurs*.

109. T. Frye and E. Zhuravskaya (2000) 'Rackets, Regulation and Rule of Law', *Journal of Law, Economics and Organization*, 16(2): 478–502.

110. Ibid.

111. Interview, Moscow, December 2003.

112. 'Central Bank Deputy Chairman Andrei Kozlov Murdered', *Kommersant*, 15 September 2006.

113. Even when suspects are brought to trial in these types of assassinations, as in the recent proceedings against two Chechens, a Moscow police officer and an FSB agent, it is often the case that they have been wrongly accused or represent the low hanging fruit of the operational chain. These latter were all acquitted ('Anna Politikovskaya Trial; Four Accused Found Not Guilty', *Guardian*, 19 February 2009).

114. M. Woodiwiss and D. Hobbs (2008) 'Organized Evil and the Atlantic Alliance: Moral Panics and the Rhetoric of Organized Crime Policing in America and Britain', *British Journal of Criminology*, 49(1): 106–28.

115. Shevtsova, *Russia Lost in Transition*, pp. 129–30.

116. Conversation with a compliance officer, October 2008.

117. G. Monbiot (2008) 'Censored by Money', *Guardian*, 15 July.

118. B. Peters (2003) 'The Media's Role: Covering or Covering Up Corruption?' *Global Corruption Report*, http://www.transparency.org/publications/gcr/gcr_2003.

CHAPTER 6

1. A. Solzhenitsyn (1972) *'One Word of Truth' – The Nobel Speech on Literature, 1970*. London, Bodley Head.

2. H. Arendt (2000) *The Portable Hannah Arendt*, ed. P. Baehr. New York, Penguin, p. 154.

3. Economic vandalism by no means overstates the appalling impact of legal economic activity on many of the world's population. As poverty, hunger and other forms of deprivation increase, and will continue to do so, it is no longer possible to engage with these conditions in the tame lexicon of 'unintended outcomes' or 'mistakes'. If vandalism implies intent then wilful (intentional) ignorance of the consequences of economic activities, even as possibilities, then this must frame some of the narratives of economic failure.

4. http://www.odccp.org/palermo.

5. http://www.thisislocallondon.co.uk/whereilive/walthamforest/display.var.1972360.0.waltham_forest_do.

6. D. Dorling (2004) 'Prime Suspect: Murder in Britain', in P. Hillyard, C. Pantazis, S. Tombs and D. Gordon (eds), *Beyond Criminology: Taking Harm Seriously*. London, Pluto Press, p. 179.

7. M. Foucault (1980) *Power/Knowledge: Selected Interviews and Other Writings 1972–1977*, ed. C. Gordon. Brighton, Harvester Press, p. 118.

8. For a summary of some of the earlier texts on organised crime in the Soviet Union, see R. Kelly, R. Schatzberg and P. Ryan (1997) 'Primitive Capitalist Accumulation: Russia as a Racket', in P. Ryan and G. Rush (eds),

Understanding Organized Crime in Global Perspective. Thousand Oaks, CA, Sage.

9. M. Woodiwiss and D. Hobbs (2008) 'Organized Evil and the Atlantic Alliance: Moral Panics and the Rhetoric of Organized Crime Policing in America and Britain', *British Journal of Criminology*, 49(1): 106–28.

10. Joseph Stiglitz, academic and former Chief Economist at the World Bank, and adviser to the Clinton administration, has been increasingly critical of the direction in which economic global policy has been evolving. Favouring a 'third way' approach, his analysis of the limitations of the free market as determined by the Washington Consensus is eloquently argued in his book *Globalization and its Discontents* (2002, London, Penguin). John Gray, an erstwhile advocate of neo-liberalism, has also produced highly critical texts on *laissez-faire* economics (see below).

11. The point to note here is that trust and accountability were confined to a geographical space in which the benefits of cooperation were more easily discernible. Unlike the small peasant commune, where it was clear that cooperation was the best means of survival as an almost instinctive form of economy, in the Soviet collective the visibility of beneficial outcomes was absent. Most important, cooperation did not come from the people *per se* but was ideologically imposed from outside.

12. K. Marx, *Estranged Labour, Economic and Philosophical Manuscripts of 1844*, Marxist archive, http://www.marxists.org/archive/marx/works/1844/manuscripts/labour.htm.

13. G. Lukacs (1923) *Reification and the Consciousness of the Proletariat*, http://www.marxists.org/archive/lukacs/works/history/hcc05.htm.

14. A. Smith (1993) *Wealth of Nations*, Book I. Oxford, Oxford University Press, p. 18.

15. Durkheim, E. (1984) *The Division of Labour in Society* (2nd edn). Basingstoke, Macmillan.

16. V. I. Lenin (1920) *The Tasks of the Youth Leagues*. Speech Delivered at the Third All-Russia Congress of the Russian Young Communist League, 2 October, http://www.marxists.org/archive/lenin/works/1920/oct/02.htm.

17. Smith, *Wealth of Nations*, Book I, p. 22.

18. S. Messner and R. Rosenfeld (2006) *Crime and the American Dream* (3rd edn). London, Wadsworth Publishing.

19. SATs are a series of compulsory national curriculum tests for school children in England to be taken at various stages of their primary and secondary education. They effectively standardise achievement, leaving little or no room for individual development and creativity. The whole ethos of continuous testing has come under increasing criticism, as teaching becomes constrained by SATs. Most significantly, SATs results have been used punitively for those schools failing to achieve the required standards, though as yet no head teachers have been sent to detention centres for failing to fulfil the 'plan'.

20. Like SATs, the Research Assessment Exercise (RAE) attempts to measure and consequently reward or punish academics and their institutions that respond successfully or not to set criteria regarding research output. What was initially intended as a means of clearing out unproductive academics has now become a major part of university life, making and breaking careers, creating divisions among institutions and staff themselves and, in many cases, prioritising research over teaching. As with SATs, league-style tables

are produced from the results of the research assessment and, if unfavourable, can close down departments. It is not only the competitive element that can be destructive in this exercise but the largely spurious means of measuring that which, for the most part, cannot be perceived in abstract positivistic terms. What is surprising is that while many academics complain about the exercise, few rarely go beyond a verbal protest (myself included) for fear of rocking the RAE boat. In this respect it acts as a subtle form of social control, ensuring a compliant production line of intellectual output, not for the sake of advancing knowledge *per se* but rather for the advancement of careers. The subsequent threat to quality research is obvious.

21. R. Reiner (2007) *Law and Order: An Honest Citizen's Guide to Crime and Control*. Cambridge, Polity, p. 18.

22. The emergence of widespread food riots in 2008 across different countries, including Egypt and other African states, parts of Central Asia and South America, is not just a result of climate change but of, *inter alia*, intensive farming and water shortages, much of which is to feed the developed world. Again this calls on a reappraisal not only of structural factors of distribution but individual responses to personal need and a macro-awareness of the impact of individual consuming habits of privileged populations on the less privileged.

23. I have discussed the use of this term with Professor Boris Kashnikov (Moscow, Higher School of Economics), who suggested the phrase 'the Patrimonialisation of the West', from Weber's use of the term 'patrimonialism'. This type of structure, which involves the use of patronage and nepotism in government and business (also known as 'crony capitalism' in market societies), best describes the similar *modus operandi* of Russian political and social structures and organised crime. My insistence on the use of 'Sovietisation' is largely connected with the concepts we in the West have of the Soviet Union whose values and practices were considered as antithetical to those we claim as realised in our liberal democracies and the market economies. It is the attempt to bridge the ideological divide and its impact of the construction of narratives on organised crime and modern economy that has prompted me to retain this nomenclature.

24. Z. Bauman (1989) *Modernity and the Holocaust*. Cambridge, Polity Press, p. 183.

25. E. Levinas (2006) *Entre Nous: Thinking-of-the-Other*. London, Continuum.

26. Reiner, *Law and Order*, p. 19.

27. S. Pemberton (2004) 'A theory of moral indifference: understanding the production of harm by capitalist society', in P. Hillyard, C. Pantazis, S. Tombs and D. Gordon (eds), *Beyond Criminology: Taking Harm Seriously*. London, Pluto Press, p. 75.

28. Bauman, *Modernity and the Holocaust*, p. 7.

29. M. Punch (1996) *Dirty Business*. London, Sage, pp. 21–3.

30. 'Decades Later, Toxic Sludge Torments Bhopal', *New York Times*, 7 July 2008.

31. E. Zamyatin (1993) *We*. London, Penguin, p. 19.

32. See D. Lyon (2001) *Surveillance Society: Monitoring Everyday Life*. Buckingham, Open University Press, and other related books by the same author. See also S. Garfinkel (2000) *Database Nation: The Death of Privacy in the 21st Century*. Sebastopol, CA, O'Reilly & Associates.

33. N. Christie (2000) *Crime Control as Industry: Towards Gulags, Western Style*. London, Routledge, pp. 15–16.

34. For the period 2007–08, Home Office statistics showed that crime fell overall by 10 per cent (according to the British Crime Survey), and by 9 per cent according to police recorded crime data, in England and Wales (see C. Kershaw, S. Nicholas and A. Walker (2008) 'Crime in England and Wales 2007/8). Findings from the British Crime Survey and Police Recorded Crime, 07/08', http://www.homeoffice.gov.uk/rds/pdfs08/hosb0708.pdf. FBI statistics for the first half of 2008 also show a decrease in crime, by 3.5 per cent for violent crime and 2.5 per cent for property crime, http://www.fbi.gov/page2/jan09/ucr_statistics011209.html.

35. In contrast to the declining crime figures (clearly open to a variety of distortions), prison figures have been moving upwards. In England and Wales the prison population has practically doubled from 1992 (44,719) to 2007 (80,216). According to the same King's College London School of Law Report, a similar trend appeared between 1992 and 2004, http://www.kcl.ac.uk/depsta/law/research/icps/worldbrief/wpb_country.php?country=190.

36. 'Blair Hints at New Powers for "Ruthless" British FBI', *Times Online*, 9 February 2004.

37. 'The YouGov survey found that almost three quarters of the public (69 per cent) support raising the detention limit from 28 days to 42 days "in exceptional circumstances". A quarter (24 per cent) oppose the plans' ('Poll: British Public Wants 42-day Terror Detention', *Daily Telegraph*, 11 June 2008).

38. R. T. Naylor (2004) *Wages of Crime: Black Markets, Illegal Finance and the Underworld Economy*. Ithaca, NY, Cornell University Press, p. 17.

39. M. Woodiwiss (1993) 'Crime's Global Reach', in F. Pearce and M. Woodiwiss (eds), *Global Crime Connections: Dynamics and Control*. London, Macmillan, p. 14.

40. V. Mitsilegas (2003) 'Countering the Chameleon Threat of Dirty Money. "Hard" and "Soft" Law in the Emergence of a Global Regime Against Money Laundering and Terrorist Finance', in A. Edwards and P. Gill (eds), *Transnational Organised Crime: Perspectives on Global Security*. London, Routledge, p. 208.

41. M. Chossudovsky (2005) *America's 'War' on Terrorism*. Pincourt, Quebec, Global Research, pp. 322–3.

42. P. Belser (2005) 'Forced Labor and Human Trafficking: Estimating the Profits', http://digitalcommons.ilr.cornell.edu/cgi/viewcontent.cgi?article=1016&context=forcedlabor

43. Naylor, *Wages of Crime*, ch. 3.

44. T. Mathiesen (2004) *Silently Silenced: Essays on the Creation of Acquiescence in Modern Society*. Winchester, Waterside Press, p. 14.

45. P. Bourdieu (1992) *Language and Symbolic Power*. Cambridge, Polity Press, p. 138.

46. Social control theorists such as Travis Hirschi have argued that social bonds and a sense of integration or 'attachment' help offset the propensity for delinquency (see T. Hirschi (1969) *Causes of Delinquency*. Berkeley, University of California Press).

47. S. Skatin and G. Tsov'janov (1994) 'Nadezhda Konstantinovn Krupskaya', *Prospects*, 24(1–2): 49–60.

48. http://www.eagleforum.org/educate/marc_tucker/.

49. M. Moore (2001) *Stupid White Men ... And Other Sorry Excuses for the State of the Nation!* New York, HarperCollins Publishers, p. 111.

50. D. Rushkoff (2000) *Why We Listen to What 'They' Say.* New York, Riverhead Books, p. 176.

51. N. Hertz (2001) *The Silent Takeover: Global Capitalism and the Death of Democracy.* London, William Heinemann, p. 67.

52. B. Roberts and A. Portes (2006) 'Coping with the Free Market City: Collective Action in Six Latin American Cities at the End of the Twentieth Century', *Latin American Research Review*, 41(2) (June): 57–83. According to World Bank data, in 2005 China was the top emigration country.

53. Zhang and Chin refute the idea that the trafficking of Chinese nationals is organised crime in the traditional sense. Instead, their findings show family members, friends and/or incidental networks operating according to opportunity rather than a dedicated criminal structure (see S. Zhang and K. Chin (2003) 'The Declining Significance of Triad Societies in Transnational Illegal Activities. A Structural Deficiency Perspective', *British Journal of Criminology*, 43(3): 469–88).

54. Willis criticises many of the often well-intentioned government job schemes to get the unemployed back into work as provoking a sense of self-blame when, after training, people are unable to find employment in a situation not of their own making. See Young, *The Vertigo of Late Modernity*, p. 125.

55. R. Sennett (2006) *Culture of the New Capitalism.* New Haven, CT, Yale University Press.

56. http://news.bbc.co.uk/1/hi/england/west_midlands/4717331.

57. 'Ex-Northern Rock Boss Gets £750,000', *Observer*, 30 March 2008.

58. L. Kaplan and S. Matteis (1968) 'The Economics of Loansharking', *American Journal of Sociology & Economics*, 27(3): 239–52.

59. Z. Bauman (1998) *Globalization: The Human Consequences.* New York, Polity.

60. Loan sharks on some Birmingham estates are crucial to the illegal drugs trade. Tony Quigley of the Birmingham Loan Shark Unit explained how the single loan shark was allowed to enter the turf of a particular crime group as his status of banker provided the cash needed by his clients for their next fix as a temporary relief from the spiral of misery (interview, 2004).

61. P. Warburton (2000) *Debt and Delusion: Central Bank Follies that Threaten Economic Disaster.* London, Penguin, p. 49.

62. George Soros, founder of the Open Society Institute, whose hedge fund activities, most notably 'playing' the devaluation of the British pound in 1992, have amassed for him a multi-billion dollar fortune, has been a severe critic of the very system he manipulated. In *The Crisis of Global Capitalism: Open Society Endangered*, published in 1998, just after the rouble crash, he writes: 'Even if we put aside the bigger moral and ethical questions and concentrate solely on the economic arena, the ideology of market funda-mentalism is profoundly and irredeemably flawed. To put the matter simply, market forces, if they are given complete authority ... could ultimately lead to the downfall of the global capitalist system' (see G. Soros (1998) *The Crisis of Global Capitalism: Open Society Endangered.* London, Little, Brown and Company, p. xxvii). Despite his contentious activities in the world markets, his numerous warnings about the future of global capitalism have come back to haunt his critics.

63. J. McMurtry (1999) *The Cancer Stage of Capitalism*. London, Pluto Press, p. 64.

64. L. Morrow (1984) 'Waiting as a Way of Life', *Time*, 23 July 1984.

65. Sennet, *Culture of the New Capitalism*, p. 49.

66. P. Hillyard, J. Sim, D. Whyte and S. Tombs (2004) 'Leaving a "Stain Upon the Silence": Contemporary Criminology and Political Dissent', *British Journal of Criminology*, 44(3): 369–90.

67. An ATL article, 'Education for Sale', describes the demoralisation within the teaching profession and the threat to employment since the 'marketisation' of education as private sector is having a more substantial presence in this sector (ATL report October 2006). This is not to imply that private funding is *per se* a bad thing, but rather that conditionality attached to funding and the profit framework within which it operates is bound to serve the interests of the companies and their shareholders over those of schools and colleges. The same applies to universities and research bias towards the needs of the funder.

68. 'NHS Staff Cheat to Hit Government Targets, MPs Say', *British Medical Journal*, 327: 179 (26 July 2003), http://www.bmj.com/cgi/reprint/327/7408/179.pdf.

69. A. Zinoviev (1986) *Homo Sovieticus*. London, Paladin, p. 48.

70. K. Simis (1982) *USSR: Secrets of a Corrupt Society*. London, J. M. Dent; V. Vaksberg (1990) *Special Correspondent*. London, Hutchinson; L. Timofeyev (1992) *Russia's Secret Rulers*. New York, Knopf.

71. E. Gaidar (1996) 'How the Russian Nomenklatura "Privatized" its Own Power', *Russian Law and Politics*, January–February: 26–32.

72. See, *inter alia*, Ledeneva (1998) *Russia's Economy of Favours: Blat, Networking and Informal Exchange*. Cambridge, Cambridge University Press; L. Holmes (1993) *The End of Communist Power: Anti-Corruption Campaigns and Legitimation Crisis (Europe and the International Order)*. Cambridge, Polity Press.

73. Ledeneva, *Russia's Economy of Favours*, p. 187.

74. Hertz, *The Silent Takeover*.

75. E. Harriman, (2005) 'Where Has All the Money Gone?', *London Review of Books*, 7 July.

76. G. Monbiot (2000) *Captive State: The Corporate Takeover of Britain*. London, Macmillan.

77. BBC News, 'Bush and Big Business', 1 May 2001, http://news.bbc.co.uk/1/hi/world/americas/1306777.stm.

78. C. Wright Mills (1956) *The Power Elite*. Oxford, Oxford University Press, p. 347.

79. 'Why the Master Tactician had to Fall on his Sword', *The Times*, 9 November 2006.

80. A. Block (1993) 'Defending the Mountaintop: A Campaign Against Environmental Crime', in F. Pearce and M. Woodiwiss (eds), *Global Crime Connections: Dynamics and Control*. London, Macmillan.

81. 'Paper Trail to Markets of the East', *Guardian*, 2 February 2000.

82. B. Bullington (1993) 'All About Eve: The Many Faces of United States Drug Policy', in F. Pearce and M. Woodiwiss (eds), *Global Crime Connections: Dynamics and Control*. London, Macmillan.

83. Chossudovsky, *America's 'War' on Terrorism*, p. 229.

84. Naylor, *Wages of Crime*, ch. 3.

85. Chossudovsky, *America's 'War' on Terrorism*, p. 119.

86. The 'trickle-down effect' was a term used by US President Ronald Reagan in relation to his tax-cutting policies for high earners. The logic ran that the wealth of the richest would trickle down to the rest of the population as jobs were created through the spending of the economic elite and prices were brought lower.

87. J. Gray (1998) *False Dawn: The Delusions of Global Capitalism*. London, Granta, p. 111.

88. Economic Institute, 'Wealth Inequality is Vast and Growing', http://www.epi.org/content.cfm/webfeatures_snapshots_20060823.

89. M. Brewer et al. (2008) *Poverty and Inequality in the UK: 2008*, Institute for Fiscal Studies, IFS Commentary No. 105.

90. 'Unexpected Results: Globalization has Widened Income Disparity', *Wall Street Journal*, 24 May 2007.

91. O. Figes (2002) *Natasha's Dance: A Cultural History of Russia*. London, Allen Lane, p. 447.

92. S. Karstedt and S. Farrell (2006) 'The Moral Economy of Everyday Crime. Markets, Consumers and Citizens', *British Journal of Criminology*, 46: 1011–36.

93. J. Baudrillard (1998) *The Consumer Society*. London, Sage, p. 88.

94. Karstedt and Farrell, 'The Moral Economy of Everyday Crime'.

95. Gray, *False Dawn*, p. 207.

CHAPTER 7

1. M. Dostoevsky (1991) *Crime and Punishment*. London, Penguin Classics, p. 34.

2. E. Sevareid (1946) *Not So Wild a Dream*. New York, Alfred A. Knopf.

3. W. Greider (2003) *The Soul of Capitalism: Opening Paths to a Moral Economy*. New York, Simon & Schuster, p. 46.

4. Stanley Milgram's now infamous experiments set out to test the impact of authority on obedience and personal moral conscience, in part as a response to the revelations at the trial of Adolf Eichmann. Eichmann was the innocuous-sounding Transport Administrator in the Third Reich, whose main task was to arrange the transportation of Jews to the death camps. During the trial, Eichmann consistently declared that he was only following orders. Milgram's experiment yielded the unpalatable results that, given certain situations, the most 'normal' and 'civilised' person would act in similar fashion, sacrificing conscience to duty. Milgram faced a barrage of criticism about the ethics of his methods, and yet the results have formed the basis of sociological and psychological debates on issues of obedience and morality.

5. P. Hillyard and S. Tombs (2004) 'Beyond Criminology?', in P. Hillyard, C. Pantazis, S. Tombs and D. Gordon (eds), *Beyond Criminology: Taking Harm Seriously*. London, Pluto Press, p. 15.

6. J. Paul and K. Wahlberg (2008) *A New Era of World Hunger? The Global Food Crisis Analyzed*. New York, FES/ Dialogue on Globalization, Briefing Paper, July, p. 2.

7. Ibid., pp. 3–5.

8. Z. Bauman (2008) *Does Ethics Have a Chance in a World of Consumers?* Cambridge, MA, Harvard University Press, pp. 52–4.

9. That we require the slaughter of animals to be a hidden event, and 'dress up' the carcass to make it look as little like the original beast as possible, yet can claim outrage at the *visible* killing of an animal, even if on television, is a banal but nonetheless clear example of this archaic form of morality. As most animal welfare campaigners point out, the inordinate level of cruelty to animals as food is driven by the desire for cheaper meat, produced away from the eyes of the consumer. Alongside commodities produced cheaply at the cost of human suffering, this marks out yet another idiosyncratic play of conscience in the consumer society's collusion of ignorance in the economic process.

10. V. Mitsilegas (2003) 'Countering the Chameleon Threat of Dirty Money. "Hard" and "Soft" Law in the Emergence of a Global Regime Against Money Laundering and Terrorist Finance', in A. Edwards and P. Gill (eds), *Transnational Organised Crime: Perspectives on Global Security*. London, Routledge, p. 208.

11. Quoted in A. Wright (2006) *Organised Crime*. Cullompton, Willan Publishing, p. 71.

12. Wright, *Organised Crime*, p. 68.

13. 'Firms' Secret Tax Avoidance Schemes Cost UK Billions', *Guardian*, 2 February 2009.

14. A. Smith (2002) *The Theory of Moral Sentiments*, ed. K. Haakonssen. Cambridge, Cambridge University Press, p. 11.

15. S. Cohen (2001) *States of Denial: Knowing about Atrocities and Suffering*. Cambridge, Polity Press p. 294.

16. Despite their good intentions, fair trade initiatives are clearly vulnerable to the vagaries of the market as currently structured unless it can offer sound competitive prices, which in turn could impact negatively on producers.

17. 'Lehman Brothers Chief Executive Grilled by Congress over Compensation', *Guardian*, 6 October 2008; 'Hubris to Nemesis: How Sir Fred Goodwin became the 'World's Worst Banker', *Times Online*, http://business.timesonline.co.uk/tol/business/economics/article5549510.eces.

18. F. Lee (2004) 'To be a Heterodox Economist: The Contested Landscape of American Economics, 1960s and 1970s', *Journal of Economic Issues*, 38(3): 747–63.

19. The collapse of Long Term Capital Management was in part due to the hubris of its owners and their confidence in the formulaic approach to inefficiencies in the bond market which allowed them effectively to 'bet' on the elimination of these inefficiencies. As its $5 billion loss testified, such a formula was, to put it mildly, flawed.

20. C. Houghton Budd (2003) *The Metamorphosis of Capitalism*. Canterbury, Associative Economics Institute, p. 95.

21. H. Arendt (1994) *Eichmann in Jerusalem: A Report on the Banality of Evil*. London, Penguin, p. 297.

22. G. Falcone and M. Padovani (1993) *Men of Honour: The Truth about the Mafia*. London: Warner, Little, Brown, and Company, p. 70.

Index

The Resort

Video of the Tycoon - corporate video
for the golf course / resort -
extolling its virtues

Alec Baldwin

---

description of Tycoon in proposal
- something to ~~suggest~~ his
vanity

— Series on 'Tammany Hall'

Pavel, the braniac maths guy,
is example of rejection of all
individual moral responsibility -
it's the ~~the~~ system, economics that
~~then~~ is the agent, which he has no
option but to serve

Vadim has girlfriend from early
teenage days, who reappears during
later sequences / chapters —
while Vadim is up, she + her
husband have slid down.
He tries to help. She is too proud
He visits her flat.
Then one day he goes over + they're not
there. Another family living there. No
sign of her. He goes looking.